Between Nothingness and Paradise

Between Nothingness and Paradise

Gerhart Niemeyer

St. Augustine's Press
South Bend, Indiana
1998

Manufactured in the United States of America.

Cataloging in Publication Data

Niemeyer, Gerhart.
Between nothingness and paradise / Gerhart Niemeyer.
p. cm.
Originally published: Baton Rouge : Louisiana State University Press, c1971
Includes bibliographical references and indexes.
ISBN 1-890318-05-1 (cloth : alk. paper)
1. Totalitarianism. 2. Ideology. I. Title.
JC480.N54 1998
321.9—dc21 97-37674
CIP

∞The paper used in this publication meets the minimum requirements of the American National Standard for Information Sciences—Permanence of Paper for Printed Materials, ANSI Z39.48-1984.

To Lucie

Preface

For many of my generation, the onslaught of totalitarian mass movements has become an all-overshadowing experience. From it have sprung a number of remarkable intellectual efforts to grasp the nature of totalitarian movements, trace their roots in the past, lay bare the structure of their ideas, and discover through self-examination wherein consists the totalitarian *fausse conscience* (the title of Joseph Gabel's book of 1962). Among the outstanding works of this kind I should like to mention here only Hannah Arendt's *The Origins of Totalitarianism* (1951), Eric Voegelin's *The New Science of Politics* (1952), Norman Cohn's *The Pursuit of the Millennium* (1957) and Ernest Tuveson's *Millennium and Utopia* (1949), J. L. Talmon's *The Origin of Totalitarian Democracy* and *Political Messianism* (both 1960), and Albert Camus' *L'homme révolté* (1951; Engl. ed. 1956).

For some time I have been interested in a feature common to all totalitarian ideologies which I have called the "total critique of society," and the corresponding activism that goes under the name of "creative destruction." Three months before the end of the war Goebbels gloated over the wholesale incineration of Germany as the road to radical newness, and a little later Hitler nodded his approval to total defeat. But these two were latecomers to a company of major and minor figures which in past and present has included Babeuf, Marx, Bakunin, Nechaev, Lenin, Trotsky, Marcuse, Cohn-Bendit, and Mark Rudd. All have made a vocation of total revolution directed not against any injustice in particular but against the "system." For them, society represents evil in general and their existential rejection of it engulfs ethics and metaphysics, politics and religion.

The ideologists' total critique stems not from indignation, the inner measure of the wrongs of others, but from idea systems placing on extant social order the stamp of unreality or falseness. A "creatively destructive" activism thus presupposes an intellectual destruction of present reality, as a result of which the believers of such ideas orient themselves no longer toward "real possibilities" but rather toward "possible realities," to use Robert Musil's terms. They put the index of reality not on what exists but on what they fancy might be brought into existence, thereby changing the character of politics from an order of "action" to a technique of "making," in Aristotle's conceptual distinction. Their denial of reality to the present society, however, forms only a part in wider circles of ontological negations—be it the annihilation of God, or the creation, or the moral order, or human nature—so that the total critique of society appears as a mere aspect of a total dissent from existence. Camus has deftly summed up the entire complex of intellectual and activist negation in the concept "metaphysical revolution."

The first three chapters of this book seek to clarify the dependence of the ideologists' total critique of society on their ontological negations. The fourth chapter is a study of the character of totalitarian activism in view of the antecedent total critique of society as well as existence as such. In the course of these critical studies, however, there arose a number of politico-philosophical questions which seemed to have received not merely inadequate attention but even insufficient formulation in political theory, and for which not even a suitable vocabulary seemed to be available. Surely the alternative to an ideological total critique of society cannot be the total acceptance of society; but on what grounds can one arrive at something like a norm regarding man's proper attitude toward society's existence? Is this existence as such to be respected as a limit or obligation? The term "existence" seems even to be out of place in this context. Generations of philosophers have worked over the problem of existence from many angles, but they have concentrated their efforts on the existence of what traditionally is called substances, leaving the applicability of the concept to relational structures in doubt. In what sense, then, could one think of a society as having "existence" or of that "existence" as having normative relevance? The problem of the limits of social critique seems to have been sadly neglected, and it is significant that Camus, who strongly calls for such limits, has nothing to say about their intellectual concretization.

The last three chapters take a step in the direction of answers to such questions. No claim to systematic completeness attaches to this attempt. I have pursued the quest through a number of inquiries into historical and theoretical materials, following each trail as far as it would take me, and there leaving the matter without trying to pull the various strands together. Each inquiry was suggested, of course, by some dubiety that I had encountered in my critical studies of the ideologists. All the same, I have felt no need, after completing the last three chapters, to return to the ideologists and to undertake a point-by-point "refutation." If the reader wishes to draw detailed conclusions, he thus has ample leeway. I personally feel that the great confrontation with political irrationality in our time has not the character of a debate or even discussion. The prerequisite for either would be a common universe of reason which is precisely what the ideologists have demolished. Vis-à-vis their great intellectual efforts on the ground of irrationality, the answer must consist in a greater effort of recollection, of recapturing the language and consciousness of reality. The re-winning of *theory* in the classical sense, the looking at phenomena in the perspective of *ratio*, is in itself the alternative to ideology. It is to this endeavor that this book hopes to make a small contribution.

GERHART NIEMEYER

Contents

Between Nothingness and Paradise

I □ Natura Ex Machina

Contemporary totalitarian movements have displayed a new political motivation, which one might call "revolution as vocation."* Revolution is no longer related to specific political objectives as a means to an end but considered a value in itself, inasmuch as it sweeps away all that exists. A kind of religious hope connected with total destruction can be found in Goebbels, Lenin, Bakunin alike. Marx's concept, "the revolution in permanence,"[1] postulated a continuing movement of unsettling change that must never be geared to any concretely attainable objective; a struggle that must not stop at removing this or that grievance, this or that institution, this or that ruling group, but claim nothing less than total renovation of human life. To the "permanent revolution" corresponds a total critique of society, the intellectual rejection or negation of the entire world of order in which men find themselves. This intellectual foundation of revolution as a way of life is very clearly formulated by Marx, for whom the radical critique of religion was the starting point of an equally radical critique "in practice." As he put it, "Thus the critique of heaven turns into a critique of the world, the critique of religion into a critique of the legal order, the critique of theology into a critique of the political order."[2] In order to carry the radical critique of society forward into a "radical revolution," Marx looks for a "negative representation of society," that is, a group representing the negation of the entire social order:

* The bulk of this chapter was published in *Politische Ordnung und menschliche Existenz: Festgabe für Eric Voegelin* (Munich, 1962). By permission of C. H. Beck, publisher.

1 Marx, "Ansprache der Zentralbehörde an den Bund," in *Karl Marx, Friedrich Engels, Werke* (40 vols.; Berlin, 1958–68), VII, 244–54. Hereinafter cited as *Marx-Engels Werke.*

2 Marx, "Zur Kritik der Hegelschen Rechtsphilosophie, Einleitung," in *ibid.,* I, 378–91.

"a class with radical chains, a class in civil society which is no class of civil society, an Estate which is the dissolution of all Estates, a sphere that has universal character because of its universal sufferings, that does not claim any particular right because no particular wrong but wrong in general is perpetrated against it, that cannot invoke any historical title but only the universal title of humanity, . . . that cannot emancipate itself without emancipating itself from all other spheres of society and thereby emancipating all other spheres of society, (a sphere) that, in one word, is the total loss of the human self and can win itself only through the total restoration of the human self. This dissolution of society as a particular Estate is the proletariat."[3]

The customary explanation of such a total rejection of the existing order is that certain men, particularly sensitive to injustice and social misery, were driven to white heat of indignation by what they observed around them, as if nothing but righteous passion had been the source of their radical schemes. In the case of Marx, this kind of explanation must certainly fail, because his critique of society was well elaborated before he even discovered the proletariat. Nor can the explanation be more successful in the cases of Goebbels, Lenin, or Bakunin. These men willed the total destruction of society not from an excess of compassion but from a certain way of thinking about order and existence. The exploration of their way of thinking and its roots in the history of ideas becomes therefore a legitimate object of exploration. How and why was a total critique of society first conceived? What is the intellectual structure of the view that sees existing society as a proper object for total destruction?

The way to discover the sources of a river is to follow its course upstream. In the case of the revolutionary movement of the Left, this is fortunately not difficult because of the continuity of its history. From the revolutionary groups active in France and England at the time of the *Communist Manifesto* a line of succession leads, through Buonarroti, to Babeuf, the author and leader of the first

[3] *Ibid.*, 390.

movement, which in its direction and organization bears striking resemblance to modern communism. Babeuf, like the Communists, preached and planned a revolution that would not stop at having accomplished the correction of any definable injustice or grievance but would continue until all of society, all of mankind, had been made new. Babeuf, mainly an agitator and pamphleteer, had not conceived such ideas himself. Whose influence prompted him to instigate such a movement? What thinkers were his spiritual mentors? In his defense before the High Court of Justice, Babeuf refers to four men whose ideas guided him more than others: Rousseau, Diderot, Mably, and Morelly.[4] It is among these men and their intellectual kinfolk, then, that we could expect to find the original experiences underlying the total critique of society.

Of the four whom Babeuf mentioned, Morelly was the one who first formulated a systematic total critique of society, in 1753, three years before Rousseau's *Discours sur l'origine de l'inégalité*. Our search for the sources of the stream may therefore move directly from the landmark of Babeuf's conspiracy to that of Morelly's *Code de la Nature*, one of the foremost documents of socialism in mid-century France. There is, however, an even earlier and equally powerful socialist thinker who both in thought and practice set forth a total critique of society—Jean Meslier. Meslier's ideas must have had considerable influence on Babeuf through Sylvain Maréchal, who published an extract of Meslier's *Testament* and who was the theoretician of the group around Babeuf. Even though Babeuf does not expressly mention him, we shall therefore first turn to Meslier, then to Morelly, and finally to Mably. Rousseau and Diderot, as will become clear in the discussion of Meslier, Morelly, and Mably, need not receive separate treatment since they did not add anything to the total critique of society already formulated by the earlier thinkers. We shall, however, at the end return to Babeuf and his chronicler Buonarroti in order to trace the influence of the earlier ideas in Babeuf's revolutionary visions.

[4] See Victor Advielle, *Histoire de Gracchus Babeuf et du Babouvisme* (2 vols.; n.p., 1884).

MESLIER

Jean Meslier (1678–1729) was a curé in the little parish of Etrépigny who, having written a three-volume testimony "against governors and kings and the gentiles" (Matt. 10:18), died in a kind of hunger strike. Before his death, he had distributed three handwritten copies of his *Testament* through which he expected both to enlighten the people about the fraud perpetrated on them by their rulers and to incite them to insurrection against "les riches, les nobles, et les grands de la terre" (the rich, the high-placed, and the powerful of the world).[5] His work was known to Voltaire as early as 1735. Condensations of it were published by Voltaire (1762), d'Holbach (1772), and Sylvain Maréchal (1789). The latter was a prominent member of Babeuf's conspiracy, so that one can assume that Meslier's ideas were not unknown to the "Tribune of the People" of 1796. Meslier was both an atheist and a communist, more than twenty years before Morelly and forty before Mably. Unlike the socialists of the middle of the century, his ideas were formed not under the influence of Locke-Condillac but of Descartes.[6] At the same time, his work is above all an attack against the Cartesians of his time, particularly Malebranche.

The Destruction of God

Meslier's ambiguous relationship to Descartes is at the core of his thought. Descartes' sharp distinction between the world of the spirit and that of extended matter is his premise. He also accepts Descartes' method and the power which it confers on "ordinary minds" to arrive at truth through a succession of simple steps from general assumptions. Taking his stand in the material half of Descartes' universe he uses Descartes' own methods to annihilate the other half. With his equipment as a preacher trained in a

[5] Meslier, *Le Testament de Jean Meslier*, ed. C. Rudolf (3 vols.; Amsterdam, 1864). Hereinafter cited as Meslier, *Testament.*

[6] On Meslier and Descartes, *cf.* Johann Haar, *Jean Meslier und die Beziehungen von Voltaire und Holbach zu ihm* (Hamburg, 1928).

seventeenth century seminary, he examines what he believes to be the Christian religion, and, by analogy, all religion. By the yardstick of what God should be like if he existed, he finds all religion not only wanting, but utterly nonsensical. God is not seen, heard, or otherwise perceived. A living God would be perfectly good, wise, and powerful. Such a God would act in certain ways which are not the actual ways of nature and history. Meslier, in eight "proofs," refutes religion, showing up its inherent contradictions, contradictions with known facts, conflicts with "Nature," "absurdities," and iniquities committed in its name. Proceeding from the logical premise which he attributes to religion, the existence of a good, wise, and powerful Being of infinite perfection, he rejects biblical Revelation in the name of *bon sens*. Why should God have made himself known to only one people instead of all mankind? Why should he have revealed himself even to this people only by the vaguest of hints? Why should a good God have punished all men for the transgression of one person, and at that for a transgression as insignificant as the eating of an apple? Why should God have to be "hanged" in order to accomplish man's salvation?

One would be inclined to dismiss such arguments as based on a distorted, literal, fundamentalist, perfectionist caricature of religion drawn by one whose theological training put him in a position to know better, had not Meslier himself revealed that he was fully aware of what he was doing: he was perpetrating what Nietzsche, a century and a half later, called the "murder of God."[7] The crucial passage shows this clearly: "En un mot, la destruction ou la négation de Dieu n'emporte pas avec elle la destruction, ni la négation, de l'être matériel et sensible; mais, au contraire, la destruction ou la négation de l'être matériel et sensible détruit en même temp l'idée de tout être sensible." (In one word, the destruction or the negation of God does not entail the destruction or the negation of material and sensible existence; on the contrary, however, the destruction or the negation of material and sensible exis-

[7] *Cf.* Eric Voegelin, "The Murder of God," in *Science, Politics, and Gnosticism* (Chicago, 1968).

tence destroys at the same time the idea of any intelligent being.)[8]

The destruction of God, in other words, can be accomplished with impunity because it will not entail the annihilation of being. We shall see whether Meslier was right in this. At any rate, the destruction of God is the key operation through which Meslier lops off, from the Cartesian universe of being, the realm of transcendence and of the spirit. Unlike later anti-Cartesians, Meslier accomplishes this not with the weapons furnished by Locke but with Descartes' own intellectual tools. His relation to Descartes resembles Feuerbach's relation to Hegel a century later. Meslier is an eighteenth century "Left Cartesian."

The truncated remnant of being is what he calls, in the philosophical jargon of the time, "Nature." Accordingly, natural being is for him the sole and entire realm of being. Extension and motion are the basic categories of all that is real. The soul is nothing but the "blood" and "vital spirits" of the body. Material being is not created. It is not purposeful; all that exists is formed by an endless series of encounters between blind and accidental material forces. Life is a "fermentation," the same in man as it is in animals and vegetative matter. Nature, accomplishing the good of some at the expense of others, is characterized by a random mixture of good and evil. As a function of extension and motion, all being is fully knowable. Science, the exploration of nature, provides reliable and certain guidance in all matters of human life. Meslier's scientism rejects as deception all knowledge that is not gained by the methods through which nature is known. He obviously heeds Descartes' postulate to regard as truth only that which can be "clearly and distinctly" known. There can therefore be no knowledge regarding something that borders on mystery and knowledge cannot go beyond controllable matter. What is real can be known "clearly and distinctly" and only what can be so known is real. Meslier agrees that religion deals with mystery but not with the ultimate mystery of being, which he does not recognize. Rather, religion is the *mystère d'iniquité,* the deliberate mystification covering up social evils.

[8] Meslier, *Testament,* II, 337.

The "Order of Nature"

Meslier's key concept is the "order of nature," in keeping with the pattern of eighteenth century social philosophy. The meaning of "nature" here is far from clear. "Order of nature" is not a term for the Newtonian laws of energy, motion, mass, and weight. Not only does it extend to human existence and society but applies almost exclusively to this problem rather than the former. It means, on the one hand, a set of principles derived by simple logical steps from simple, general, and self-evident premises. On the other hand, it is the kind of order so derived from the general premise that human life is essentially a set of relations with a view to man's dependence on nature and purposes regarding nature. The "order of nature" thus does not refer to human nature, in the sense of a philosophical anthropology. It connotes, rather, a set of external relationships of men with one another, by and with the only reality they are supposed to have in common—material nature. It connotes the idea that community among men is realized in and through things, in their production and use.

"Order of nature" precludes rather than implies any transcendent purpose in the structure of being. Nature itself is merely regular, the result of the interaction of blind and purposeless forces. "Order of nature" as connoting social order, however, assumes actions and relations ordered toward conscious ends. These ends, the only ones there are, are set by the minds of men. In dealing with material nature, men act purposefully. Nature's own productions fashion themselves by their own motion. Men, however, form their products with materials that have themselves no movement. The motion is supplied by human hands, according to human purposes. It is in connection with these human "works of art," in the relations existing between men for the sake of the changes they want to produce in matter, that the concept "order of nature" becomes Meslier's formula for a social order of self-evident simplicity. Social order is the order of human relations in dealing with nature's materials, on the basis of nature's regularities. Meslier speaks of three basic relationships between men, with regard to natural materials: labor, possession, and consumption. Thus man is seen essentially as an artificer, both a dependent part of nature and nature's master. Given this fundamental premise, labor, possession, and consumption are indeed the only relevant problems of a social order. They are, for the same reason, as characteristic of Locke as of Marx.

Meslier's communism follows directly from these premises. His outline of a communistic society is not in the nature of a utopia, a deliberate attempt of the human mind to conceive of an ideal of future perfection. For Meslier, communism is the natural order of human life, an order which he takes for granted in its self-evident truth as he castigates the rulers of the present society for their "unnatural" political practices. His outline of a communistic society is not the final and crowning chapter of Meslier's work—that place is held by his call to insurrection—but rather a "commonsense" criterion by which he judges and condemns existing society, which judgment is in turn part of his sixth proof of the absurdity of religion. Essentially, Meslier's communism can be reduced to three propositions: universal obligation to work, common property, equality in consumption. These are indeed self-evident conclusions from an anthropology that sees man's dependence on and mastery of nature as his essential being. Labor is for Meslier, as for Marx, the central problem of human life. Labor being necessarily social, all individuality appears both irrelevant and accidental in its context. The important concern is compact solidarity in the accomplishment of man's purposed changes of nature. Property must be common, because nature is the common material ground on which man's purposes are to be realized. Participation in common labor takes the place of man's essential humanity. On the other hand, man as a dependent part of nature is a type rather than individuality, a type of being characterized by the "same kinds of organs and the same physical needs." Consumption, the satisfaction of these needs, can therefore be measured out only in equal shares. Inequality of possession must appear as a denial of the very concept of man. Rather, the place of a concept of man is taken by the concept of common life and work. This accounts for the fact that Meslier does not present his outline of a communistic society as a bold new program but as the underlying "natural" order of human existence which is hidden and buried under the existing "false" order of politics based on unequal property and religion.

The Ideological Annihilation of Existing Society

The contrast between a true but hidden "order of nature" and the false but extant structure of political power is the real axis of Meslier's revolutionary thoughts. As communism is not an ideal of future perfection but is the self-evident truth of human life, its realization is not a problem of history but rather of discovery, or rediscovery. Meslier is therefore neither a moralist like Mably nor a historicist like Condorcet and Fourier. The "order of nature" is already real. It does not come to fruition as the accomplishment of a particular age of historical development nor as a result of moral discipline. The crucial fact is, rather, that while the "order of nature" is real, men are actually subject to a regime that in all respects runs counter to the order of nature. That regime upholds and defends the inequality of possessions and rank, lays the burden of work on some and maintains others in leisure, keeps the masses in misery and a few in splendor, practices violence and warfare, deceives the people through religion, and enforces these conditions by harsh and punitive power. In other words, the political regime of the present, being diametrically opposed to the "order of nature," is totally "false," devoid of reality. This annihilation of existing society is the corollary of Meslier's destruction of God. He denies reality to man's present social existence. As the destruction of God became the vehicle by which he conferred the name of being exclusively on material nature, so the annihilation of existing society confers the attribute of reality on an "order of nature" which according to Meslier himself has no actuality anywhere. It cannot be experienced. It can be grasped only by that pure mind that has cleansed itself of all "prejudices," that is, influences and experiences of surrounding society. Meslier's entire social thought is thus projected from the Archimedean point of a hidden or rather clandestinely known reality, the full and public recovery of which appears as a work of redemption from falsehood, error, and evil.

What or who stands in the way of such public recovery of the hidden reality? Since the existing order is totally "false," the powers-that-be are necessarily tyrannous. Meslier applies the term "tyranny" to all governments in the world, refusing to make any distinctions of legitimacy or justice between them. Existing governments are tyrannies inasmuch as they are not founded on the "order of nature," as evidenced by their upholding of religion, unequal property, and privileges. As the entire political regime is evil, those who maintain it are wicked persons. Their wickedness consists in their identification with public falsehood and tyranny. Hence Meslier's formula "les riches, les nobles, and les grands de la terre" which totally condemns all who have power, rank, and benefits in the existing regimes. The formula explicitly includes not only the actual rulers but also their helpers and "flatterers." The entire company of the powerful—a concept which is reminiscent of Hitler's indictment of "the System"—constitutes a living obstacle to the recovery of reality and must therefore be overthrown.

Religion as Ideology

How is the fact of such evil power to be explained? Power, says Meslier, consists in the compliance of those who are ruled. The necessary basis of false power is therefore the blindness of the subjects who are being kept in error. It is the characteristic function of religion to accomplish this end. The "absurdity," falsehood, and inherent contradictoriness of religion is the fitting and indispensable basis on which alone a power regime contrary to the "order of nature" can exist. In other words, religion is to Meslier above all ideology, the deliberate blinding of human minds to truth with the intention to justify unjustifiable power interests. The false teachers of the people are the priests, "who do not themselves believe what they preach." If it were not for the *vaines superstitions* in which the priests keep the people, the *grands de la terre* would have no authority. The force which keeps false power in existence is thus *aveuglement*, public blindness. This can be remedied only by *lumières*, by enlightenment. The task of enlightenment is to destroy the prejudices inherited from generations of false living, so as to rediscover the "order of nature" in its marvelous simplicity and clarity. Meslier's strategy becomes obvious at this point. He himself, having cleared his mind of "prejudices," clandestinely knows nature's real order. His knowledge is necessarily clandestine, since he is entirely surrounded by the powers of falsehood and unreality. His knowledge of true reality must therefore be clandestinely spread. This Meslier accomplishes by writing in his own hand three copies of a work, which in print now covers more than a thousand pages, and by depositing these copies at three different points so that at least one of them would eventually be discovered. The removal of error by means of rational argument rather than the organization of a political movement is Meslier's revolutionary strategy. Once the blindness is dispelled, the position of the powers-that-be will become untenable. The people will no longer bend their necks under the "yoke of tyranny" (one of Meslier's favorite terms) and will drive out all kings, nobles, wealthy men, their retinue, and the priests.

The Causes of Evil

What would such a revolution accomplish? The existing regime is far more than just oppressive power: it is the source of all evil. "La source . . . de tous les maux . . . n'est autre que cette détestable politique des hommes." (The source of all evil is only that detestable system of human politics.)[9]

The existing regime is called by the name of "politics," implying that the characteristics of political power are found only in the presence of unequal possessions—an implication which led Marx and Engels later to anticipate the "withering away" of the state in

[9] *Ibid.*, I, 7.

a classless society. The system, by maintaining inequality of possessions, engenders and promotes cupidity. Private property induces men to amass as much wealth as they can, by means fair or foul. The ones who succeed are necessarily the most ruthless and malicious of all. The others are driven by their misery to seek an improvement of their condition, likewise by any means, fair or foul. The *Testament* begins with a bitter complaint of the *méchanceté,* the wickedness which Meslier had seen in his life. Cupidity, the passion aroused by property, is its sole cause. "De là naissent ensuite les murmures, les plaintes, les troubles, les séditions et les guerres qui causent une infinité de maux parmis les hommes. . . . De là viennent les fraudes, les tromperies, les fourbières, les injustices, les rapines, les vols, les larcines, les meurtres, les assassins, et les brigandages . . . ." (This is the source of the discontents, the complaints, the disorders, the rebellions, and the wars which cause countless evils among men . . . . From that root issue frauds, deceits, knaveries, injustices, robberies, thefts, pilferings, murders, manslaughters, and hold-ups. . . .)[10]

Property, the key institution of the existing power regime, is the motive of all crimes. The evil in the world is then the product of the false system prevailing in the world. Its maintenance is the chief concern of those who in this regime are rich, high-ranking, and powerful.

The Revolutionary Destruction of the Political Order

From this derives the division of all men into something like two camps. Meslier addressed the *Testament* to his parishioners, common people whom he exhorted to combine with other folk "similar to them" to overthrow "les riches, les nobles, et les grands de la terre." The parishioners of Étrépigny are thus representative of all common people. On the other side are the beneficiaries of the false regime. All men are thereby divided into those who have an interest in the prevailing system and those who do not. The former, by virtue of their identification with a tyrannical power, are

[10] *Ibid.*, II, 215.

evil. Their institutions and their rule are the very cause of evil. Their subjects, by contrast, are absolved from blame. Even though they are engaged in evil practices, they are victims rather than active defenders of the false regime. The existential fact of their subjection constitutes the seal of their innocence. Having no share in power, being the passive objects of public deception and pillage, they represent no evil but rather, by contrast, the only hope of mankind to recover nature's real order. Meslier's bipolarization of all social forces foreshadows Marx's later definition of the "only really revolutionary" class:

> . . . since in the living conditions of the proletariat all the living conditions of existing society are pointed up to their maximum inhumanity, since man in the proletariat has lost himself but at the same time gained . . . the theoretical consciousness of this loss . . . (and also, by circumstances,) is compelled to rebel against this inhumanity, the proletariat can and must free itself. It can, however, not free itself without abolishing its own living conditions. It cannot abolish its own living conditions without abolishing *all* inhuman living conditions in existing society, which are summed up in its own situation.[11]

This revolution of the victims against their spoilers will be the result of the victims' liberation from error. The fruit of their revolution will be not only emancipation from error but also from human evil. The insurrection of the people is thus a redemptive act—*the* act of human redemption.

It is the combined refusal of all the victims to continue in subjection to the false regime which removes the basis on which evil power has so far maintained itself. Unity is therefore the foremost requirement of the insurrection. Once the people unite in negation of the political order, false power will no longer have a foundation. It will collapse and vanish into thin air. Revolutionary unity, in turn, demands the universal enlightenment of the people about the error of religion in which the priests have kept the people through the centuries. Like Marx, Meslier sees the combination of

[11] Marx, "Die heilige Familie," in *Marx-Engels Werke*, II, 38.

correct (i.e., enlightened) consciousness and revolutionary solidarity as the two requirements of redemptive revolution. Once these requirements are met, the world's evil will be vanquished in the "death of the last tyrant, strangled by the entrails of the last priest."[12] The destruction of the prevailing political order through universal insurrection is the third of Meslier's great concepts of negation, a fitting corollary to the ideological destruction of God and the annihilation of society's reality. Like Bakunin, he sees in the sweeping away of the institutions and incumbents of power a creative act of salvation from evil, the only hope of truth. The total falseness of the prevailing system of power cannot be reformed. A return to reality is possible only through the destructive action of the only members of mankind who, not having shared evil power, are untainted and innocent. The force they practice is by its nature wholesome and creative.

Nothingness

Meslier felt that it was possible to destroy God, for the "destruction of God does not involve the destruction of material and rational being." Yet one wonders whether, having destroyed God, Meslier does not end up precisely without any being at all. The destruction of God leads him to annihilate all existential social reality: the forms in which men have lived, acted, and striven are for Meslier nothing but a snare and a delusion, a total falsehood. Man is for Meslier a part of a labor process, a typified link in the chain of productive activities. There is for him no essence of man and hence no essential significance of the concrete, living individuality. Nature, not being created, slips through his fingers as something without inherent direction, the accidental result of blind forces. History is utterly without meaning in a world unguided by Providence. What is left to him is the clandestine knowledge of a reality he perceives apart from experience, in the realm of speculation about the "order of nature," plus the hope in liberation from false power by the upheaval of the saintly masses. One wonders whether he, at the end of his labors, began to realize the void into which he had

[12] The phase is actually used in the *Testament,* although Meslier did not coin it.

maneuvered himself. The *Testament* ends with a sentence expressing despair, not a mere despair of historical success, but metaphysical despair, the "black mood" of Pascal: "Je finirai donc ceci par le rien, aussi ne suis-je guères plus que rien, et bientôt je ne serai rien, etc." (I shall finish this with nothingness; but then I am hardly anything more than nothing, and soon I shall be nothing, etc.)[13]

The thrice repeated emphasis of the word "nothing" is a profoundly eloquent outburst declaring a nihilism that has enveloped the man who thought it safe to destroy God.

Meslier's revolution is neither utopian nor futuristic. He does not see human life as moving toward perfection in the course of history. Perfection is not the fruit of either automatic progress or the continued process of divine creation in partnership with finite man. Perfection, if it has any relation to time, lies in the past; but, more properly speaking, it is contemporaneous reality, although it is not actualized in historical societies. Hence, it is grasped not in the experiences of this life nor through any hints in man's actual existence, but only by the speculative mind which attains and maintains its knowledge in secret opposition to the powers and the prejudices of this world. The insurrection of which Meslier dreams is meant to be a victory of a secretly known reality over the unreal works and structures of historical societies. Into the present world of falsehood, the Truth will irrupt and its power will sweep the thrones and the palaces before it. Meslier and the Truth are allied in the revolutionary rejection of all that is. "Whatever is, is wrong," said Louis Blanc more than a hundred years later. Meslier could have replied: "Whatever is wrong, is not; but what is can be known by the insurrectionist mind." Meslier's knowledge of the invisible reality is the justification of a permanent and total revolution.

MORELLY

The person and life of the author of the *Code de la Nature* (1755) have remained obscure to this day. For a while, the public attributed the book to Diderot. Now it is known as the work of

[13] Meslier, *Testament,* III, 398.

Morelly, the author of the allegorical poem *Basiliade* (1753). There is a question whether the author of these two books was the same Morelly who published in 1743 the *Essai sur l'esprit humain*, in 1745 the *Essai sur le cœur humain*, and in 1751 *Le Prince*. Lichtenberger assumes that there are two Morellys, father and son, while Dolléans and Chinard attribute all of these works to the same person. Without going into the details of the controversy, I shall take my stand with Lichtenberger, on the ground that, even though some common ideas seem to run through all five books, the *Basiliade* and the *Code* utterly differ from the other three books in their philosophy. The earlier works accept the existing political order, and analyze it within the framework of Locke's and Hobbes's political theories. The *Basiliade* and the *Code*, by contrast, consider the existing society as totally false and unreal and point to the all but forgotten "order of nature" as the sole reality. The appearance of common ideas running through all five books is easily explained as the intellectual pattern of the time which imposed itself on even the most divergent philosophies. Underneath the surface similarity, the basic outlook of the earlier three books is simply incompatible with that of the *Basiliade* and the *Code*, nor is there any indication that the author of the former was developing in a direction that could have allowed him to conceive of the world as the author of the latter did. It is, then, the mind that created the *Basiliade* and the *Code* who concerns us here, even though the question of his true identity may remain unsolved.

The message of these two works—the confrontation of the real "order of nature" with the unreal regime of civilization—is fully contained in the *Basiliade*,[14] which Morelly presented to the public in poetic form. The reason for this form is part of the argument itself, for, as he said, the general state of reason in existing society is so deplorable that "one must make a thousand efforts, use a thousand stratagems, in order to tear away the veil that blinds it (reason) and to make it turn its eyes toward the true interests of

[14] Morelly, *Naufrage des Isles Flottantes ou Basiliade du célèbre Pilpai* (2 vols.; n.p., 1753). Hereinafter cited as *Basiliade*.

humanity." His "stratagems" are the devices of a fantastic tale attributed to the "famous Indian sage, Pilpai," concerning two kingdoms, one, happy, representing the true order and governed by a prince named Zeinzemin, the other a miserable and strife-torn country subject to a false morality and false political regime. The plot of the tale turns around the conflict between two groups of allegorical "genies" (*dives*) who intervene in the human events with supernatural powers. On the one side are Nature and Truth (Nature, "the mother of Truth"), on the other side, Interest, Error, and Falsehood. Nature and Truth are worshipped in the kingdom of Zeinzemin, the Vices in the "Floating Islands," the place where the other regime prevails. The tale ends with the victory of Nature and Truth and the destruction, not only of the Floating Islands, but also of the false genies, in a natural catastrophe. The *Code* expressly and repeatedly refers to the *Basiliade* in the way of a commentary on the lessons of the poem, and it seems intended to be chiefly a discursive explanation of the underlying philosophy of man and society. In any study of Morelly, the accent should therefore be on the *Basiliade* and its symbolism, even though it is useful to resort to the explicit formulations of the *Code* for purposes of interpretation.

The Destruction of the Moral Order

It is obvious that the regime under the sway of "Interest, Error, and Falsehood" is supposed to portray the order of things as it has prevailed in history for "6–7000 years"—that is, for the entire duration of history. Its core is the false "cult of Interest" which, aided by Error and Falsehood, "governs the earth by a multitude of prejudices." Reason, "seduced or oppressed, languishes under the yoke of these tyrants, or lends itself cowardly to their whims."[15] The "multitude of prejudices" is a reference to "vulgar morality"—that is, the moral order governing men and their institutions. Morelly identifies the historical world, that is, society as it has been known for "6–7000 years," with this "vulgar morality" and its erroneous

[15] Morelly, *Basiliade*, II, 33, 43.

assumptions concerning man and order. The entire world of human society thus has been ruled by Error and Falsehood. The symbolism of the *Basiliade* must be taken seriously. "Vulgar morality" bears down on sin, though in reality there is no sin. Morality's precepts are based on false premises. As normative commands designed to repress natural inclinations, they introduce into human existence the alienation of ought from is, of thought and action. This conflict between precept and nature is itself the source of needless tensions, so that morality, far from being a cure for human evils, actually is their cause. In the truth of "natural order"—an order which is not reflected in the historical world—human needs, forces, and passions are arranged in perfect harmony and require no specific moral regime.

Morelly believes in God, but in a God who is twice removed from human existence and human action. Human existence is for Morelly entirely bound up within the world-immanent setting of "Nature." To be sure, nature itself has been created. Morelly explicity rejects the kind of materialism which is Meslier's credo.[16] But the author of nature is not the judge of human beings or the Providence in human history. In fact, he is so much beyond human reach that there is no possibility of a theology above and beyond a science of nature. In the half-ruined and forgotten temple of Truth, which Zeinzemin, in the *Basiliade*, happens to discover in a desolate part of the Floating Islands, a line is drawn all around the wall, with the inscription: "Jusqu'ici peuvent s'étendre les sages conjectures sur les bontés de l'Être Suprême à ton égard; mais tu tenterais en vain de pénétrer au delà." (Thus far can one push cautious guesses about the Supreme Being's kindnesses regarding you; but any attempt to penetrate further will be in vain.)[17] God, in other words, is nothing but the prime mover of the world. Man, in his quest for order, can only turn to the equilibrium of nature. Morelly thus reduces the problem of order to that of existence, and existence itself to its world-immanent aspects. First, he eliminates the very concept of a final cause, an order of *summum bonum* of con-

[16] *Ibid.*, 211.

[17] *Ibid.*, 238.

scious actions. God is not the source nor the end of any moral order. Morelly ridicules the notion that God could be offended or that he would punish transgressors.[18] Nor does he consider it permissible to link the problem of good with any future life and the hopes and fears pertaining to it. Rather, the sole object of wisdom is man's "present happiness."[19] Having severed man's actions from any transcendent end, he then limits man's existence to the world-immanent framework of nature. The notion of a divine prime mover has no other significance than the assurance that nature in itself is orderly and harmonious. The order and harmony of nature, that is, of inanimate, animal, and vegetative being, thus becomes man's sole source of authority. Reason, in other words, is reduced to the faculty of learning and observing the secrets of animals, plants, and stones. Human order is the "extension . . . of the regularity and the beautiful order of inanimate things."[20] Both works of Morelly, but particularly the *Basiliade*, abound in pointed references to the way in which trees, mammals, and insects exist in harmony with their kind and their environment. Morelly thus reverses Aristotle's hierarchy of being which recognizes human reason as the specific faculty through which human life, though dependent on the animal, vegetative, and inanimate levels, ranks higher than and rules above the lower orders of nature. His elevation of the animal, vegetative, and inanimate realms of being to ruling rank destroys both the specific quality of human life and the orientation of human actions towards a highest good, the moral order.

Morelly's annihilation of the moral order results in a radical divorce between the divinely established potential order he calls "Nature" and the actual world of history. The historical world does not in any way reflect God and his order, it contains no evidence of the truth of existence. Still, the historical world, too, is a creation. It is the work of "human reason, this created deity."[21] As a creation having the semblance of order it is, however, senseless, evil, devoid

[18] Morelly, *Code de la Nature,* ed. Gilbert Chinard (Paris, 1950), 261 *passim.* Hereinafter cited as *Code.*

[19] *Ibid.*, 283.

[20] Morelly, *Basiliade*, I, 106.

[21] Morelly, *Code*, 261.

of reality. Morelly thus finds himself in a world that has been created by an evil demiurge. Evil, he says, cannot come from any other source but rational creatures—that is, misguided rational creatures. God has established in nature an "infallible principle of innocence." Hence the historical world has no part in God or nature, and man is a stranger to this society and to himself. He is separated from God, nature, and true existence by the very world he has created and in which he finds himself. This historical world roots in the negation of knowledge, it is shaped by institutionalized Error. Having no link with man's true self through knowledge, the world is actually nothing but an alien power. It tyrannizes both man's mind and man's existence. "Vulgar morality" is known by the harsh authority with which it imposes its precepts. Similarly, political authority, being unable to ally itself with man's natural inclinations, maintains itself by senseless insistence on rank and by the brute wielding of force.

The "Order of Nature"

So far, the structure of Morelly's thought bears strong resemblance to the radical dualism characteristic of the Gnosis of the first three centuries. In Gnostic thought, man, too, feels radically separated from the world in which he finds himself, but believes himself linked to a nonexistential God through the knowledge of *pneuma*, the spirit, so that God and man are, in a sense, allied against that which separates them, the world of existence.[22] The significant difference is that the true knowledge, in which Morelly as well as the Gnostics saw man's reality, is, in Morelly's case, not knowledge of a radically transcendent God but of the immanent "order of nature." God is beyond knowledge and reach, life after death must be discounted; man's concern is with "present happiness," which, in the context, means life in the setting of nature.[23]

It is Morelly's Deism which induces him to look to nature for the potential and yet alone real order that is "not of this world," although at times it may appear that Locke's sensationalism might

[22] *Cf.* Hans Jonas, *The Gnostic Religion* (2nd ed.; Boston, 1963), 320.
[23] Morelly, *Code*, 283.

have suggested to him that man is at birth, and thus essentially, a creature solely aware of his physical needs and their satisfaction. At any rate, this satisfaction is and remains the central concern of man. "The true political freedom of man consists in the enjoyment, without obstacle or fear, of anything that can satisfy his natural and very legitimate appetities."[24] Man, in need of physical objects, finds also that he is individually weak and subject to manyfold dangers. He is therefore dependent on help and feels himself attracted to whatever or whoever helps him. This *attraction morale* is the natural bond of society. Society is not a contract between independent individuals but a tightly knit and unified "whole" (*un Tout*), which only as a collectivity can realize man's purposes in relation with nature.[25] The realization of man's purposes in nature requires *prévoyance unanime*[26]—that is, collective planning for a "common utility." Man can thus exist in harmony with his appetites and with nature only when performing collective work on nature's materials, which ought to be nobody's private property, and by a rigidly enforced scheme of divided labor. Only the consumption of the products thus obtained must be in common, nature having made sure, through the variety of tastes and the staggering of momentary needs, that there will never be any material want.[27] In this natural order of existence, it could not occur to any one individual to do another harm. Man's goodness is thus simply an aspect of his daily functional dependence; so is his religion. In the *Basiliade*, Zeinzemin's subjects worship God not by specific prayers of praise and

[24] *Ibid.*, 219.

[25] "Ce n'étoit point là les intentions de la suprême Sagesse; elles vouloit faire de l'espèce humaine un Tout intelligent qui s'arrangeât lui-même par un méchanisme aussi simple que merveilleux; ses parties étoient préparées, et, pour ainsi dire, taillées pour former le plus bel assemblage." (The intentions of the Highest Wisdom aimed at something else: they wanted to make of the human race an intelligent Whole that would order itself by a simple and wonderful mechanism; the parts of which were prepared and, as it were, tailor-made to fit together in the most beautiful assemblage.) *Ibid.*, 166. Here are all the basic concepts of Morelly's "order of nature": Humanity as a whole is a "mechanism," the parts of which are by nature fitted to interlock. At other places Morelly speaks of the "merveilleux *automate* de la société" (the wonderful automaton of society). *Ibid.*, 169. These remarks prefigure the Feuerbach-Marxian concept of man as a "species being."

[26] *Ibid.*, 178. [27] *Ibid.*, 167.

supplication but through the daily functions of work in harmonious sociability. In this society, rulership is not power. Zeinzemin is described as an "expert in the things of nature." He guides his people not by moral precepts or punitive laws but by his personal charm and heart-winning attraction, an ancient art the "seductive secrets" of which have been passed down in his family.[28] The passions of man are the prime causes of sociability, since they are innocent by nature and become vicious only when distorted by "false necessities"—the necessities caused by private property. Such are the features of the real order, the sole order whose principles can be "mathematically demonstrated"—that is, discovered by the mind that succeeds in elevating himself above the "prejudices," the moral laws of historical society.[29] To exist apart from this natural order means to live "outside of truth," which has been the characteristic feature of the entire history of civilization.[30] At a few places, Morelly does find in the world of experience an example of the kind of society which is a copy of the true order. Thus, he compares it in the *Basiliade* with the state of the bees[31] and, more significantly, with the managerial totalitarianism of the Incas in ancient Peru.[32]

The Rejection of Historical Society

For six to seven thousand years, as long as mankind has lived under laws, the natural order has been "contradicted" by the rulers of human societies.[33] The original sin which brought about man's divorce from the divine order was the "partage monstrueux des productions de la Nature et des élements même en divisant ce qui

[28] Morelly, *Basiliade,* I, 39. [29] *Ibid.*, I, p. xxxvii.

[30] " . . . dans l'ordre moral, la Nature est une, constante, invariable, . . . ses loix ne changent point, et . . . sont en général tout ce qui produit dans les créatures animees des inclinations paisibles, et tout ce qui en détermine les mouvements; . . . au contraire, tout ce qui éloigne des ces doux panchans, est dénaturé, c'est à dire, sort de la Nature." (In the moral order, nature is one, constant, invariable, . . . its laws never change and . . . are in general what produces in animated creatures peaceful inclinations; whatever causes contrary movements, whatever draws away from such gentle bents is denatured, in other words, outside of nature. Morelly, *Code*, 184.

[31] *Ibid.*, 7. [32] *Ibid.*, xxxvii.

[33] *Ibid.*, 178.

devoit rester dans son entier," the monstrous division of nature's products and even its elements.[34] In other words, private property is the basic act of man's rebellion against nature, the equivalent of Adam's sin of pride in wanting to be like God. From this basic disobedience have flowed all the evils known to humanity, above all the root vice, avarice. "The only vice which I know in the universe is avarice . . . this is the Proteus, the Mercury, the foundation, the vehicle of all the vices."[35] The "false necessities" created by private property have corrupted the original innocent passions, above all that of self-love (*amour de soi, amour propre*). Self-love, by nature the innocent desire to preserve one's existence, is in the order of nature the source of an *affection bienfaisante*, and thus of sociability. Private property corrupts this passion into unlimited greed. The *désire d'avoir*, the lust of possession, is the "knife which cuts the social bond." Thus, in the presence of private property, there can be no society. What takes its place is a structure of power, without any obligating normative significance. The corruption of man's innocent passions into raging monsters driving men to evil actions is the characteristic product of this alien regime.

Morality pretends to stem the tide of such corrupted passions by its teachings but its claim is a lie. "There can be no virtue, no wisdom other than that which restrains not the passions but the prejudices that cause passions to be impetuous and harmful."[36] In order to justify itself, morality teaches a false concept of man. It makes men believe that evil is rooted in their hearts. In so doing, it presents man "not as he has been formed by nature, but as he has become as the result of many centuries of obedience to laws."[37] Just as false and senseless is the focusing of all social norms on the problem of distributive justice.[38] The historical social regimes carry no inner obligation because they are instructed by false teachers. Their usurpation of authority has produced nothing but a body of

[34] Morelly, *Code*, 206.
[35] *Ibid.*, 171.
[36] Morelly, *Basiliade*, II, 27n.
[37] Morelly, *Code*, 183.
[38] ". . . le bel axiom, *Cuique suum,* c'est dommage que les parts n'en puissent jamais être égales: à quoi servent donc les balances de la justice?" (. . . regarding the fine principle, *suum cuique*, what a pity that the parts can never be equal; what, then, is the use of the balance of justice?) Morelly, *Basiliade*, I, 189.

preachings and rules that is lugubrious, harsh, life-destroying, and contrary to man's natural inclinations. The entire system is therefore effectual power but power that is meaningless and not obligating. More: it is harmful power. It engenders "a multitude of interests, of various prejudices which are perennial subjects of discord and of crimes otherwise unheard of."[39] On his visit to the Floating Islands, Zeinzemin, in the *Basiliade*, speaks of the "terrible menace of your laws."[40] The historical regimes have "divided humanity," their citizens feel that "the interests of the country are no longer ours."[41] Their life is nothing but "an ocean of evils."[42] The citizens of these regimes cannot even be called human. In the *Basiliade*, a group of them is described as "une foule d'hommes, ou plutôt de monstres de différentes figures, qui ne ressemblent à l'homme que par la tête" (a crowd of men or, rather, monsters of various shapes, resembling men only in the head).[43] Even their awareness of God is distorted in proportion as property corrupts man's innate inclination to *bienfaisance*. Hence in a false regime, God is dishonored by religion's "ridiculous proofs."[44] The regime of laws, in which men find themselves, bears thus no evidence whatsoever of reality and truth. Men persist in it in a state of blindness, a kind of death-sleep of their minds, in which they mistake the effectiveness of the regime's power for existential reality. They have forgotten and neglected the temple of Truth, as they pay homage to the idol "Interest, the child of Property and Luck." The social world is here in effect, but it fails to speak to human hearts or minds, it cannot bind their wills or loyalties. It is a world of nonexistence. Its location, the Floating Islands, is a fitting symbol of its insubstantiality.

The Destruction of Historical Society

The way of salvation requires the dethronement of "vulgar morality" and the destruction of the entire regime based on it.[45] This

[39] *Ibid.*, I, 45.
[40] *Ibid.*, II, 99.
[41] *Ibid.*, II, 67.
[42] *Ibid.*, II, 77.
[43] *Ibid.*, II, 9. The reference to the "head" is obviously a symbol indicating that man's essence is in his faculty of knowledge, his *gnosis*.
[44] Morelly, *Code*, 200.
[45] "De plus, comme je prétens que la Morale vulgaire s'est établie sur les ruines

is the task of the exceptional man who, in the midst of a world of blindness, possesses knowledge of the truth. In the *Basiliade*, it is Fadilah, a citizen of the Floating Islands but Zeinzemin's friend, who, together with a few primitive fishermen (another significant symbol!), is the only one to grasp Zeinzemin's wisdom of Nature. It is Fadilah who, on a visit to the Islands, leads Zeinzemin to the hidden and forgotten temple of Truth where are encarved the ruined remnants of forgotten knowledge. There is no need to emphasize that Fadilah is Morelly, the rediscoverer of the "wisdom of all time."[46] Hence, the *Basiliade* is a tale attributed to the pen of one Pilpai, "la perle des philosophes et de toute la terre,"[47] and the title page of Morelly's second book reads: "Code de la Nature, ou le véritable Esprit de ses Loix. De tout temps négligé ou méconnu. Par-Tout. Chez le Vrai Sage." ("Code of Nature, or the True Spirit of its Laws. At all times unheeded and unacknowledged. Everywhere. Publ. by The Real Sage.") The opening sentence of this book likewise speaks of "verities which, in spite of their simplicity and obviousness, have remained in oblivion through almost all time." Salvation, in other words, is through the rekindled light of knowledge, of *gnosis*. The discovery, or rediscovery of the real order, in opposition to the historical world, is an awakening of man from the sleep of error to an awareness to the true order. There can be no question for Morelly that such enlightenment will sweep the false regime of property and morality away: "Begin by allowing full freedom for the true sages to attack the errors and prejudices which maintain the spirit of property: once this monster is cornered, see that education should fortify this happy reform; it will not be difficult any more to get your peoples to adopt laws . . . in order to keep them from becoming wicked."[48] The power of knowledge here must be understood not merely in psychological terms. The liberating effect of the rediscovery of nature comes from the

---

des loix de la Nature, il faudroit entièrement renverser celle-là pour rétablir celles-ci." (Moreover, since I maintain that vulgar morality has been established on the ruins of the laws of nature, one must wholly overturn the former in order to reestablish the latter.) *Ibid.*, 180.

[46] Morelly, *Basiliade*, I, p. viii.

[47] *Ibid.*, I, p. v.

[48] Morelly, *Code*, 284.

joining of forces between man's *pneuma* and the forces of divinity, both strangers to the world of history. Once man's mind makes contact with reality, the false world will inevitably go down. It is no empty figure of speech but a highly significant symbol that the Floating Islands, where the false regime is located, are vanquished in an act of physical destruction wrought by the genie Nature, after Fadilah and his fishermen have made their commitment to the true order.

The victory won and the false world once destroyed, this "happy reform" must be fortified. The task is to be accomplished by a totally new legislation which is no longer based on the morality of distributive justice but on the logic of divided labor and common consumption. The object of this legislation is the same as that of Morelly's writings: "To find an arrangement [*une situation*] in which it would be almost impossible for man to be depraved or wicked, or, at least, *minima de malis*."[49] Accordingly, the fourth part of his *Code* consists of a model of such rules. The first three laws read as follows:

> I
>
> Nothing in society is held in private property, except those things of which a person may make use either for his daily needs, his pleasure, or his daily work.
>
> II
>
> Every citizen will be maintained and employed at public expense.
>
> III
>
> Every citizen will contribute to the public utility whatever he can, in accordance with his strength, his talents, and his age; on these factors will be based his duties, as regulated by the Distributive Laws.[50]

The destruction of the historical regime and the "fortification" of this victory will guarantee the work of salvation: "There will be no more furious passions, no more ferocious actions, no more prejudice, no more idea of moral evil."[51] Man will be restored to his *probité naturelle*. He will once again acknowledge God and remain free from atheism, for "neither happiness nor innocence have ever

[49] *Ibid.*, 160.
[50] *Ibid.*, 286.
[51] *Ibid.*, 247.

lead anyone to atheism."[52] The harmony of man with nature, God, his fellow beings, and himself will be perfect, nevermore to be endangered.

MABLY

The Abbé de Mably (1709–1785), a brother of the philosopher Condillac, was the most widely read teacher of the socialist gospel in the immediate prerevolutionary period. His best known work, the *Entretiens de Phocion*, was published in 1763, his *De la Législation ou Principes des Loix* in 1776, his *Principes de Morale* and *Étude de l'Histoire* a year before his death. Like Meslier and Morelly, he could conceive of the "natural order of society" only as a socialist egalitarian community. Unlike his two predecessors, however, this premise did not lead him to a total critique of society or radical revolution. Since Mably's thought follows the by now familiar pattern, a shorter treatment of his ideas will suffice to explain these similarities and dissimilarities.

The "Order of Nature" and the Fall of Man

"Nature," says Mably, "has established the law of equality to our forefathers and has declared her intentions so clearly that it is impossible not to understand it. . . . Has she not given to all men the same organs, the same needs, the same reason? Did not the good with which she has strewn the earth belong to all in common? Where did one find a principle of inequality?"[53] Mably's reference to "men as they emerge from the hands of nature" does not connote a concept of natural existence, an existence ordered by the relations between man's physical needs and the materials nature offers for their satisfaction. On the contrary, he expressly rejects a derivation of society from the needs of physical subsistence or the satisfaction of natural desires. "Social institutions," he insists, "are not established because man is an animal that must be nourished,

[52] *Ibid.*, 282.
[53] Gabriel B. de Mably, "De la législation ou des principes des loix," in Mably, *Oeuvres complètes* (12 vols.; Lyon, 1792), IX, 43.

but because he is intelligent and has feeling [*sensible*]."[54] It is thus significant that he emphasizes not collective labor but rather equality as the salient feature of the "order of nature." Natural equality, moreover, is not a fact but a principle which can be realized only by a conscious rational effort. "The physical and moral qualities of individuals are not equal, and if one leaves individuals to themselves, equality would soon be destroyed."[55] Mably also refuses to imitate Morelly in comparing human affairs with the realm of animal or vegetative being: "It is bizarre to want to compare the physical equilibrium and the moral equilibrium, or to think that their effects are the same."[56] Mably's equality in the state of nature must thus be understood as a moral postulate, and the "order of nature," accordingly, as a rational ideal rather than a latent existential reality.

Even though it may at times appear as if Mably had joined Morelly in the deification of Nature (nature "has intentions," "wisdom," is *bienfaisante*, has created individual *amour propre* in perfect harmony with society, etc.), there is a decisive difference between Mably and Morelly. For Mably, "nature" is not a concept denoting the whole of reality, as it is for Morelly. Mably recognizes that both faith and reason point to realities beyond nature. God is not identified with nature, nor is the moral order. The order of society belongs to the realm of morality and religion, not to that of animal and vegetative nature. "Order of nature" is for Mably therefore nothing but a formula that expresses belief in the potential social harmony of rational and sentient beings here on earth, the element of "nature" emphasizing the immanent character of this possible perfection of society. The harmony, moreover, is under no circumstances automatic or instinctive but depends on the awareness and conscious actualization of the moral precepts of reason, precepts that are derived from a divine source. This is eighteenth century rationalism in its purest form; a rationalism that may toy with the idea of a "state of nature" in which passions are imagined to have been more harmonious than they are in the pres-

[54] Mably, "Doutes proposés aux philosophes économistes sur l'ordre naturel et essentiel des sociétés politiques," in *ibid.*, XI, 25.

[55] *Ibid.*, 18.

[56] *Ibid.*, 231.

ent state of civilization, but nevertheless puts its ultimate trust not in a natural equilibrium of the passions but in the rule of moral principle over them. "The passions are as old as the world and have always been at strife with each other as well as consistent in their errors."[57]

The "state of nature" of Mably need therefore not be taken too seriously as the image of a golden age to which mankind should return. It should, however, be taken most seriously as an indispensable concept in a new version of the fall of man. Mably very clearly understands the present corruption of society as the result of definite historical occurrences. At a certain time in history, mankind departed from a past condition of harmony which in its original form can still be found "in the forests of Africa and America,"[58] and thus must have been historical reality elsewhere. This construction serves Mably as a vehicle to analyze the present society as a fallen society without having to trace the fall to a rupture of man's relation with the divinity. The fall is, nevertheless, a story, the beginning of a drama in which we are still involved, a historical event with continuing consequences. According to his version, however, it resulted from man's disobedience not to God but rather to the rules of a perfect immanent society. If the drama began within the framework of world-immanent society, it can also be brought to a happy conclusion within the same framework. Salvation, in other words, can be achieved by society through a return to the true order of society.

Man's departure from the correct rules of social order, the cause of the present evil and misery, occurred with the introduction of "inequality" or unequal property which set off a chain reaction of bad institutions and sinister passions.[59] Human corruption thus stems from incorrect institutions and mistaken laws. Under the

[57] Mably, "Principes de Morale," in *Oeuvres complètes*, X, 208.

[58] Mably, "De la législation," 84.

[59] ". . . l'inégalité des fortunes et des conditions décompose, pour ainsi dire, l'homme et altère les sentiments naturels de son coeur . . ." ". . . cette chaîne de tous nos vices, dont le premier anneau tient à l'inégalité des fortunes . . . ." (. . . the inequality of financial and social positions distorts man, as it were, and changes the natural inclinations of his heart . . . that chain of all our vices of which the first link is attached to the inequality of estate.) *Ibid.*, 37, 40.

influence of the institution of inequality, man's psychology has changed. There appeared new vices of which the arch-vice is, of course, avarice. It is not ambition that has bred avarice, but rather avarice ambition.[60] Ambition could be said to root in man's pretensions against God but avarice is exclusively a sin against equality. Ambition can be said to inhere in man's heart but avarice can be blamed on the external condition of inequality. The derivation of ambition from avarice is the corollary of Mably's new story of the fall. The laws of historical societies, insofar as they have been dictated by these passions, have left a record of misery, calamities, and disasters which is the characteristic of history.[61] Morelly, contrasting the "false political world" with the "order of nature," found the former not merely corrupted but altogether unreal. Mably, for whom the "order of nature" is above all a rational moral ideal, finds it wicked but unfortunately real.

Morality and Religion

Even though the historical world is a fallen world, it is, for Mably, not devoid of reality. There is a moral order, an order of reason, which is real since God has taught us our duties.[62] The reality of the moral order thus hinges on the reality of God. Unlike Morelly, who sees God as nothing but the prime mover of nature, Mably knows of God as our judge and as the "master of all things." God is real in history because he has instructed our reason and motivates our moral obligation. Apart from divine reward and punishment, men would have no cause to behave morally. "If there were no God, there would be no morality."[63] Mably's God is not the God who miraculously reveals himself to man nor the God who offers man the gift of his grace, but rather the God who is seen as identified with man's practical reason. He is the God who speaks through the mouth of the moralist. Morality is the pivot on which Mably's entire concept of society turns, and his authority as a

[60] *Ibid.*, 59.
[61] *Ibid.*, 151.
[62] Mably, "Des droits et des devoirs du citoyen," in Mably, *Oeuvres complètes*, XI, 264.
[63] Mably, "De la législation," 324.

moralist depends on religion. No wonder that this eighteenth century egalitarian demands that governments be intolerant regarding religion: they should give their full attention to preventing any change in religion or the rise of a new faith.[64] Even in fallen society, the voice of real order is thus still heard by man, as God is still known. In the midst of vices, there are some people "of character," men who cultivate their reason and listen to it.[65] The reality of God and of the moral order confers, in turn, reality on the laws of society. Men could not live without laws. The "order of nature" is not a self-executing harmony of existence in which the passions would beneficially equilibrate man's actions. The passions, rather, dispose men often not to listen to the voice of reason. This creates the need for a public authority.[66] Laws are both necessary and real; the trouble with present society is not that its laws establish no order but that they do not make for a good order. All that is needed is, therefore, to instruct the legislators in the right principles of legislation. Society and its laws are not nothing, they are merely wrongly oriented. Rather than being destroyed, they must be reformed.

The Reform of Society

It becomes clear why Mably indulges neither in a total critique of society nor in revolutionary schemes. The "order of nature" for him is not an alternative reality or even the exclusive reality but a principle to be injected into the very real legal institutions of the historical world. Nor is nature a "golden age" to which mankind could return. The present world, corrupt as it is, is the only one which exists for us. Hence Mably, unlike Morelly, does not feel that there is any magic power in the spreading of knowledge about the order of nature, or that awareness of nature's principles would

[64] *Ibid.*, 389.
[65] Mably, "Principes de Morale," 260.
[66] Mably, "De la législation," 57. Mably expressly rejects also the sufficiency of Morelly's order of collective labor when he says: "(l'homme) peut se passer de cultiver la terre; mais rien ne peut le dispenser de faire des lois." (Man may do without cultivating the ground; but nothing can relieve him from the making of laws.) Mably, "Doutes proposés," 25.

destroy the illusory world of politics. Such preaching, he felt, would necessarily remain ineffectual, for the rich would not listen to it, and even if they might, the poor would reject it as something to which they are unaccustomed.[67] What, then, is the hope of improvement for this world?

The laws are real, meaningful, and have effect, so are the institutions created by them. The reform of society must thus be a work of legislated change. The model Mably has ultimately in mind is the authoritarian regime established by the Jesuits in Paraguay.[68] The greatest possibly equality should prevail among men, mainly as regards their wealth and their dignity. In order to accomplish this ideal, the laws must make strategic use of the now corrupted passions—a point of great importance which shows clearly that Mably accepted the world as it is as the real setting of human existence. Envy, jealousy, ambition, pride, vanity may through proper institutional devices be turned into competition, patriotism, prudence, firmness, heroism.[69] The reform of society is thus not a reform of the individual human heart but the creation of institutions that are capable of turning individual malice into public blessings. This typical eighteenth century trust in institutions is the logical consequence of the idea that an original moral harmony has been disturbed by nothing else but mistaken institutions. Institutions have brought about the fall, institutions can now save. Meantime, while men are still under the influence of avarice and ambition, the most important safeguard against the passions of those who make laws is to establish "countervailing forces."[70] The study of this device is recommended to political scientists as their most important business. The changes that are to be legislated are deep and pervading; the legislators cannot proceed by force but must as often as not resort to ruse, in dealing with resisting forces. All in all, Mably feels, the needed changes can most easily be accomplished where there is self-government,[71] so that democracy is here advocated not

[67] Mably, "De la législation," 80. [68] Mably, "Doutes proposés," 7.
[69] Mably, "Entretiens de Phocion," in Mably, *Oeuvres complètes*, X, 186.
[70] Mably, "Étude de l'histoire," in *ibid.*, XII, 277.
[71] *Ibid.*

because it entails human freedom but because it lends itself best to sweeping programs of legislated change.

Mably is conventionally numbered among the precursors of communism. There is some superficial justification for such a judgment, since Mably preached absolute egalitarianism and blamed private property for being the source of all historical evils. However, it is significant that if Mably was a communist or socialist, he was not a revolutionary nor an adherent of a total critique of society. He cannot be listed among those who inspired the movements of total destruction characteristic of revolutionary communism. It becomes clear, in the case of Mably, that socialist premises need not lead to revolutionary conclusions but may issue in the political program of modern democratic liberalism: separation of powers, governments elected by universal franchise, progressively egalitarian legislation. Mably parts company with the revolutionists Meslier and Morelly when he acknowledges the reality of the moral order and on this basis conceives the world of historical society as the proper field of activity. Man, no matter how wicked, is still susceptible to discipline and improvement.[72] Nature is not a hidden reality but the ideal yardstick by which legislation ought to be guided. Legislation itself becomes the foremost instrument of human formation. "If they would let me do it, I would give them much more rigid laws than Plato."[73] Mably demands not the total power of gnostic destruction but a moralistic dictatorship run by the public planner of human virtue.

There is no need to add a detailed study of Diderot and Rousseau to that of Mably, for neither of these two contributed any new element to the already mentioned influences on Babeuf. When Babeuf mentions Diderot, he actually often means Morelly, whose *Code de la Nature* he still attributed, with most of his contemporaries, to Diderot. Even discounting the *Code*, however, Diderot looked upon the dualism between nature and society very much like Mably. Like Mably, he believed that "where the laws of nature prevail, there can be no crime," so that corruption of man is the

[72] Mably, "Principes de Morale," 231. [73] Mably, "De la législation," 77.

fault of institutions and bad laws. Rousseau's ideas are close to those of Mably. Like Mably, he emphasizes morality, austerity, and equality. He, too, considers the public authority the moderator of the passions. He, like Mably, felt that once man had "fallen from nature," he could never be fully restored and could be led back in the direction of nature only by the authority of the state. Rousseau likewise assumed that wealth is the ultimate source of human corruption and human slavery, so that the public control of wealth is the requisite of virtue. Most of the men of the mid-eighteenth century had ideas about labor closely resembling those of Mably. Montesquieu speaks of salutary institutions which "owe to all citizens, in exchange for their work, assurance of maintenance, food, suitable clothing, and a kind of life that is not harmful to health."[74] There was a widespread inclination to regard anyone who did not work with his hands as belonging to the depraved part of mankind. The prevailing ideas among the French rationalists, then, were predominantly of the socialist or communist variety.[75] But even though much of this thought implied a wholesale condemnation of civilization, it did not also imply a denial of the reality and significance of the world in which men lived. It accepted the moral order as real. Frequently, it recognized the inescapability of religion. And it generally turned toward the state and the laws as the instrument by which to correct society's flaws. This correction, in general, was conceived in terms of either a repartition of property or else an authoritative arrangement of institutions with the aim of preventing extremes of wealth and property. In all this, we can therefore instruct ourselves sufficiently by taking Mably as the representative of rationalist eighteenth century socialism, a socialism that issued in concrete legislative aims rather than in an indefinite and permanent "radical" revolution. At this point, then, we must return to Babeuf and the underlying motives of his conspirational movement of the Equals.

[74] Montesquieu, *Esprit des Lois,* XXIII, XXIX.
[75] A. V. Espinas, *La philosophie sociale du XVIIIe siècle et la révolution* (n.p., 1898), 109.

BABEUF

Gracchus Babeuf (1760–1797) was a revolutionary pamphleteer and conspirator who was tried and executed as the leader of an abortive revolutionary movement. He published his views mostly in a newspaper called *Tribun du Peuple* of which he was the editor. Among his closest associates was F. M. Buonarroti, whose history of Babeuf's conspiracy became, after 1830, a revolutionists' Bible, particularly on the European continent. Other prominent members of the group were Sylvain Maréchal, the author of the *Manifeste des Egaux*, the first revolutionary manifesto of modern times, and Darthé, who alone was executed together with Babeuf. It has been said that Babeuf's main importance lies in the contribution he has made to revolutionary techniques, particularly "the attention to preparation by propaganda, the use of methods of infiltration and permeation through local cells of activist supporters, the direction of operations by a small central committee," and other similar methods.[76] In this context, the question of Babeuf's contribution to any subsequent enterprise does not interest us as much as the character which Babeuf's movement assumed in the light of the ideas he derived from the socialist thinkers of the eighteenth century.

Nature and Equality

Babeuf's ideas were undoubtedly socialist or communist, but they were also eclectic and frequently inconsistent. The influence of Mably often seems to predominate, since he emphasizes most strongly the perfect equality of nature with the inequality of existing society. However, Mably's ideas appear side by side with those of Morelly, Rousseau, and others. Of nature, for instance, Babeuf speaks as "an eternal code," "an original contract," "the source of eternal rights," a "pure state," but also a condition "corrupted by force and cunning." Babeuf's main assumption emerges, however, like a refrain: equality, collective work, and "common enjoyment"

[76] David Thomson, *The Babeuf Plot* (London, 1947), 51.

are primordial and sacred principles which are being violated by existing society and must be restored for the happiness of all men. Babeuf's emphasis is on plans for the future, rather than on happenings of the past, although even in this respect he combines mutually exclusive ideas. Thus legislation, on the one hand, is to be reduced to a few simple elementary principles, in fact, to the art of augmenting the knowledge and pleasures of society.[77] On the other hand, Babeuf envisages a complete *administration de subsistances,* a regime of public economy which certainly would entail a host of detailed and complicated laws. He sounds very much like Mably when he demands full powers for the *régenérateur,* the regenerative legislator who uses the laws to turn society around to a new direction, but he reminds us of Meslier when he speaks of the utter demolition of the governments which "still disquiet us,"[78] and of the "sacred duty of insurrection."[79] Neither Babeuf's ideas about nature nor his plans for the future, however, can account for the permanent character of his revolution and the underlying total critique of society. Mably, Rousseau, Diderot could be quoted as authorities for both Babeuf's concept of nature and his *administration de subsistances,* but not for the permanence of his revolution. There can be no question that Babeuf and his group considered themselves engaged in the same enterprise which Marx called "the revolution in permanence." Most groups in the French Revolution, said Buonarroti, sought to secure their selfish advantage, while a small group alone fought for a "real radical reform of society."[80] The "radical" revolution is a struggle not merely against the order then existing in France, but against the "prejudices engendered by the political systems which have preceded the revolution in which, in all ages, bequeathed to the earth only calamities and crimes."[81] The French Revolution itself is described as the forerunner of "an-

[77] Babeuf's reply to a letter signed "M. V.," quoted in Philippe M. Buonarroti, *Buonarroti's History of Babeuf's Conspiracy for Equality,* tr. by Bronterre (London, 1836), 372. Hereinafter cited as *Buonarroti.*

[78] *Ibid.,* 374.

[79] Haute Cour de Justice. *Suite de la Copie des Pièces Saisies dans le local que Baboeuf occupoit lors de son arrestation* (Paris, an V.), 244.

[80] *Buonarroti,* 5.

[81] *Ibid.,* 29.

other revolution far more grand, far more solemn, and which will be the last."[82] The people of France, to whom the call to this last revolution is addressed, are destined to act in this as the representatives of all humanity.[83] The time for this ultimate revolution is at hand, and the fight is against all the evil of all times and places: "The moment for great measures has arrived. Evil is at its height; it has reached its maximum, and covers the face of the earth. Chaos, under the name of politics, has too long reigned over it. Let everything revert to order, and resume its proper place. . . . "[84] This is not the language of Mably but that of Meslier or Morelly, the refusal to see any reality of order in the existing "chaos," the identification of politics with evil, the reversion of everything to a "proper place" which is conceived in radical opposition to anything society has ever known. Nor is this ultimate revolution destined simply to "make one order or government prevail over another."[85] It is aimed at ignorance, the real source of all slavery.[86] Again we can hear the voice of Meslier and Morelly who believed in the magic power of *gnosis* as a revolutionary force. Babeuf believed in *gnosis* not any the less for having planned armed action: "Je vais maintenant vous offrir les grandes clartés de la nature . . . la justice originelle . . . la vérité premiere." ("I shall now offer you the great lucidities of nature . . . prime justice . . . original truth.")[87] In the above quoted *Reply to a letter signed "M. V."* he speaks of our "monstrous societies," the "present grand organized and perpetual anarchy."[88] All our institutions and transactions are nothing but a perpetual robbery authorized by barbarous laws.[89] Against this alien, meaningless, and tyrannous system of power there is one remedy: the people's insurrectionist refusal to obey. This is Meslier's concept of the destruction of the political order by disobedience. For Babeuf,

[82] *Ibid.*, 315. The passage is from the *Manifeste des Egaux.*
[83] *Ibid.*, 316.
[84] *Ibid.*, from the *Manifeste des Egaux.*
[85] *Ibid.*, 6.
[86] *Ibid.*, 9.
[87] Quoted in Maurice Dommanget, *Pages choisies de Babeuf* (Paris, 1935), 230. From the *Tribun du Peuple*, No. 1.
[88] *Buonarroti*, 364, 373.
[89] Advielle, *Histoire de Gracchus Babeuf*, II, 39.

too, insurrection is a "sacred duty" of the people. A public appeal of his directing committee declared the people to be "in insurrection." This is meant to be the end of all political order, for, as Babeuf explicitly states, if the revolutionists aimed merely at "setting up their rule in the place of another, or if the revolution were to be finished, it (the revolution) would have been nothing but a grand crime."[90] The only revolution which is justified is thus a permanent one which has no practical end but leaves the people in a permanent state of insurrection.

But surely Babeuf wanted to establish a government? He did, indeed, and made the most painstaking preparations therefore. But a revolutionary government, in Babeuf's eyes, is not the same as a government presiding over an established political order. The concept of a "revolutionary government" as an instrument of terror in an indefinite period of transition was well established in the French Revolution and is at the core of Babeuf's ideas about public power. The concept is perhaps best epitomized by the reply Trinchard made to an accusation by St. Just: "A revolutionary jury is not an ordinary jury; we were not men of law; we were good sansculottes, pure men, men of nature [*hommes de la nature*]."[91] Babeuf considered the men of the permanent revolution pure, virtuous, fully justified in anything they might do to destroy their enemies. For from their power would result "a universal happiness," the end of all "fences, hedges, walls, doorlocks, disputes, lawsuits, thefts, murders, of all crimes, of law-courts, prisons, gallows, pains, despairs, . . . of envy, jealousy, . . . finally of all vices. . . ."[92] This is but a paraphrase both of Marx's call to revolution "not against any wrong in particular but against wrong as such," and Meslier's insurrection as mankind's redemption. Let us remember that it was the annihilation of religion and the moral order which deprived actual society, in the eyes of Meslier and Morelly, of reality, so that

[90] *Ibid.*, 30.
[91] Quoted by Espinas, *La philosophie sociale*, 269.
[92] Babeuf's defense before the court, quoted by Advielle, *Histoire de Gracchus Babeuf*, II, 41. The passage was originally published in the *Tribun du Peuple*, no. 35.

the true reality could be regained only by the total intellectual rejection and physical destruction of actual society. Let us remember also that this gnostic attitude toward the world in which we live is by no means the necessary result of blaming private property for humanity's vices, as became clear in the case of Mably. What Babeuf and his friends had inherited from the eighteenth century philosophers was not primarily their socialism—although this legacy was also found in their baggage—but their gnosticism, the idea of a hidden or forgotten truth irrupting devastatingly into an unreal world. It was the total critique of all existing society which made them reject any definable goal of the revolution in favor of a general movement of destruction. It was, finally, the resulting denial of any responsibility toward the world and its citizens that inspired them to endorse the notion of terror, as reflected in Darthé's notorious instruction to the followers of Babeuf: "Kill the five, the seven ministers, the General of the Interior and his general staff, occupy the halls of the Five Hundred and of the Ancients, seize everyone who presents himself there, put to death every public official who exercizes his functions, every foreigner who does not submit himself to provisional arrest, every citizen who, after a rigorous search of his house, is still found having flour, vegetables and other edibles he has not declared, every wine merchant who does not distribute his merchandise; hang on the first lamp-post every baker who does not bake; persecute with fire and sword anyone who offers resistance."[93]

After the total critique of society—total hostility, total suspicion, total terror: totalitarian power.

AN ARCHETYPAL SOCIALISM

It was not primarily curiosity about the eighteenth century that prompted this study of certain second-rank figures of the Enlightenment, but rather the hope of finding through them, as originators, an archetypal pattern of total critique. It may be true that the

[93] Quoted by Espinas, *La philosophie sociale*, 302.

ultimate type of alienation must be located in Gnosticism, but modern ideologies differ from ancient Gnosticism in their emphasis on the transformation of political society which in the Gnostic religion was wholly subordinate to the redemption of the entire cosmos. We are here concerned with that special type in the general class of Gnostic outlooks which has converted the Gnostic "radical transcendence" into a social metastasis. One may circumscribe its general features as follows:

(1) Its total critique of society is rooted in theological or ontological revolution, be it a rejection of God or of goodness, at least of experienceable goodness. Mably serves as a controlling counterexample on this point, since his refusal to deny either God or the moral order induced him to espouse social reform rather than total revolution.

(2) This particular pattern of "total critique" is characteristically ahistorical and antihistorical. It does not criticize society as a temporary evil phase, in the name of process and its ultimate outcome; rather, it rejects all the products of recorded history as antirational, false, and unreal.

(3) This particular pattern of total critique invokes as its title the perfection of a logical construct concerning social order. Here we have the introduction of "value" in the form of abstract ideal propositions, so that this particular pattern of total critique should be named *axiological total critique.*

(4) The content of the "value" invoked as revolutionary justification goes under the name of "nature" which connotes social order beyond good and evil, be it the order of labor or the order of natural passions. Nature serves as the antithesis to history, everything of historically concrete configuration, and thus all moral, political, and legal concretions known to experience.

(5) The "value" of nature appears wholly alien to human existence and experience in history. It can be grasped only by virtue of a specific and secret knowledge made manifest by the thinker as a messenger. At this point the eighteenth century total critique most closely resembles Gnosticism.

(6) The secret knowledge, once it takes hold of the masses, will of itself cause the historical world of law and order to come tumbling down. Here knowledge as such is conceived as redeeming, and the false world understood as resting solely on ignorance about true "values."

Because we are familiar with socialism mainly in the form that Marx gave it, the tracing of socialist conclusions to this eighteenth century pattern throws considerable light on the nature of the socialist critique. One cannot deny to either Meslier or Morelly the name of socialist, but in their premises we look in vain for the proletariat, the "social question," the industrial revolution, or even a self-conscious materialism, not to speak of the dialectic of history or the class struggle. What we find, rather, is socialism as a concept of abstract though world-immanent perfection rooted in an antihistorical idea of nature as harmony beyond good and evil. Inasmuch as the modern total critique of society makes prominent use of the dialectic of history, we must now turn to another archetype of radical negation.

II□The "Laws of History"

TURGOT AND CONDORCET

In 1750 at the age of twenty-three, when he was Prior of the Sorbonne, Turgot delivered two Latin addresses, the first a "Discourse on the Advantages which the Establishment of Christianity has Procured for Mankind" and the second a "Philosophical Tableau on the Successive Advancements [*progrès successifs*] of the Human Mind." These addresses systematically developed for the first time a doctrine of history as progress impelled by natural causation. For Turgot progress is the unfolding of the human mind chiefly in the sciences, spearheaded by mathematics and physics. Men of genius are the agents of progress. While genius is always present, it can bear fruit only in the right kind of environment, for which a rich and flexible language is the most important factor facilitating the growth of higher ideas. Language, in turn, develops through the merging of various cultures and idioms, which merging is brought about by such historical vicissitudes as wars and revolutions issuing from human self-seeking passions.

The concepts which Turgot here created became stock-in-trade among all the varieties of the immanentist, progressivist view of history. They are significant in the context of this study because out of them developed a total critique of society based not on the criterion of a perfect order of nature but rather on that of a movement from dark beginnings to a perfect future. The critic, taking his stand in that perfection-yet-to-be, finds the past alien, repulsive, hostile, and totally depraved and extends that condemnation to the society in which he lives insofar as it embodies the past. Such attitudes require certain intellectual foundations enabling the modern mind to believe in the certainty of a future perfection and the utter worthlessness of the past, accepting the possibility that history as a whole can be known like a datum and that from impersonal and imperfect causes the production of good could follow along the lines of "laws."

History as a Given Whole

The very title of Turgot's second discourse implies that one can see history as a whole given to experience. "Tableau" suggests a completed picture, an arrangement of parts within a framework so that each part adds to the overall meaning. In the first discourse Turgot rhetorically raises the question of whether mankind has a "childhood." In answering affirmatively he postulates that the whole of human history can be arranged into childhood, adolescence, and maturity—that is, as a movement of steady growth toward a fulfillment within the framework of time.[1] The term "tableau" posits a pattern of seemingly unrelated and meaningless events, something which previous historiography used to cover with the term "Providence," the difference being that "Providence" acknowledges a mystery in the pattern while Turgot claims it is empirically knowable. There are, then, two presuppositions which combine in this view of history. The first is the assertion that historical causation can be known and that history constitutes a course of events subject to full empirical analysis. The second is the assumption that this analyzable course of events moves from low to high, from initial cultural chaos to eventual cultural perfection, which movement constitutes the whole of human destiny. The "goal" is known rather than embraced by faith and love and this knowledge is rooted in the supposedly empirical analysis of the succession of developmental phases.

On the point of man's world-immanent destiny Turgot is quite explicit, nowhere more so than in his discourse on the "advantages of Christianity." He conceived these "advantages" wholly in the nature of contributions to the advancement of the sciences and mundane civilization. Thus, he praises religion for moving and

[1] Turgot, *Oeuvres de Turgot,* ed. G. Schelle (5 vols.; 1913–23), I, 198.

stimulating the human mind at a time when science was not yet able to penetrate the darkness of mankind's infant centuries.[2] It may be noted at this point that Turgot, in attributing to religion and philosophy the function of having nudged the human mind to higher levels from its original barbaric coarseness, divides history into a barbaric, a religious-philosophical, and a scientific phase, the latter being the phase of fulfillment. Another "advantage" of Christianity is that it preserved the "intelligence of the ancient languages" through its divine services. This for Turgot is supremely important because mixture of languages prepares the ground for progress, and the modern languages are essentially a rich combination of ancient with barbaric tongues. Then again he finds that Christianity has proved useful in overcoming the political parochialism of men and setting before them the "rights of humanity," so that now men's "preference" for their own society is combined with a "general love of humanity." Finally, Christianity has influenced the development of the *moeurs,* the "inner laws" of morality which are stronger than civil laws and have softened men's conduct toward one another.[3] All of Christianity's gifts are thus judged by the onward and upward movement of human civilization, more precisely defined in terms of the improvement of the sciences, the expansion of a uniform social order, and man's love for the whole of "humanity." Humanity here emerges as a new and immanentist human love and loyalty, in the sense that only where this kind of loyalty prevails do nations qualify for the distinction of "civilization." Thus Turgot, a young but already prominent member of the clergy, can eulogize the Christian religion without mentioning Jesus Christ or "having in remembrance his blessed passion and precious death, his mighty resurrection and glorious ascension" and "the innumerable benefits procured to us by the same," as the *Book of Common Prayer* expresses itself on the same subject. For the young Prior of the Sorbonne the "advantages of Christianity" center in man's worldly progress rather than in "the redemption of

[2] *Ibid.*
[3] *Ibid.*, 199, 210, 212.

the world by our Lord Jesus Christ, the means of grace and the hope of glory."

Turgot thus subordinates religion to the higher end of perfecting civilization which he conceives as man's ultimate destiny. In scattered remarks Turgot indicates what kind of perfection he envisages. The perfect world of the future is one linked through the bonds of commerce, in which all nations resemble one single vast republic, united in the light of fully developed human reason enlightened by a mature science of both nature and society.[4] History's goal is a fully developed scientific mind in a world united by commerce; in such a world inequalities would disappear and equal conditions would promote an even spread of civilization.

Progress through Natural Causation

Turgot's most important conceptual innovation was that the progressive fulfillment of man's destiny results from impersonal and unintended (i.e., natural) causes. The causes can be called natural inasmuch as external stimuli—either events or environmental factors—call forth "natural" responses of human beings, for instance, appetites, passions, self-interest, which in turn lead to necessary social actions. "Interest, ambition, vainglory change every moment the scene of the world and flood the earth with blood; and in their midst, customs (morals) become softer, the human mind clearer, the isolated nations approach one another; commerce and politics finally united the parts of the globe, and the total mass of mankind marches, through alternative phases of quiet and disturbance, of good and bad, slowly but steadily toward ever greater perfection."[5] In this combination of blind and accidental external forces with the lower, self-centered motives of human action, man, as it were, is improved *malgré soi*. Turgot conceives progress resulting not from any human yearning, upward glance, response to the pull from transcendence, but rather statistically, in the interaction of meaningless stimuli with unreflective reactions. The sole requirement of progress is that the stimuli be strong and the reac-

[4] *Ibid.*, 206, 215, 220, 232.

[5] *Ibid.*, 215.

tive part vigorous. For this reason Turgot considers inequality among men an important cause of progress. Nature, he says, distributes her gifts unequally, particularly the gift of talent. Hence, some nations advance faster and become the spearheads of higher civilization. From inequality among nations result conquests, empires, revolutions, and all kinds of disturbances, by the means of which national cultures and languages interpenetrate and enrich each other. Thus arise new and complex cultures in which knowledge can move to higher levels. There may of course be long periods of seeming retrogression which, however, are the necessary price of progress. Turgot compares the process to the mixing of two liqueurs which first yield a cloudy and troubled fluid that eventually settles down to a new and richer transparency.[6]

A chief preoccupation among all eighteenth century thinkers was the discovery of the "order of nature." Turgot is no exception. Where others were looking for nature's normative principles, however, Turgot looked for the overall statistical pattern of causes and effects. This was the orientation typical of the Physiocrats, a school that considered him a member and founding father. The Physiocrats' advocacy of *laissez faire, laissez aller* follows logically from the assumption that environmental factors and the "normal" responses of human passions add up to a pattern of order besides which no other source of order need to be considered. To know the true social order one needs to study man's physical constitution and the conditions for satisfying his physical needs. "There is thus a *natural order*," wrote Dupont de Nemours, "which embodies the constitutive fundamental laws of all societies. . . . Nature . . . does not confine her physical laws to those that have so far been studied in our colleges and academies . . . . If she gives to ants, bees, and beavers the faculty to submit themselves by common accord and for their own interest to a good, stable, and uniform government, she does not refuse to man the power to elevate himself to the enjoyment of the same advantage. . . . The study of the physical laws concerning society . . . became a very new doctrine, wholly

[6] *Ibid.*, 229, 232.

different from the generally accepted prejudices."[7] On this general assumption, the Physiocrats believed that there could be "nothing arbitrary in physical acts aiming at a definite end," because men's ends are "essentially determined by their nature . . . . Their physical constitution and those of other beings surrounding them do not permit that the means to attain these ends be arbitrary."[8] Man, said the Marquis de Mirabeau, another prominent member of the Physiocrat school, is by nature not destined to "aspire to anything but his advantages and constantly obey his needs."[9] And Dupont quoted the Margrave of Baden as saying: "There exists . . . a concatenation [*un enchaînement*] of all human interests, a fixed point of unity of interests between men."[10] The full significance of such assumptions becomes clear when the Marquis de Mirabeau proclaims, "There are not two moralities, one Christian and the other economic; they are but one," and Badeau calls Physiocracy "the true theology."[11]

Such statements by the men who claimed Turgot as their coreligionist throw a sharp light on the doctrine that the blind hazards of self-regarding human activities add up to meaningful forward movement of life through history. As early as 1748 Turgot had formulated his views about the chain of causality in these words: "Nature sows at all times and in all places a certain number of geniuses at about equal intervals, which the hazards of education and of events either allow to develop or bury in the ground of obscurity. The hazards of circumstances and events vary continuously, their interactions must in the long run cancel each other out, and consequently the always active [factor of] genius must in the course of centuries produce its rational effects (*effets sensibles*)." The role that external forces play in man's progress is again pointed up: "Only through upheavals and ravages do nations expand and

[7] Dupont de Nemours, *De l'origine et des progrès d'une science novelle* (London and Paris, 1768), 7, 9.

[8] *Ibid.*, 6.

[9] Quoted in G. Weulersse, *La Physiocratie à la fin du regne de Louis XV* (Paris, 1950), 105.

[10] *Ibid.*, 106.

[11] *Ibid.*, 112.

are political systems and governments perfected in the long run."[12] Turgot thus justifies the evil of any given historical moment as the cause of eventual historical good, which means that present-to-be-loathed makes sense in view of a future-to-be-attained. The happiness of coming generations thus replaces any value criterion anchored in the present lives of individuals.

The Phases of History

Mention has already been made of the three ages into which Turgot divided mankind's history. The three phases emerge rather indistinctly in Turgot's writings; but he does consistently set off barbarism from a civilization dominated by Greek philosophy and Christian religion, and the latter from contemporary civilization dominated, since Bacon and Descartes, by science. This is essentially the same three-phase doctrine later elaborated by Comte. Comte and Turgot differ mainly in the dialectic of forward movement, Turgot's relying chiefly on inequality. The first period, barbarism, equalizes all men.[13] In the second period marked inequalities between nations prevail. These inequalities are the very stuff of progress because they cause some nations to take the lead over others. In the third phase mankind again returns to equality, this time on the highest level of existence. "Soon baneful discords will tear the whole of Europe apart; audacious men have shaken the foundations of faith as well as of empires; do the flowering stems of the arts grow only as they are watered by blood? A day will arrive, and it is not far away, when they will embellish all parts of Europe. . . . Century of Louis the Great, may your enlightenment adorn the precious reign of your successor! May it last forever, may it extend over the entire universe!"[14] The future world will be united by a single civilization, that of France under Louis XV. No narrow parochialism will refuse to adopt cultural achievements on the grounds that they are of foreign origin. The peoples will learn to "know each other, to unite, they will plant the seeds

[12] Turgot, *Oeuvres*, I, 117, 285.
[13] *Ibid.*, 217.
[14] *Ibid.*, 233, 235.

of that modern political order through which the nations seem to make up one vast republic."[15] The spiral movement of Turgot's construction of history thus prefigures that of Marx, from primitive communal property through the divisions and inequalities of private property to the future communal property.

It was Turgot's friend and biographer Condorcet who elaborated this hinted periodization into a full-blown schedule of ten phases or ages, some of which are defined by advances in human skill or learning and others simply by well-known dates, for example, "Descartes to the French Republic." From what he called "observation of the succession of generations" Condorcet derived the "knowledge" that enabled him to set up a table of progress with the "precision of an empirical science." And he maintains: "This progress is subject to the same general laws which can be observed in the individual's development of his faculties, since it is the result of that development as one considers simultaneously a great number of individuals united in society."[16] The succession of phases is explained as a causal necessity so that the table of progress, like a table of chemical elements, "exposes the influence which each instant exercises on that which replaces it, and shows through the modifications of its existence . . . mankind's march . . . toward the truth or happiness."[17] Consequently the "laws of history" become the chief object in the study of man. Here is another "new science" to stake its claim besides the many discoveries of "hitherto hidden knowledge" that mark this period of pseudoscientific dilettantism.

The Self-Propellant Movement

This particular "new science," the discovery of which Condorcet attributes to "Turgot, Price and Priestley," goes under the name of the "infinite perfectibility" of mankind.[18] "Infinite perfectibility"

[15] *Ibid.*, 232.
[16] Marquis de Condorcet, *Esquisse d'un tableau historique des progrès de l'esprit humain* (3rd ed.; Paris, 1797), 3.
[17] *Ibid.*, 3.
[18] *Ibid.*, 271. *Cf.* Richard Price, *The Evidence for a Future Period of Improvement in the State of Mankind, with the Means and Duty of Promoting It* (1787), and Joseph Priestley, *Disquisitions Relating to Matter and Spirit* (1777). The

connotes a development without a terminal point, final cause, or high source of attraction. Man's existence rather is pushed to higher and higher levels by blind forces without purpose or end. The causes of human progress are inferior to man, his rise to ever higher forms of existence is engendered by pressure from below rather than a pull from above. The concept of creative hazard assumes the place of a demiurge, but the idea of a self-generating rise strictly speaking precludes any knowledge of an end, because the upward movement is not elicited from above. In Aristotelian language, this amounts to the elimination of any *summum bonum* or even final cause, leaving only efficient causes and those without any "prime mover." By the same token, an analysis of impersonal forces supplants the awareness of essences. Where man and society are seen as the product of impersonal thrusts and whirls there can be no natures.

This view of history logically calls for the end of philosophy. Philosophy, the love of truth which man experiences as drawing him beyond himself, must give way to the possession of positive information of how we got so high, so that sociological history becomes the key to human order. Condorcet, prefiguring Marx and Engels, proclaims the end of philosophy: "Philosophy has no need to speculate any more [*n'a plus rien à déviner*], it does not have to formulate any more hypothetical combinations; nothing more is needed than to assemble and order the facts and show the useful truths [*les vérités utiles*] that flow from their interaction and combination [*ensemble*]."[19] Here is an already self-conscious positivism, albeit without the religious pretenses later added by Saint-Simon and Comte. All the same, even here the religious overtones are not wholly absent, for Condorcet takes it on faith that the self-propellant progress will move ahead faster or slower but will "never retrogress."[20] Moreover, even though in strict logic the upward thrust of blind force should be open-ended, Condorcet takes it for

latter said in his "Essay on the First Principles of Government": Whatever the beginning of the world, the end will be paradisaical, beyond what our imagination can conceive."

[19] *Ibid.*, 14.

[20] *Ibid.*, 4.

granted that history will move toward ultimate happiness. One might call this faith, if Condorcet's general attitude toward reality were one of faith, which it is not. Instead, it is an eschatology unsupported by reason or experience but nevertheless postulated as the *telos* of historical causality and thus also of action in history. Here emerges a prototype of modern historical determinism which is never encountered as a doctrine of mere causality but always as a combination of seemingly empirical information with the pretense of "absolute knowledge" concerning the goal of all historical change. Condorcet was not even vague about the future: "Our hopes regarding the future state of mankind may be reduced to these three important points: the destruction of the inequality between nations, the progress of equality within the nations, and finally, the real perfection of man."[21] What the "real perfection of man" meant, Condorcet had already learned from Turgot, who was "convinced that the perfection of the social order would bring about an equal perfection of morality, that men would become continually better in the same measure in which they become more enlightened."[22] The interaction of blind and purposeless forces will result in the improvement of the sciences, the perfection of the sciences implies the perfection of practical reason, and this "enlightenment" of man amounts to perfect goodness and happiness. Man's destiny is hereby circumscribed within the framework of world-immanent causes and effects, his self-fulfillment to be the crowning product of the momentum created by a chain of causal accidents.

Once the question of history's world-immanent *telos* is raised, the problem of greatest urgency is to know just where on history's path one happens to be at a given moment. Each moment of history must therefore be defined in terms of the preceding and the coming stages of development, according to the "table of progress." Condorcet asks rhetorically, "Are we at the point where we have nothing more to fear?" For the first time[23] he answers this

[21] *Ibid.*, 333.

[22] Condorcet, *Vie de M. Turgot* (London and Paris, 1786), 274.

[23] Except for a much less self-assured formulation of the same idea in Turgot's *Plan de deux discours sur l'histoire universelle* of 1751, to wit: "Thus the *univer-*

question in terms of a "series of revolutions" through which the progress of the "total mass of mankind" is achieved: "Everything tells us that we are entering the period of one of mankind's great revolutions. What could better enlighten us on what to expect, what could offer us surer guidance for our conduct in the midst of these movements than the table of revolutions which has preceded and prepared the present time?"[24] The "table of progress" is here identified with the "table of revolutions" which serves as the "guide to conduct" in the same way in which Marxism later claimed to have discovered a "scientific" key to socialist activism. From the study of this table one can obtain indisputable knowledge of "what obstacles we still have to fear, and what means we have to overcome them."

History as an Object of Knowledge

Since Turgot and Condorcet formulated their views of progress and its causes, intellectuals in the West have developed the habit of identifying history with forces moving men and bringing forth "ages" or "stages," as a schedule of events past and future imposing on any living generation the inexorable necessity of "the next step." Our daily vocabulary resounds with such phrases as "history compels us," "to be in step with history," "according to history," "catching up with the age," "trying to move the clock of history back." The fact that such language can attain public standing can be understood if one keeps in mind that our civilization has always centered in a concept of history as a pilgrimage toward a goal of ultimate fulfillment of human destiny. Augustine's creation of a philosophy of history, however, did not look on history as a process

---

sal history embraces the consideration of the successive advancements [*progrès successifs*] of mankind and the detailed causes which have contributed to this progress. The first beginnings of men, the formation and merging of nations, the origin and the revolutions of governments, the progress of languages, of physics, of morality, of morals, of sciences and arts, the revolutions which made empires succeed empires, nations succeed nations, religions succeed religions,—mankind [*le genre humain*], always the same through its upheavals, like the water of the sea through the storms, and always advancing toward its perfection." Turgot, *Oeuvres*, I, 276.

24 Condorcet, *Esquisse d'un tableau*, 19.

that can be observed from without and in which one can perceive "factors" which operate as "causes" with predictable "effects," producing a development in "stages" or "phases." Rather Augustine illumined from within man's experience of participation not only in a timeless order of being but also in a time that is created and has meaning. Machiavelli was the first political thinker of rank to propose a way of looking at human life that leaves out the question of what ought to be and merely observes "what is"—a view from without reducing political science to the analysis of phenomena. Since Turgot and Condorcet, this idea of political theory has been applied also to history. Insofar as it is applied to history as a whole, it postulates the whole of history as a phenomenon, an object given to perception, an ensemble of statistically normal effects which admit of valid generalizations about the efficient causes.

Augustine knew of no history formulated in such terms. He could formulate a concept of order in time because certain events dispersed over many centuries appeared related by a common inner meaning and a continuous human experience of a dimension transcending time. In the chaotic multitude of fleeting moments, some were lifted above oblivion and statistical insignificance through the experience of holiness. Those moments in time have an abiding quality eliciting human responses and inducing a newness of life.[25] Augustine's perception of the inner meaning that links these moments to each other added up to a concept of time-directed-to-a-goal which in turn enables men to conceive of history as a whole. But Augustine never posited history as either an object or a datum. He merely pointed to perspectives that can be discerned through the moments when the Eternal irrupts into time, perspectives of consciousness as men articulate their understanding of participation. These perspectives established by past moments of connected meaning point to a future but tell nothing about causes and effects, and least of all about the concrete configuration of coming events that have not yet occurred. Augustine

[25] Eric Voegelin speaks of them as "representative centers of reception from which revelation is communicated to the rest of mankind." Voegelin, "History and Gnosis," in B. W. Anderson (ed.), *The Old Testament and Christian Faith* (New York, 1963), 75.

does not pretend to view history from the vantage point of a being beyond time who surveys all that was and will be, but from the position of man who is embedded in time but can orient his consciousness through moments on which the Eternal has impressed its mark. He comprehended the movement of human order in time through the experience of human participation in the divine and divine participation in time-bound humanity, but he postulated no manipulation of mankind to push it in the desired direction. The goal of all movements in time must lie beyond time, history is meaningful only in the light of a transcendent fulfillment, and all that is mutable can be comprehended as a "continuous creation." Augustine could never have conceived that history is something "made," because there is no subject playing the role of the "factor." God's irrupting grace is not tantamount to an "authorship" of history. Man in his freedom to respond to or to resist the irruption of the Eternal cannot be called history's master. Nothing moves history, history moves nothing. Inasmuch as human souls, in the dimension of time, open to inspired newness of life, mankind *has* history.

When Voltaire demolished Bossuet, the Augustinian understanding of history as time illumined from within was destroyed. What survived for the moment was a caricatured notion of Providence and an eschatological teleology without content. These concepts remained as a hollow shell calling for some substance which was supplied by various thinkers in the seventeenth and eighteenth centuries, most emphatically by Turgot.[26] An orderly succession of events and an ultimate fulfillment being taken for granted, the only question was how to account for them. Turgot, Physiocrat and positivist, naturally looked for "physiological factors." He thus postulated a history that could be known through methods suited to the explanation of natural objects. Thus, his-

[26] It seems that one of the first to combine the Christian eschatology with a scheme of evolutionary progress was Thomas Burnet, whose various books, especially *The Excellency of Theology* (1674) and *Theory of the Earth* (1684) enjoyed wide reading. *Cf.* E. L. Tuveson, *Millennium and Utopia* (Berkeley, 1949).

tory was viewed as a process of causation, with mankind as that which was being caused to move. In this view history happens only to "the total mass of mankind." Particular persons figure only statistically or as instruments. Human responses and experiences count only insofar as they can be reduced to an average. The upward trend of the causative process is assumed. When it comes to an explanation, the human response to irruptions of divine grace is ignored, but subhuman factors operating independently of any human understanding or experience are emphasized. True, Turgot assigned a creative role to genius. In his scheme, however, genius is a natural capacity that is everywhere available in statistical quantities. It contributes to progress each time that conditions favor it. These latter again produce themselves on a statistical average as the result of social turmoil. Turgot's history is a mechanism automatically working for beneficent change.

The cumulation of change then must amount to an accumulation of value. What Turgot described is no mere change but rather a "becoming." Who is "becoming"? Turgot answers, "la masse totale de l'humanité," the "total mass of humanity." Conceived apart from divine grace and the opening of the human soul one can construe "becoming" only as something comparable to a subject, with mankind as the object. It is self-generating, requiring, at most, subsidiary action, and moves beyond good and evil. Progress piles upon progress, no intelligent being willing or intending it. Turgot shifted history's "becoming" from the human soul and human consciousness to something construed as an objective world which all the same appeared as if suffused with wisdom. History moves both forward and upward, the upward direction going under the eighteenth century name of "civilization," the world-immanent refinement of manners, mind, and technology, the elimination of poverty, disease, and war. "Becoming," then, means ultimately the arrival of civilization conceived as the work and purpose of mechanical and blind causation. The entire process is not only beneficent but also planful. It has "phases" supposedly occurring on a schedule, "forces" which can be known, and effects capable of prediction. An entirely new relation between memory, hope, and human purpose developed from this "new science." The past now appears as something that deserves to be dismissed as contemptible, possibly even rejected and combated. Destiny is wholly concentrated in the future, a future conceived in militant opposition to the past. History has a dialectic in that periods of turbulence and misery serve as the required instrument of progress. It is the schedule of history as a whole and its goal of world-immanent perfection that provides the yardstick for political action, action particularly directed against "prejudices"—that is, the eggshells of the rejected past. History is the growth of mankind and thus the new allegiance is to "humanity as a whole." Hence a new trinitarian formula characterizes modernity: *History* the author of creation, *Humanity* the royalty of our allegiance, *Civilization* the spirit of life.

An Ersatz *Religion*

Turgot-Condorcet's table of history appears to rest on empirical foundations. Upon looking closer, though, a concealed metaphysics, the metaphysics of immanentism, is discernible. On the surface one might consider Turgot's argument incontrovertible. For it is true that in the course of millennia mankind's store of knowledge and skill has grown, that an evolution of civilization has taken place, that wars and other disasters have often spread languages and civilizational achievements. The metaphysical character of the "new science" of history consists in the generalization of some facts into the alleged structure of a universal history and the combination of empirical material with pseudoreligious speculation. Attributing the capacity to produce order to an interaction of blind forces and "natural" human reactions is a piece of metaphysics, although a metaphysics from which the perennial human experience of divine grace has been removed. It is also a piece of metaphysics when one assumes certain foreknowledge of the ultimately happy culmination of history, but again a contracted metaphysics which has eliminated from human life the happiness of participation. It is a piece of metaphysics when history is hypostatized into something like a subject with its own will, intention, and plan into which men have to fit their thoughts and actions. Precisely because of these metaphysical features, the hypostatization of history has in the last two hundred years served many as a substitute for religion—that is, as an explanation of the meaning of life, a focus of loyalty, and a guide to action. It has substituted the love of progress for the love of wisdom or truth. It has replaced the awareness of the human condition with the confidence assurance of man's unlimited possibilities. Rather than looking on change as something to be judged, it has elevated change itself to the criterion of judgment, particularly as a devastating judgment on the past and an implicit enthronement of the future as the *summum bonum*.

Marx later fused philosophical materialism with immanentist progressivism, so that one could gain the impression that the salient features of the Marxist view of history might stem from the materialist premise. In the Marxist sense, Turgot and Condorcet were no materialists. Nevertheless, in all essential respects the structure of their view of history as the true scientific knowledge of man is congruous with that of Marx. This suggests that it is less materialism than historical immanentism which accounts for the outlook that characterizes Marx. The decisive element is the attribution of creative ordering powers to immanent forces and the assumption of immanent perfection in the onward and upward march of human history, so that the drama of time centers wholly on man's collective existence. The knower of this process then turns into the knowledgeable helpmate of history who identifies himself or his group with the irresistible and alone valuable creation of future perfection. History's knower thus is also the sole competent helmsman to steer the ship of society through the turbulent waters of time.

FOURIER

Those who claim that history as a whole can be "scientifically known" do not necessarily assert knowledge of all causal links between particular events. They are concerned not so much with particulars as with "phases" or "ages" and the alleged necessity governing their succession. A phase or age, according to them, has a governing characteristic structure, a form into which all life is pressed at a time; but there is also a motion from one phase to the next and this is allegedly governed by knowable "laws." Hence "the next step" can be known, so that which "is bound to come" constitutes the sole meaningful content of human action. Turgot did not elaborate the bare hint of phases contained in his early works. However, his disciple Condorcet expanded Turgot's three phases to ten of which many, though, consisted of no more than divisions by memorable dates. While Turgot and Condorcet emphasized causation by impersonal forces and automatic progress, they did little to formulate any "laws" of history, the concept that characterized the works of Hegel, Comte, and Marx. But the one first to introduce this concept was Charles Fourier.

Fourier's Significance

Fourier first conceived of "phases of history" not merely as taxonomic conveniences but as etiological categories, each harboring the force required to move life to the next higher step. Fourier is particularly instructive, because he claimed to have originated his ideas exclusively out of his own experiences. His *Théorie des quatre mouvements* was published in 1808 but, as he said, was sketched in his mind before the turn of the century. He thus antedated Saint-Simon by several years. He prided himself in having read next to nothing. Furthermore, he adopted as his starting point the *écart absolu*, the total rejection of everything that had been thought before. Accordingly, the underlying experiences generating a totally new "science of history" can be discerned better in him than in others. Besides, Fourier exercised very great, though not always manifest, influence on the revolutionary mystics following him. In Russia his enthusiastic followers at one time or another included Herzen, Petrachevski, Belinsky, and even Dostoevsky. The Left-Hegelian Cieszkowski recommended him. Engels, in his *Origin of the Family, Private Property and the State*, acknowledges that this speculation on the natural history of mankind owes a debt to three men: Lewis Morgan, Karl Marx, and Charles Fourier. Marx praised Fourier in the *Communist Manifesto* and other writings for his exemplary total critique of the present-day society. As late as 1949 the surrealist André Breton praised Fourier in his *Ode à Charles Fourier*. In the movement of revolutionary students in the France of 1968, Fourier was again repeatedly invoked.

Contemporary references to Fourier mostly dwell on a description of his plan for agricultural community life, the *Phalanstère*, for which Fourier is classified among the socialists even though he did not propose the abolition of property. Fourier's view of history is hardly mentioned, probably for the same reason for which Auguste Comte's foundation of a new religion is usually passed over in embarrassed silence. In both cases, the two parts belong integrally together. Fourier's community project and scheme of history stem from his metaphysics and psychology. In our estimation the most frequently mentioned part of Fourier's thought deserves least attention; it was tried, failed, and passed on, without leaving any trace except brief mentions in history books. Fourier's ideas about history, on the other hand, introduced the notion of the *aetia* of history, phases that generate their own laws of succession, a notion that is representative for most of nineteenth century historicism.

The Course of Mankind's Life

Fourier's discontent with life expressed itself in the inference that because human life passes in conflicts between passion and obligation, the present form of existence must be totally false and a movement toward the right kind of existence must be expected. Looking back in a desire to find the cause of all this, he decided that the five or six thousand years of recorded history constitute merely a preparatory phase for a more perfect future. First, he distinguished in the past the ages of savagery, patriarchism, and barbarism, to which he later added a still more primitive age of bliss, Edenism. Thus the present is the fifth age, civilization. It belongs to a group of seven historical ages which together constitute mankind's "infancy," a period scheduled to last about five thousand years. Then come longer periods of maturity, eventual decline, and finally a period of senescence. Unlike Turgot who, from the assumption that mankind had an infancy, concluded only that there would be an age of maturity, Fourier carries the analogy to its end and predicts a natural death of the human race. The total scheme looks as follows:

Ascending Vibration	
Infancy or ascending incoherence	5,000 years
Growth of ascending combination	35,000 years
Descending Vibration	
Decline or descending combination	35,000 years
Decrepitude or descending incoherence	5,000 years

Each of the two periods of incoherence comprises seven ages of different structure. The two periods of combination are each composed of nine ages, so that the full cycle consists of thirty-two ages or phases with a total duration of eighty thousand years. The social patterns of incoherence are torn by discord and are called mankind's unhappy times, while the ages of "cohesion" make up the happy phases. Unfortunately, because the "uncertain sciences" of ethics and politics taught error for so long, mankind is now more than a thousand years behind schedule. Fourier, however, has finally discovered the way out of the impasse and presents it in the form of his "new science." Had mankind only found out earlier that savagery and barbarism are mere transitional phases, it could have accelerated its development by passing directly, let us say, from the fourth to the seventh age. "Nothing is easier than to make truth triumph in the whole world; one must only leave societies 2, 3, 4, 5, and even 6, and enter into the societies organized in series."[27]

It is noteworthy that the movement from the unhappy to the happy ages results from deliberate changes in human society. Once mankind has entered its "destinies," with the attainment of the eighth age, however, further historical movements will come from new creations of nature that will occur periodically and which are characterized in the following passage: "Every creation takes place

[27] Charles Fourier, *Oeuvres Complètes* (6 vols.; Paris, 1846–48), I, 34.

by the conjunction of a boreal fluid, which is male, with an austral fluid, which is female. A planet is a being which has two souls and two sexes, and which procreates like an animal or vegetable by the union of two generating substances." Thus the stage for nature's successive creations can be set only by man's completion of certain social phases. Once mankind has fully organized and exploited the globe beyond sixty degrees north, a fundamental change in nature will produce itself through the appearance of a "boreal crown" (*couronne boréale*)—that is, a luminous ring around the pole that will equalize climatic conditions all over the earth. Among other effects of this boreal crown will be a change of the sea water by means of a "boreal citric acid" which will give the ocean a taste resembling lemonade.[28] Malicious animals will vanish and adverse natural conditions will no longer bar the realization of perfect social harmony. After the period of mankind's infancy, when man has attained full harmony with nature, there will be no more evil until the period of senescence.

The Mechanism of Cosmic and Social Change

While the progressivists, with their "infinite perfectibility of man," sketched history along lines receding to the farthest horizon, Fourier circumscribes all history within the compass of a limited duration, so that history as a whole fully comes into sight. Within the total span of years one discerns something like history's timetable. Having run the course of a phase, mankind can no longer dwell in it because the schedule calls for onward motion. Mankind's destiny is identified with some of these phases, while the others appear as a negation of human destiny. After having attained it, mankind will again fall from the existence for which it is meant. Human destiny is harmony with nature, which alone makes possible social harmony without any evil.

The mutual dependence of nature's and social movements is characteristic for Fourier. On the one hand, nature's creations must wait until mankind has completed the first cycle of ages. On the

[28] *Ibid.*, 38, 41, 45.

other hand, once the happy ages are attained, historical change will occur only as the result of some new creation of nature. At one point, the key to the whole of history is entirely in human hands: the decisive movement from civilization (the present age) to the ages of bliss consists in a human decision to discard error and embrace the truth of social organization. Thus the entire world, now comprising savagery, barbarism, and civilization, will be "transformed by an undertaking [*essai*] confined to one square mile and 1800 persons" (i.e., a Phalanstery).[29] Once this social action has terminated the reign of misery and evil, nature will take on the role of the mover.

Fourier reversed the value predicate which until then was attached to the concept "civilization." In the eighteenth century the term "civilization" was a synonym for what was growing in the advanced nations of Europe under the leadership of men of the Enlightenment. In that sense, civilization connoted man's hope, a destiny to be desired. For Voltaire, civilization constituted the central meaning of history. The voices of inchoate Romanticism cast a certain amount of doubt on civilization, and Rousseau put civilization in opposition to nature, with the value accent exclusively on the latter. But Fourier went beyond Rousseau. In his series of historical ages, civilization marked the nadir of mankind's life, a synonym for the worst possible distortion, utter falsehood, negation of humanity, alienation from God and nature. "The vice of our so-called reformers is to indict this or that defect, instead of indicting civilization as a whole, inasmuch as it is nothing but a vicious circle of evil in all its parts; one must get out of this hell."[30] Fourier's intent is the same as that of Meslier and Morelly, to annihilate present-day society, but he employs the machinery of time to attain this effect. He needs not even postulate an insurrection against the false powers-that-be. All that is required is someone to initiate and finance the enterprise (the *phalanstère*) which will push the wheel of history beyond its present stance, so that the evil of the present will cease because time has marched on.

[29] *Ibid.*, VI, p. xv.
[30] *Ibid.*

This worst of all ages is characteristically not a dwelling place but a transition. With Fourier the important symbol of the present-day society as a phase of transition is introduced into political thought. Fourier's civilization is a threshold age, much as capitalism is for Marx; an age in which mankind will take the decisive step forward to its "destinies." Such ages of transition are necessarily miserable, but their misery is vindicated by the bliss-to-come. "What are four or five thousand years of misery compared with eighty thousand of happiness?" asked Fourier. The quantity of happy years here takes the place of the symbol of the precious pearl for which everything else is the justified price. Fourier is one of the first to give expression to that dialectic view which believes that real man will exist only in the future and sees history as the process of man's coming-to-be, a process in which all presence is provisional and the future is the queen of necessity. Fourier is here first cousin to Marx and anticipates Lenin in attributing a key role to the "period of transition" from nonbeing to being, from inhumanity to humanity. "Transitions are either painful or physically ugly."[31] Those who know history's necessity and can manage the period of transition are mankind's true liberators. They occupy a rank of unique distinction. It is not a slip of the pen when Fourier's editor's, writing in 1846, called him "the God of an unknown world."[32]

Fourier's Metaphysics

"Nature," in Fourier's scheme, characteristically straddles physics and metaphysics. Many eighteenth century minds had begun to speculate on a universal substance to which all causation could ultimately be attributed. Some called this prime cause "attraction," others an "elementary fire," still others discovered the "phlogiston," light, animal magnetism, electricity, the "prime fluid," or other real or imaginative substances at the root of all things. Those who defined the prime mover in terms of matter declared matter to be coeternal with God. Most eighteenth century thinkers were quite far

[31] A. Brisbane, *Social Destiny of Man* (Philadelphia, 1840), 229.
[32] Fourier, *Oeuvres Complètes*, I, p. iii.

from abandoning their belief in God. They merely assigned to Him a new, rather auxiliary position as not the mover but only the architect of the universe. All creation in this view results from the combination of raw material energies with a principle of form and order. There emerged a new trinitarian formula with God the architect, matter the energy, and the third being "the force which partakes of matter by its origin and of the Supreme Intelligence by its laws."[33] This third being of the trinity is nature, the force unifying substance with form, the "soul of the intelligible world," the main object of knowledge as contrasted with the unknowable deity. "One would not go wrong in thinking that during the 18th century there were more Frenchmen who were taught the doctrine of the naturalist trinity than the mysteries of the Christian Trinity."[34]

Fourier claims not to have read anything but he manifestly had absorbed this doctrine of the century in which he was born. "Nature," he taught, "is composed of three eternal principles which are not created and are indestructible: 1) God, or Spirit, an active and moving principle, 2) Matter, a passive and moved principle, 3) Justice or Mathematics, a principle regulating the movement. In order to establish harmony between the three principles, it is necessary that God, moving and modifying matter, should conform to mathematics; without that he would be arbitrary . . . in so far as he would not observe a sure justice independent of him. But if God subjects himself to mathematical rules which he cannot change he finds in that accord his glory and his interest."[35] Thus Fourier finds the key to God's mind in one of the precise sciences. He scathingly criticizes the "uncertain sciences" which had hitherto occupied themselves with the problems of human existence and action and accuses them for not having produced any reliable knowledge of God. Those who disclaim God are in turn derided for their "bastard opinion." It is the foremost task of the sciences to penetrate God's mind. In view of the "miracles of our technology," which, given man's backward political condition, are still

33 A. Le Flamanc, *Les utopies prérévolutionnaries et la philosophie du 18ème siècle* (Brest, 1934), 42.
34 *Ibid.*, 47.
35 Fourier, *Oeuvres Complètes,* I, 30n.

"premature," how can one possibly assume, cries Fourier, that God would have denied us knowledge of the "social art," without which all the other arts come to nothing?

The "New Science"

It is, of course, Fourier who was the first to discover that science. Like Newton, he found it in connection with an apple. Once, eating an apple in a city restaurant, he suddenly became aware of the difference between its price and the price of apples in the countryside. "I was so struck by this price difference between regions of the same temperature that I began to suspect a fundamental disorder in the industrial mechanism, and thus initiated studies which, in the course of four years, led to the discovery of the theory of industrial groups in series, and subsequently of the law of universal movement that Newton had missed. . . . I have said since that time that one may speak of four famous apples: two which have caused disasters—that of Adam and that of Paris,—and two that have rendered service to science,—that of Newton and mine. These four famous apples—do they not deserve a page in history?"[36] One should not dismiss such remarks as those of a man with a probable touch of mental disorder. Fourier's life and work testify to a precise, almost pedantic and orderly mind. What speaks here is the spiritual excitement of a man living in an age of spiritual disorder who feels that he has broken through the hitherto impenetrable secret of the Creation. It is the celebration of a newly found *gnosis*, a hitherto hidden knowledge of the supernatural. This man, otherwise very modest in his personal habits and demands on life, bursts into a hymn to the newly gained possession: "I alone will have confounded twenty centuries of political imbecility, and to me alone will the present and future generations owe the beginning of their immense happiness. Before me mankind had lost several thousand years in foolishly fighting against Nature; I was the first to bow to her in studying attraction, the organ of her decrees; she has deigned to smile on the sole mortal who has worshipped her [*encensé*]; she

[36] Quoted by F. Armand and R. Maublanc, *Fourier* (Paris, 1937), 46.

has given up to me all her treasures. In possession of the book of Destinies I shall dissipate the political and moral darkness, and on the ruin of the uncertain sciences I shall establish the theory of universal harmony."[37] The language of the new knowledge is that of the positive natural sciences, but its meaning is the discovery of God's hitherto secret plan for the Creation.

The Natural Order of the Passions

Fourier's rejection of civilization included the rejection of the entire recorded experience of mankind. "Hardly seven thousand years have elapsed since the creation of man, and in all this time we have gone only from torment to torment."[38] From this totally negative judgment, a comprehensive discontent with life, flows Fourier's conviction that the real life of man still lies ahead of us. This conviction, as we have seen, expressed itself not as a vague hope but as a precise plan of history. From where did Fourier draw the elements of this plan and the design of his Phalanstery? Not, like Isaiah, from the voice of grace flooding him with hope but rather from the discovery of "positive science," psychology. Fourier's psychology has curious dimensions, being neither fully nor wholly human. Of man it takes only the passions as it ascribes to them the true human essence. The passions, however, are not confined to man; they govern the entire universe with a strength that is second only to God's. In fact, they even make up the very essence of God.[39] In other words, the passions are a force that is fundamental to everything and brackets God with man and the universe with this globe. Neither God nor man can change them.[40] When frustrated, they turn from harmonious drives into "ferocious tigers." All one can do is to recognize them for what they are and to provide proper channels for them through adequate human institutions. "The problem is to give free reign to the twelve root passions."[41]

[37] Fourier, *Théorie des quatre mouvements* (n.p., 1841), 285.
[38] Fourier, *Oeuvres Complètes*, I, 52.
[39] *Ibid.*, VI, 445.
[40] *Ibid.*, I, 14.
[41] *Ibid.*, VI, 55.

Knowledge of the passions is Fourier's key to the knowledge of order as well as to the knowledge of God. He divides them into five "sensitive passions" (sight, hearing, smell, taste, touch), four "affective passions" (friendship, love, ambition, paternity), and three organizing or "distributive passions" (emulation, alternation, combination), the latter functioning as the "pivots" for the harmonious arrangement of the others. Misunderstanding the passions as something deserving repression is the root mistake in man's present existence, his rebellion against God. If man could only accept his natural drives as unquestioningly as those animals in whom God has instilled a passionate love for the work on which their existence depends![42] Not reason but rather the unreflecting forces in human nature are considered as that in and through which man is closest to God. Here we can discover a line from Hobbes through La Rochefoucauld, Morelly, and Fourier, to Freud.

Marx attributed basic reality to matter, Fourier to the passions. Both reduce all being to a force that they see as both ontic and phenomenal, something construed both as the root of everything and as knowable through the methods of natural science. The knowability implies eventual mastery over all the forces of being. Fourier believes that through a "positive" science he has gained precise knowledge of the transcendence which is thus potentially brought into the range of human manipulation. In other respects, though, Marx's and Fourier's constructions differ significantly. What Fourier obtained through his table of passions is some concept of human nature, a latent and yet unrealized essence which must and will attain future actuality. Marx, on the other hand, put in lieu of any concept of human essence only his awareness of alienation. Politically, Marx's concept was more powerful. Philosophically, however, it provided no Archimedian point from which to contruct a history that would make man come-to-be. Once one accepts Fourier's premise that man's soul is coextensive with his passions, that the passions must be beneficent and, should they appear destructive, can only have been perverted, it follows that an

[42] *Ibid.*, III, 250.

existence in the full harmony of the passions is still in store for mankind. It also follows that no violent revolution needs to put things right, because the passions already are more potent forces than any other. Thus "to do away with crime and what is termed moral depravity we have not to change man's nature, create a new being or a new race . . . we have only to change the social organization and the vicious direction which the passions receive from it."[43] With nothing more than a financial benefactor who would supply the funds for the first Phalanstery, mankind could thus expect to take the "leap from chaos to harmony."[44]

God on Trial

Fourier believed in God. He heaped scorn on the atheists, their "bastard opinion," their superficiality and inconsistency. To know God's will was to him man's first and foremost task. But the knowledge of God, in spite of man's professions of humility, is not something he expects to derive from God's revelation of Himself. Fourier's God is less than almighty. He "cannot create something from nothing."[45] Whatever it is that He formed human souls of exists independently of God and limits God's will. The knowledge of that which, existing independently, confines God is possible through "positive science," which thus becomes man's chief access to the knowledge of God himself. Fourier, finding the "true order of the passions," had attained this knowledge. From this vantage point he then proceeded to demand of God why mankind's lot has been so miserable. True, the earth had labored under an error about the passions which amounted to rebellion against God. God, however, had permitted this debasement of man and Himself. The misdoings of civilization thus are ultimately the misdoings of God. In an article called "Égarement de la raison"[46] Fourier drew up an "act of indictment" against God, pushing it to the conclusion that God is

43 Brisbane, *Social Destiny of Man*, 260.
44 Fourier, *Oeuvres Complètes, III*, 246.
45 *Ibid.*, 304.
46 Quoted by Paul Janet, "Le socialisme au XIX siècle," *Revue des deux mondes*, XXXV (1879), 628.

the "equivalent of the devil." Before Fourier, like an open book, lies the scheme of the relation between God and man as it should be, from which he repeatedly specifies the tasks and duties of either part, particularly those of God. "God's duty is to give us a code, man's duty is to find it."[47] As God has made us to be happy, there must be a plan for our happiness: this plan must be discovered. After seven thousand years of error Fourier has finally discovered it. "God is the exclusive possessor of the most powerful force, the talisman of attraction."[48] This "magic lever" is what moves the universe. God could not be so inconsistent as to deny it to man nor would God be so stupid to give us passions that were not useful.

Armed with this newly gained knowledge of what God really wanted or should have wanted, Fourier perceives mankind's scheduled movement through the thirty-two ages of its life cycle. His thought now moves in eons. A mere four to five thousand years of misery are dismissed as unimportant in comparison with eighty thousand of bliss. Assuming God's point of view, he builds with the planner's large blocks. "Do you take God for a cad who busies himself in each household, for a meddler who pokes his nose into every person's affairs?"[49] God is concerned with the globe and not with particulars. The whole of history is His plan to which the generations living at an unhappy time are logically sacrificed. "God has willed that the theory of universal movement fell to the lot of an illiterate man," Fourier seemingly humbles himself.[50] Once in possession of his "theory," however, he turns its searching power on God Himself. He puts Him "on trial," prescribes to God His duties, imputes to God His plan of history. Fourier's repeated use of the terms "magic," "talisman," "most powerful force of nature" is no accident. God, limited as He is, can be known and controlled. The "leap from chaos into harmony" is not God's work but man's, under Fourier's guidance. Positive science plays here the role of the Cabbala.

[47] *Ibid.*, 630.
[48] Fourier, *Oeuvres Complètes*, III, 248.
[49] Janet, "Le socialisme au XIX siècle," 632.
[50] Fourier, *Théorie des quatre mouvements*, 151.

Paradise

From beginning to end, mankind's cycle of life is known to Fourier. It does not move anywhere except back to its beginning. The rise to paradise is followed by a final fall. Similar cycles, says Fourier, occur on other globes. The whole, like the intake and release of breath, has no meaning. But there is meaning in the movement from phase to phase of history, so that these phases are truly mankind's "destinies." The plural is significant in that there is no human destiny except that of passing through a number of historical phases. Human striving finds its direction in each respective future phase, so that the order of time provides the order of action.

Among the thirty-two phases of the cycle there is one unique in hope and significance. It is the present moment of history, the age from which mankind will suddenly enter into its destinies. "We shall witness a spectacle which can be seen only once on each globe: the sudden passage from social incoherence to social combination; this is the most brilliant motional effect [*effet du mouvement*] that can occur in the universe; its attainment must console the living generation for all its misfortunes."[51] While history as a whole is cyclically meaningless, this step from the fifth age to the next higher one is full of hope. Unlike other passages from one phase to the next, this one is entirely man's work. Nature has no part in it, God's grace is not required. History is pushed forward by a social action which not only reorganizes human existence but also unloosens the power of nature subsequently to confer its beneficent creations on the race. Out of the time-ocean of meaninglessness, a time-island of hope-in-action thus arises. It is the present moment in which man's own decision to bring about the next phase snatches sense from a total cycle of absurdity.

This unique movement at the end of the fifth phase leaves behind a regime of reflective reason and initiates one of harmony with natural forces. Such works of human reason as are born from reflection on transcendent norms—the state, law, morality—will disappear. Up to this point Fourier agrees with the later Marx who

[51] Fourier, *Oeuvres Complètes,* I, 17.

also dismissed the political order as a mere illusion. Marx attributed a creative role to violence, a conclusion which he could hardly escape as long as he did not see any beneficent elements in this world. Violent destruction of the false world of the present alone could pave the way for the paradise of the future. Fourier's psychology, however, allowed him to demand that the passions only be given a "new chance" whereupon they would develop three and four times the strength they had in the present "incoherent" condition.[52] In other words, Marx hoped for salvation through external force while Fourier looked for the elimination of internal restraints. In both cases, however, human freedom is implicitly denied. Fourier sees it as a disturbing feature only during the "incoherent" ages, and expects that his new science "will change the lot of mankind, it flatters the passions that are common to all men and seduces them by the lures of gain and lust; there is the guarantee of its success with the savages and the barbarians as with civilized people, because the passions are the same everywhere."[53] The future will consist of social engineering in the form of manipulation of the passions. The age of bliss is also the age of total planning, the planning not only of "combination" but also of the individual human personality. A century after Fourier's death, a modern writer, about whom nobody is laughing, cast Fourier's paradise into the form of fiction. Aldous Huxley's *Brave New World* spelled out the inhumanity of an order in which the lever of human passions dispenses the planners from any need to resort to normative compulsion.

AN ARCHETYPAL PROGRESSIVISM

A new type of total critique has now emerged in addition to the axiological variety. The axiological total critique operated with a very simple juxtaposition of an abstract logical scheme of social perfection called "nature" and the actual societies of history, attributing value only to the former and convicting the latter of total

[52] *Ibid.*, 15.
[53] Fourier, *Théorie des quatre mouvements*, 12.

unvalue and unreality. The new pattern is more complex and less apparently logical. One can distinguish the following components:

(1) In general, we find that history is construed as a necessary process resulting from "natural" (i.e., nonintelligent) causes, a process which, by means of evolution or revolution, moves through a series of "phases" or "stages" of social order. In this way, the concept of "laws of history" takes the place of the former concept of Providence.

(2) The speculative view of this process includes not merely the "laws" of change but also an ultimate goal of the entire process. Both the causality of change and the "goal" are assumed to lie within the purview of world-immanent conditions. Thus the goal is a social order in time and on earth, the ultimate or "final" in a series of successive societies. It is depicted as a social order of harmony beyond good and evil.

(3) The crucial and by no means logical point in the process-oriented outlook is the attribution of sole value to the goal phase of history. In the light of this explanation, the entire process appears as the "becoming" of ultimate value, which may be conceived in terms of being, or freedom, or true humanity, or harmony of man and nature.

(4) As one attributes value only to the goal stage of the historical process, all stages other than the ultimate stand condemned of inherent imperfection, unvalue, or unreality. In other words, every society except the last one is subject to total critique. We may name this pattern the *teleological* total critique, in which the *telos* of future value serves as the Archimedian point from which the world of present and past experience is lifted off of its hinges. Camus called this the substitution of "horizontal" for "vertical" transcendence—the use of the future as a transcendence to which all presents are subordinated as mere preparatory stages.

(5) Not logically but rather gratuitously, the present age or society is frequently seen as the extreme antithesis to the future, so that it can be construed as an age of total alienation. In other words, the value of the goal age appears as the total negation of the

present age, and vice versa. The historical process then can be seen not merely as the "becoming" of value but also as the "overcoming" of present conditions of unvalue.

(6) The value of the goal stage of the entire process cannot be construed as the good of now living men or societies nor as that of past generations. Nor would it do to construe it as the good of any particular people or nation, unless a people or nation can be identified with a future universal "destiny." Thus the goal stage is assigned to humanity ("the total mass of humanity," in Turgot's words). As a result, humanity becomes the subject whose becoming takes place in and through history, and humanity moves into the place of all other transcendent loyalties.

(7) As history is the "becoming" process occasioned by causative "laws," the knowledge of these laws not only discloses the ultimate destination of mankind but also is instrumental in history's forward motion. Hence, the most important political distinction is between those who "know" and the others who are ignorant, in the sense that mankind's destiny appears to depend wholly on the former, with their power and political efficacy.

Marxist socialism fits this pattern, but it is not the only type of total critique to be found there. The same pattern can be observed in Comte's Positivism, Nietzsche's view of history, and a number of other ideologies of the historicist variety. The particular modalities may differ. It matters relatively little whether one identifies the mechanism of progress as that of economic invention, or scientific thought, or natural selection, or the operation of genius. The decisive step is the substitution of a future condition for all value, present or past, and the absorption of moral judgment by the requirements of historical process. The pretense of positive knowledge of the future is the key to an attitude that considers itself an alien in any kind of present. In Marx we can observe the combination of this type of total critique with the previous one.

III □ Total Critique and Total Revolution

Fourier's interest in the historical process was missing in Meslier and Morelly, and the latters' speculation on a perennially valid order of nature is not found in Fourier. Nevertheless, the total rejection of existing society is common to all three. There are, then, two different patterns of total critique of society which should be further compared, with the help of some theoretical concepts.

AXIOLOGICAL AND TELEOLOGICAL CRITIQUE OF SOCIETY

As Meslier and Morelly reduced the existing order to nothingness, they took their stand in what they called "nature." They used this term in three different senses. First, they meant by nature something roughly equivalent to "the nature of man"—the idea of a built-in structure either of an organism or a community or relationship. In a second sense, the term "nature" connoted the content of that structure, its model in the inanimate, vegetative, or animate environment of man, or in the vital forces observable in the cosmos as well as in man himself. This second meaning approximated that of *physis* as the Sophists used the term in opposition to *nomos*—vital and causal necessity opposed to the order of the human mind and human institutions, with a preference for norms derived from nature rather than from human awareness of God or goodness. In this second meaning one can distinguish three subdivisions: nature as a norm may be found in the world of animals, in the "naturally" (i.e., unconsciously or subconsciously) potent human drives or passions, or in man's relation with nature through labor. The third meaning of nature opposed a phantasmal but rationally perfect order to whatever has grown in history, the latter being characterized as haphazard, irrational, and characterized by "prejudices," so that all of history appeared as a deviation from "nature." The verdict of being a product of history then fell particularly on the existing order, so that salvation was seen as the destruction of "prejudices" by enlightenment, which would constitute man's turning from history to nature. This type of total critique of society therefore demanded no revolutionary action other than an awakening to the "long-lost truth" of nature, from which awakening would automatically follow the dissolution of allegiance to the existing society. In other words, what Meslier and Morelly sought is, in the contemporary vernacular, a "dropping out" of the people from society. The emphasis is wholly negative but not necessarily violent.

In Turgot, Condorcet, and Fourier, by contrast, the emphasis was precisely on history rather than timeless nature, the term "history" again being used in a variety of meanings. "History" connoted, first, a succession of distinct phases of order, including the idea that this succession occurs according to knowable laws, so that the knowledge of these laws extends to the not-yet-actualized future. Second, "history" meant a long-extended process through which true humanity will come to be at some future time, having not yet existed either in the past or the present. Third, history was used to describe the dramatic turning from the *summum malum* of the past and present to the *summum bonum* of the future. This particular meaning again has three subdivisions: it denoted either the inescapable necessity of the movement from nonbeing to being, or the "mission" incumbent on some social element to accomplish this movement, or else the normative character of this movement as the supreme yardstick for rational conduct. A total critique of society based on these meanings of "history," then, is conceived in terms of process rather than timeless being. Some doubt has been expressed whether, for instance, Marx really accepted history as the measure of his thought on society, the doubt having been raised by Marx's condemnation of the order which has historically grown in the past. It seems to be a general characteristic of the total critics who are oriented toward history that they divide time into two parts, an acceptable and a nonacceptable one, the first containing being and the second nonbeing, the first identified with the future and the second with the past. A certain rejection of history can thus be found in thinkers of this type. All the same, their total critique should be called historicist because the process by which mankind supposedly moves from nonbeing to being is construed as an historical sequence of action, including active struggle against the past. The good is for them necessarily in the future, as the evil belongs to the past, so that their negation is focused on the present as a product of the past.

We have called the first type of total critique *axiological* and the second *teleological.* In both cases a contraction of human life, particularly human experience, is postulated. As in the case of the Sophists, "nature" can be accepted as a norm only to the exclusion of the divine, but in addition also to the exclusion of the historical. It is, of course, true that human life is embedded in nature and that man's relation with nature is inescapable. All the same, to treat man's relation and participation in nature as all there is to human life is a reductionism. It is also a reductionism, on the other hand, to exclude the timeless from the historical and to consider the flux of things the sole reality in which human life takes shape and order. Man has an historical existence, but he also transcends history, which is precisely why he has been able to become conscious of history. Thus, both types of total critique maintain themselves by excluding from their evidence certain human experiences which have been central to the problem of order, calling these experiences illusory.[1] The various ideological types of total critique have assumed an Archimedian point beyond the realm of experience from which the world of experience can be surveyed, criticized and even declared a nothingness. The Archimedian point, in turn, a realm of phantasmal perfection, appears as paradise when viewed from the point of view of the actual nothingness. A polarity between nothingness and paradise is characteristic of every ideologi-

[1] On the rejection of experience as "illusory," *cf.* Eric Voegelin "Immortality: Experience and Symbol," *Harvard Theological Review*, LX, 251.

cal total critique of society, which always extends to a critique of all experienced reality.

Since the axiological critique is deficient on the historical side, and likewise the teleological critique on the axiological side, the idea could occur to someone to combine these two in one system. The idea did in fact occur to Marx. We shall see whether combining the two helped to remedy the defects of either critique. Marx began with speculations about an order that in contrast to the false society of experience would be true to nature. He later proceeded to speculations about ages or phases of history and the necessity of their succession, combining the two speculations in his "scientific socialism" which postulated the eventual attainment of an order true to nature as the result of a causally necessary succession of time segments. But Marx also replaced philosophy with revolutionary action: "The philosophers have only *interpreted* the world in different ways; the point is, to *change* it." We shall now look into the question of whether the replacement of total critique by total revolution had anything to do with the combination of the two critiques.

HEGELIAN CHILIASM

Two prophets in mid-nineteenth century converted the total critique of society into a call to arms: Marx and Bakunin.[2] Both came from Hegel in the sense that they joined in the wave of chiliastic enthusiasm, the anticipation of a new world, that characterized the Hegelians after 1834. It has now become customary to make a clear distinction between Saint-Simon and the Saint-Simonians, the latter being inspired by their master but carrying his ideas into new territory and even developing new ideas of their own. Hegel scholarship has not yet begun to treat the Hegelians as a separate ideological phenomenon, although there are beginnings of a distinction of the Hegelians similar to that of the Saint-

[2] Others still carried on the revolutionary enterprise of Babeuf, which generated a latter-day community of faithful around Blanqui.

Simonians.[3] Such a distinction makes eminent sense, chiefly in terms of the underlying experience. Hegel's dominant experience was twofold: Christianity and the French Revolution; the central experience of the Hegelians was Hegel himself, the philosopher who in their eyes had finally penetrated the mysteries of heaven and earth, who had secured for man the ultimate goal of "absolute knowledge," and who had proven that history was the dialectic of man's redemption. His message appeared to them as a terminal one: the entire previous experience of mankind was wound up in it, a line was drawn and the sum total was added, and now something wholly new would begin.

The experience of an imminent "new world" elicited the counter-concept of an "old world" which Hegel's achievement had supposedly done away with. Since the "new world" would center in the full rationality of "absolute knowledge," the characteristic of the "old world" must be its irrationality. From a post-Hegelian point of view, this conceptual opposition applied above all to Hegelianism and Christianity. In 1833 the Hegelian Friedrich Richter called for the systematic destruction of Christian symbolism, chiefly the symbolism of life after death and of the end of time. True, other Hegelians rushed forward to prove that the master's philosophy was compatible with Christianity, but in the course of this attempt their leader Göschel had to admit that "Christianity and speculative philosophy are distinct not only in form but also in content."[4] Another group of Hegelians, led by Strauss, heeded Richter's call and began dismantling the "old world" by substituting Hegelian for Christian symbolism and planning action for the practical realization of the Hegelian *logos*. Their common attitude was one that looked on Hegel's task as one as yet uncompleted. Michelet spoke for them when he rephrased that philosopher's famous sentence, "What is real is rational—but not everything that is rational is real." The task, therefore, was to remake reality in the image of Hegel's rationality. As one of the enthusiastic followers put it: "The

[3] *Cf.*, for instance, Jürgen Gebhardt, *Politik und Eschatologie: Studien zur Geschichte der Hegelschen Schule* . . . (Munich, 1963), and Nicholas Lobkowicz, *Theory and Practice*, (South Bend, 1967).

[4] According to Michelet, as quoted by Gebhardt, *Politik und Eschatologie*, 79.

Beyond has become immanent," to which he added, "All this darkness little by little will turn to ashes."[5]

THE "DESTRUCTION OF EVERYTHING THAT EXISTS"

All Hegelians, Marx included, thus lived in the expectation of a new world in which, the crust of past irrationality broken, Hegelian rationality and practical life would be fully reconciled, and this, while it would occur "little by little," to be realized within a few years. On this common basis the Hegelians began to unfold their various versions of what were the irrationalities which most effectively blocked the advent of absolute knowledge and what should be done to remove them. These variations, therefore, center on the common theme of a critique of actuality in the name of "possible reality," the latter being the Archimedian point used to lift the world from its hinges. The assumption of an imminent, as well as immanent, transfiguration of human existence, was the "living point," in Göschel's words, which no one can learn and which precedes philosophy as a "Pentecost," a "rebirth," without which no philosopher "can climb from the sphere of natural reason to the speculative heights of the living concept."[6]

The process, however, had also its negative aspect which consisted in converting "all this darkness" to "ashes." It was not Marx alone who thought of this negative process in terms of "revolution." Before him, Bruno Bauer had called for a "revolution against everything positive" and had spoken of the "terrorism of the true theory." Edgar Bauer saw the struggle of Hegelian philosophy not as a struggle of "ideas against ideas," but of "men against men."[7] As there are "a thousand ways of saying no," Left Hegelianism moved at a feverish pace from one variety of negation to another. Bauer's vaunted "Critique" resembled Meslier's method, the "unmasking" of irrationality of whatever exists, with the assumption that whatever had been so unmasked had thereby been effectively destroyed. Arnold Ruge rejected such merely intellectual destruc-

[5] Wilhelm Vatke, as quoted by Gebhardt, *Politik und Eschatologie*, 53.
[6] As quoted by Gebhardt, *Politik und Eschatologie*, 55.
[7] Lobkowicz, *Theory and Practice*, 274.

tion as inadequate and demanded "political emancipation." Marx in turn was dissatisfied with political revolution and called for a total "human emancipation." It would be idle to arrange these various "positions" in terms of influences and developments, and any such attempt would only obscure the nature of what was occurring among the Left Hegelians. Rejecting actual reality in the name of "possible realities" could take on many forms, violent and nonviolent, intellectual and practical, religious and secular, political and economic. The fundamental irrationality of assuming an Archimedian point outside of the world to be at some men's disposal would lend an element of inadequacy to every one of these attempts. Thus, there would be a tendency to rush from one to another, and, still finding the goal unaccomplished, to yet another, and this to happen within a closely knit group or even within one person's mind.

Marx's own position was originally formulated in March, 1843, in a letter to Ruge, in which we read, "one might perhaps allow a ship of fools to drift a while before the wind; but it would drift towards its destiny precisely because the fools did not believe it. That destiny is the imminent revolution."[8] On the basis of this assumption he then arrives at the conclusion: "The school [i.e., Left Hegelianism] has this advantage, that we do not dogmatically anticipate the world but want to find the new world out of the critique of the old . . . . Philosophy has become worldly . . . . What we must accomplish is the ruthless critique of everything that exists . . . . Reason has always existed, but not always in rational form. The critic therefore can begin with any form of theoretical or practical consciousness and, out of existing reality's own forms, develop the true reality at its norm and its ultimate goal. . . . Out of the principles of the world we develop the new principles for the world."[9] In Bruno Bauer's sense, critique meant destruction, as we have seen. The "ruthless" destruction of "everything that exists" becomes in Marx's eyes not merely a negative aspect of a

[8] Marx, "Ein Briefwechsel von 1843," in Marx, *Frühe Schriften*, ed. H. J. Lieber and Peter Furth (2 vols.; Stuttgart, 1962), I, 428.

[9] *Ibid.*, 447–49.

"rebirth" (in Göschel's sense) but rather the *via negativa* of a new creation. In radical negation alone can be found the knowledge of the as yet hidden "norm of reason." It was only a year earlier that Bakunin had formulated the sentence: "The urge of destruction is at the same time a creative urge."

"TAKING BACK" ONE'S OWN

The movement to which Friedrich Richter had supplied the first articulate impulse considered itself engaged in removing the remnants of the "old world," which had become obsolete through Hegel's attainment of "Absolute Knowledge." What precisely was this "old world"? How could one distinguish its "oldness" from the "newness" to come? Richter himself had decided that the essential difference must be seen in terms of transcendence and immanence, when he demanded a "clear and comprehensible refutation of the Beyond [*Jenseits*]," so that in its place could be established "the higher world of Immanence [*Diesseits*]."[10] Why would the refutation of the transcendent be experienced as a liberating salvation? Feuerbach provided the answer to this question in his *Essence of Christianity* which made the divine appear as a fantastic production of the human mind as it bestowed on a nonexistent being its own most noble qualities. The change from transcendence to immanence then would call for man to "take back" what essentially belonged to him and which religion had separated and alienated from him.

This was a new twist given to Hegel's reconciliation, the mind's "coming to himself," a twist that defined reconciliation as the recovery of the "lost" products of man's own freedom which confronted him as an alien necessity.[11] The same movement of recovery can be seen in Marx's contrast between the "abstract citizen" and the "real man." Marx had pushed the transcendence-immanence problem one step further back, discovering in Hegel's

[10] As quoted by Gebhardt, *Politik und Eschatologie*, 72.
[11] Johann G. Fichte, "Wissenschaftslehre," in Fichte, *Werke*, ed. R. Lauth and H. Jacob (6 vols.; Stuttgart-Bad Camstatt, 1964–68), II.

state, and consequently also in the "citizen," that same transcendence which Feuerbach had found only in God. Marx's "emancipation" thus required a "restoration" (*Zurückführung*) of the world to "man himself." In the same way in which Feuerbach demanded that man take back the God whom he had created, so Marx could see salvation only as man took back into his "real self" the abstraction of the "political citizen."[12] Richter, Feuerbach, and Marx alike saw the "old world" essentially as that of some kind of transcendence and the "new" as that of a radically consistent immanence. Each of these three variations on the same theme had become a little more radical from what preceded it. Marx, having gone furthest of all, smelled "transcendence" not merely in Christianity or religion as such, but in Hegel's Concept. As he turned against it, he took his stand in that other aspect of the world as Hegel had constructed it, in the sphere of concrete particularities, separate persons and their self-centered activities which Hegel had designated "civil society."[13] This, the immanent part of Hegel's universe, Marx now acclaimed as the sole reality, accusing Hegel of building in the Idea a "second reality," a fantasy of mystifying imagination and a product of human alienation the same as Feuerbach's God.[14] Thus, the thrust of Marx's only work on political theory is his determination to "take back" the attribute of reality from the embodiment of Hegel's idea, the state, and to reserve it exclusively for what Hegel considered a mere attribute, namely, the "civil society." Marx considered himself the champion of the "real" reality, the sensuous setting of human existence here and now, the

[12] Marx, "Zur Judenfrage," in Marx, *Frühe Schriften,* I, 479.

[13] Hegel, *Grundlinien der Philosophie des Rechts*, ed. H. Glockner (Stuttgart, 1928).

[14] Marx, "Kritik des Hegelschen Staatsrechts," in Marx, *Frühe Schriften*: "Reality is approached [by Hegel] not as it is but as a second reality [*andere Wirklichkeit*]." (p. 262) "The 'concept' is the Son in the 'Idea' [which is] God the Father." (p. 272) [The political state, the constitution] "developed as the universal reason vis-à-vis the other spheres [of society], as their transcendence [*Jenseitiges*]. . . . but the particular spheres are not conscious of their transcendence [*jenseitiges Dasein*], being nothing else but the affirmation of their own alienation. Until now the political constitution was the religious sphere, the religion of the people's life, the heaven of its universality as contrasted with the wordly existence of its reality. . . . Political life in the modern state is the scholasticism of the people's existence." (p. 295)

tangible concreteness which Hegel had "contemptuously"[15] treated as if it were a mere predicate of the alone real Idea. In his turn, Marx treated the Idea, and, indeed, everything pertaining to the mind, with even more contempt. Together with Hegel's Idea, Marx cut off from his notion of reality the entire political order, calling it a "mere illusion." He reduced reality to what Hegel had termed "civil society" minus the state and thus faced the task of construing this contracted reality as something like a social order. This he attempted to do with the help of two concepts, private property and labor. The attempt, however, was not successful.

A SOCIETY OF "PRIVATE MEN"?

"The *real* man is the *private man* of the present constitution."[16] This private man is the same as Hegel's "concrete person who is himself the object of his particular aims, . . . a totality of wants and a mixture of willfulness and natural necessity," an existentially isolated being whom Hegel saw joined to some kind of universality through the state. For Marx, however, the state is transcendence, "alienation." There is no such thing as universality in the political order which actually is composed of bureaucrats, who are mere careerhounds, and a monarch, who himself is a particular natural person with his own concrete interests.[17] Thus the real society is the field of self-seeking economic activities rather than the political order. Man as such is not, there are only men. In the place of the banished universal Marx put a metastatic substitute, "species life."

Let us accompany Marx as he sets out to construct, in lieu of Hegel's reality of the Idea, the reality of man founded in practical, sensuous activity. The private sphere, which he sees as the only social reality there is, appeared to both Hegel and Marx as determined by private property. Hegel looked on private property as one of the concrete determinants of the state as the universal idea; Marx, reversing the construction, considers private property the actual constitution, the "highest political spirit." He maintains:

[15] *Ibid.*, 335.
[16] *Ibid.*, 363.
[17] *Ibid.*, 316, 346.

"Independent private property or the '*real* private property' is . . . not only the 'pillar of the constitution' but the '*very constitution*' " [*die Verfassung selbst*]. Now the pillar of the constitution must be the constitution of constitutions, the prime and real constitution."[18] And further, "The *reality* of the ethical idea is seen here as the *religion of private property*."[19] So far it sounds as if Marx regarded men's economic orientation as the chief ordering principle in society. At this point, however, he moves from men to forces. "Private property is secured against the arbitrary will [Willkür] of the owner in that the sphere of his will has been transformed from a general human will to the specific arbitrariness [Willkür] of private property so that private property has become the subject of will and the [human] will is nothing more than the predicate of private property."[20] What Marx considered the "real" constitution has turned out to be something impersonal to which men and their wills are subject. The impersonal something, however, may possibly turn out to hold men together in something like social unity.

The reader will have noticed that Marx, in reversing Hegel, continued to operate with Hegel's concepts. Hegel had described "civil society" as a sphere of conflicting and separate private wills which required mediation and obtained it through the state. Marx, having declared Hegel's mediations both illusory and nonnecessary, is left with the separateness of the many particulars. "Comprehension consists not, as Hegel thinks, in finding everywhere the attributes of the logical concept but rather in grasping the peculiar logic of each particular object."[21] These "particular objects," be they "private men" or private properties or both, would not form any kind of unity for Marx: "Real extremes cannot be mediated, precisely because they are real extremes. Nor do they need mediation, because they are essentially opposites. They have nothing in common with each other. . . . [It is an error to think] that the adamancy of *real* opposites, their development into extremes, which means nothing but their self-awareness and their excitement to a decisive

[18] *Ibid.*, 387, 398.
[19] *Ibid.*, 392.
[20] *Ibid.*, 389.
[21] *Ibid.*, 377.

combat, is something one could prevent or even consider detrimental."[22] Where Marx hoped to find the structure of a "real" constitution, he came up only with a battleground between "particular objects" which have "nothing in common" and instead are getting ready for final combat.

THE ORDER OF COLLECTIVE LABOR

Marx fared no better with his other concept of order—labor. Here he relied mainly on the concepts of Adam Smith who, two generations before Hegel, had already treated of "civil society" as a sphere of order somewhat independent of the state. Smith, possibly following Locke in this respect, saw in labor the measure of all economic value, the ultimate yardstick of exchange. He praised the division of labor, that is, the development of functional specialization, as the greatest advance in labor productivity but attributed it not to technical innovation as rather to the fundamental human propensity for exchange, which he in turn traced to the faculty of reason and speech.[23] One recalls that Aristotle, too, regarded exchange as the most fundamental principle of human association, the "bond that holds men together."[24] Both the division of labor and exchange mediated, in Adam Smith's eyes, between human individuality and society. Labor time appeared to him a suitable universal criterion of value measurement, not as an objective factor but because the subjective sacrifice of "ease, liberty, and happiness," involved in any labor process, remained the same for every worker.[25]

Adam Smith, as the subsequent development of the new science of economics proves, was not wholly unsuccessful in developing concepts of an order that held together "civil society" apart from political constitutions and rulers. Marx rejected this construction of nonpolitical order no less decisively than Hegel's construction

22 *Ibid.*, 373.
23 Adam Smith, *The Wealth of Nations* (New York; Modern Library, 1937), Book I, chapter 2.
24 Aristotle, *Nicomachean Ethics,* 1132b32, 1133a5.
25 Smith, *Wealth of Nations*, I, 5.

of the state. What Marx rejected was Smith's central notion of exchange. Smith spoke of labor as the original "money" with which man purchased his products, in view of which all commodities now had a real and a nominal price, the latter a money value. Marx objected: "The labor of each individual, considered in the act of production, is the money with which he purchases the product or the object of his specific activity; but it is a specific money which purchases only this particular product. In order to be money in general it would have to be not specific but general labor, i.e., it would have to be posited from the outset as a link in the chain of common production."[26] The term Marx here uses is *allgemein,* which can mean either "general" or "common" or "collective." The ambiguity is essential to Marx's argument which posits a metastatic in lieu of Adam Smith's reality-oriented concept of labor. In the world of experience, labor has always been performed by particular persons, and by "their mutual contributions men are held together" in "reciprocal exchange" (Aristotle). Marx eliminates both the division of labor and exchange as he posits social labor as if it were performed by a single subject. As such labor cannot be found anywhere in experience, Marx postulates it as a future reality, in which "not exchange will give its general [*allgemein*-communal, collective] character, but the presupposed communal character would govern the sharing of the products . . . . Labor would be presupposed as general [common, collective] before the exchange. . . . The labor of each individual is postulated as social from the outset. . . . Therefore, he has no particular product to exchange. His product is not an exchange value. . . . Instead of a division of labor which arises necessarily as a result of exchange, there would be an organization of labor resulting in each individual having a share in the common consumption."[27]

"Postulating" such a condition might be a *jeu d'esprit,* even though a somewhat frivolous one, but it could hardly apply to the conceptual construction of social reality, a construction intended to be more "realistic" than Hegel's idea. In the first volume of *Cap-*

[26] Marx, *Grundrisse der politischen Oekonomie* (Berlin, 1953), 88.
[27] *Ibid.*

ital, however, Marx makes clear that he has indeed substituted his own fanciful "second reality" for the perception of the experiential world. In chapter 1, section 4, he compares five different modes of production, of which the first is that of Robinson Crusoe, who "knows that his labor, whatever its form, is but the activity of one and the same Robinson. . . . All the relations between Robinson and the objects that form his wealth of his own creation, are here so simple and clear." Two pages later, this literary model furnishes Marx with the key for the understanding of "a community of free individuals, carrying on their work with the means of production in common, in which the labor-power of all the different individuals is consciously applied as the combined labor-power of the community. All the characteristics of Robinson's labor are here repeated, but with this difference, that they are social, instead of individual." Since he "postulates" a community producing like a single individual, Marx believes he can dismiss the division of labor and exchange. At this point Marx becomes the prisoner of his own fanciful flight of the imagination when he transfers it into the world of experience: ". . . the life-process of society, which is based on the process of material production, does not strip off its mystical veil until it is treated as production by freely associated men"—that is, as if it were the production of a Robinson Crusoe.

A DREAM "REALITY"

Two kinds of observations have been made regarding the fundamental character of Marx's endeavor. Some students say that Marx above all sought to establish the reality of the here and now, to bring the concept of man back from the clouds of spirit and idealism and to locate it in the practical, sensuous activities and conditions that characterize human existence within, and upon the basis of, material nature. Others maintain that Marx focused attention on the particularity of man as the producer and consumer of things in order to show forth the utter inhumanity especially of the condition of modern society, where things could be produced and acquired only as commodities, so that commodity production attained an ontological character governing the being of humans. Both of these views agree that Marx was concerned not with attributes of man or human existence but with the basic question of reality as such. Both agree, moreover, that Marx was concerned with reality not in the general context of metaphysics but as centered in man, human activities, and human society. It is further customary among most political writers to dwell on the power and accuracy of Marx's critique, either of Hegel or of modern society, and to allow his alternatives to appear justified by the profundity of the critique. Marx's critique has demonstrated a pervasive power, to be sure; other modern total critiques as, for instance, the national myth, Freudian psychoanalysis, Existentialism, have found it impossible long to continue their negation without entering into some kind of alliance or merger with Marxism. There is, therefore, some justification in treating Marx's critique as the core of the total critique of society in modern times, so that an investigation of its structure could well serve purposes of insight into other types of total critique.

To what extent did Marx succeed in establishing reality on a radically new conceptual basis? Marx's new concept was the "private man," the man who changed nature by means of his labor, who "created his own life" through the objects which his labor fashioned, who in all this was a *Naturwesen,* a being of nature pertaining to nature, whose mind and spirit were wholly derivative from his functional and ontological connection with nature. This being, then, could be social only in and through the order of production, so that Hegel's "civil society" appeared as the concept closest to man's true reality. The shift from a philosophy of man's political order to one of man's economic order was indeed a kind of Copernican turn; but it could be considered successful only if it could be demonstrated that economic activities considered by themselves, and apart from the products of man's contemplation, amount to some kind of order, indeed, to all the order there is. This Marx did not accomplish. While he claimed that "the *entire so-called world history* is nothing but the creation [*Erzeugung*] of man through human labor and the coming-to-be of nature for man,"[28] his verdict on the result was that in historical societies man "feels that he is free only in his animal functions—eating, drinking, and procreating— . . . while in his human functions he feels only like an animal."[29] Marx applies the epithet "animal society" now to the Middle Ages and then also to modern capitalism. If labor, under such different conditions, has produced nothing but an animal reality, then there never has been any human reality. Quite consistently Marx puts his account of what he considers a human order of production in the subjunctive mood throughout, indicating that he is treating not of a reality of experience but merely of a "possible reality."

Marx fares not much better when we consider him as the critic of human "self-alienation" in this economic order which he sought to establish as the sole reality. In this reality of sensuous, practical activity he found only "craftsmen but no men, thinkers, but no men, priests, but no men, masters and servants, young people and settled ones, but no men," (Hölderlin) and with the poet he could regard the whole only as a "battlefield, where hands and arms and all members lie scattered about in fragments, while the spilled life's blood trickles into the sand." Because the experience of fragmentation in particularity is real and widespread and undoubtedly reflects an aspect of the human condition, Marx had hit a note that was bound to reverberate in many hearts. Again, however, he drew from experience and the historical world nothing but the evidence of human nonbeing. So far as experiencing an existence as fragmented, less-than-human, and incomplete presupposes an experience of human wholeness, Marx failed to account for any example of the latter. No society had ever allowed man to be himself, for self-alienation, rooted in the division of labor, had emerged so early that Marx attributed its beginning to the sexual act. Aristotle, too, had noted that the particularities of their economic situation may so dominate men's minds that they are unable to see each other as

[28] Marx, "Ökonomisch-philosophische Manuskripte," in Marx, *Frühe Schriften*, I, 607.

[29] *Ibid.*, 565.

human beings, but he also had allowed that there were always some men in whom the various particularities so balanced each other that they were capable of an awareness of human nature and the nature of things. Marx saw no evidence whatsoever of such men. Self-alienation to him appeared as a general ontological characteristic of humanity as far as history's record went. While he concentrated his critique on bourgeois society, the "present-day society," he held all other previous societies to be subject to the same judgment.

Nonalienated man could be found not in historical societies, with their division of labor, systems of economic exchange, separation of mental from physical labor, contradictions between thought and action, and differences between town and country, but only in a society in which none of these conditions prevailed. Thus Marx, who could not find human reality in terms of record or experienced actuality, postulated a reality which would "negate the negation." His possible reality centers in a mystical integration of labor, of which Robinson Crusoe is the prototype, "which makes it possible for me to do one thing today and another to-morrow, to hunt in the morning, fish in the afternoon, rear cattle in the evening, criticize after dinner, just as I have a mind, without ever becoming hunter, fisherman, shepherd, or critic."[30] Not only the particularity of function in the production process, but also the particularity of individual personality as such will give way to a oneness of thought and action, town and country, man and nature, society and state, the individual and the species.

Marx no doubt speaks the language of mysticism, the language of a unitive process or reality. Mysticism is the experience of actual or potential unity with a greater reality from which particularity ordinarily separates us. Zaehner recently has carefully elaborated the differences between mysticism sacred and profane, the latter centered in nature, the whole of everything that exists in the tangible world.[31] Marx's observation about the origin of the division of

[30] Marx, "Deutsche Ideologie," in *Karl Marx. Die Frühschriften*, ed. S. Landshut (Stuttgart, 1953), 361.
[31] R. C. Zaehner, *Mysticism, Sacred and Profane* (New York and Oxford, 1957).

labor in the sex act contains at least a hint at a potential androgynous oneness of humanity. All the same, his is not another version of nature mysticism. Not only is there a total lack of any kind of mystical experience in Marx's writings but there is also the positive statement in which he sees man the worker estranged from himself by nature: "Thus the more the worker by his labor *appropriates* the external world, the more he deprives himself of *means of life* in [that] double sense [i.e., of objects of his needs, and the means of subsistence]."[32] The worker, operating on nature, is actually "the slave of his object." The extremity of this bondage is that it is only as a "*worker* that he can maintain himself as a *physical subject,* and only as a *physical subject* can he be a worker." Lest one consider this passage an isolated remark in his early work, one should read with it Marx's observation in the third volume of *Capital,* where he speaks of his postulated future society: "Freedom in this field can only consist in socialized man, the associated producers, rationally regulating their interchange with Nature, bringing it under their common control, instead of being ruled by it as by the blind forces of Nature; and achieving this with the least expenditure of energy and under conditions most favorable to, and worthy of, their human nature. But it nonetheless still remains a realm of necessity."[33]

These passages exclude any construction of Marx's mysticism as a nature mysticism. Nature for him was something either controlling man or to be controlled by man and in any case it was a realm of odious necessity. Any thought of sacred mysticism is, of course, inconceivable. In fact, Marx at no point gives any hint of a greater reality of which he knows and to which he yearns to be united. Meslier and Morelly spoke of nature as an overarching superior reality to which man should conform. Helvétius and d'Holbach saw matter as a kind of demiurge, the basis of all being and thus an ultimate reality. Marx shared neither view. The only ultimate reality to which he alludes is one of his own intellectual fabrication, the Robinson Crusoe type of unitive labor, the society

[32] Marx, "Ökonomisch-philosophische Manuskripte," 562.
[33] Marx, *Capital* (3 vols.; Moscow, 1954), III, 800.

without political order, activity without contemplation, a species without individuals, a countryside without towns and cities without countryside, a world with no basis or potentiality rooted in experience, a dream world. Marx's criticism of Hegel applies to himself *a fortiori*: far more than Hegel, Marx is open to the charge that his "posited" essence is a pseudoessence, his man a "hidden and unreal man," and his "negation of the negation" nothing but the confirmation of a "mystical subject-object."

ALIENATION

Marx's critique of society thus does not confront an imperfect human reality with a more fundamental truth of being. This is what one might say, *cum grano salis,* of Meslier, Morelly, Hegel, and even Bruno Bauer, all of whom claimed to have attained insight into what true being is and on this premise rightly assumed that the proclamation of the truth of being to men would suffice to convert people from their mistaken perspectives. For all of them, true being is a present potency capable of actualization by men who are rightly oriented. Marx confronted the facts of social existence not with real potency but rather with fancied desirability, unsupported by any supposed or actual reality of cosmos, heaven, or earth. Marx's "second reality" is not so much speculation, which always regards the profundities and mysteries of actual reality, but pure projection of will and design. He could not, therefore, rely on the truth to make its own impact on men's hearts, but he must engage in plans how to bring his design about. Marx's notion of alienation thus has a peculiar structure, distinct from that of Hegel's and Feuerbach's alienation.

Marx himself called it a "contradiction," and "a dynamic relationship moving inexorably to its resolution." The German for "dynamic" is *energisch*, so that Marx attributes energy, the energy that ultimately creates reality, to something that he designated as "negation." Negativity as creative energy is the device that Marx assumes will bring about the reality which he fancies as possible and desirable. His alienation therefore appears as the very acme of negativity. In this he goes radically further than either Hegel or Feuerbach. Hegel, who in a neo-Platonic fashion began and ended with the One (Absolute Spirit or Mind) conceived alienation as the *kenosis* of Absolute Mind, the self-emptying of the Absolute into the contingent world, on the model of Christ's *Entäusserung* (= alienation, Luther's translation of Phil. 2:7) of himself as he became man. Seen from the human side, alienation is experienced as "the contrast between the Unknown which men seek without being conscious of it and the existence which is offered and permitted to them . . . the need to become conscious about what holds them captive and the Unknown which they desire."[34] In another work of the same period Hegel characterized this tension between "the finite life and the infinite life" as the basic strangeness between the mutable and the constant, the concrete and the universal. Hegel's alienation, then, is an integral feature of the human condition, an experienced deficiency which in its suffering bespeaks man's unknowing knowledge of the ground of being. For Feuerbach alienation is a self-deprivation by means of a self-deception, something to be overcome and corrected because it is a mistake. But the mistake in its time was unavoidable and even desirable, so that Feuerbach might have spoken of a *felix error*. Happy or not, the mistake was one which Feuerbach felt would correct itself simply by a confrontation with the truth, which consisted of only two ultimate realities, nature and man.

By contrast, Marx's alienation has the character of an ontological negativity, antibeing which of its own lack of reality drives towards being. Marx, however, adds yet another note that assumes sinister significance later, for he depicts alienation not merely as a condition shared by all men, but also as a kind of crime. In the *Economic and Philosophical Manuscripts of 1844*, Marx still talks of alienation as a kind of universal curse upon all human existence, but already in *The Holy Family*, and much more in later writings, alienation appears as something in which one class finds "its power and its good," so that this class is pronounced guilty of perpetrating

[34] Hegel, "Freiheit und Schicksal," in Hegel, *Sämtliche Werke*, ed. A. Lasson (20 vols.; Leipzig, 1928–29), VII, 138.

"wrong in general" against the rest of mankind by their very mode of existence. From 1847 on the term "alienation" disappears from Marx's works, to be replaced by "exploitation," the latter having a clearly more transitive meaning than the former. Thus alienation is constructed not merely as a contradiction with an inherent dynamism driving towards its own dissolution, but also as justification for a general attack on a human target, with the inherent promise that the struggle, if successful, will result in the removal of "wrong in general."

MORAL INDICTMENT

Here we find the locus of the moral indictment that has so powerfully appealed to Marx's readers. Massive blows of judgment fall on the whole of society, even when Marx indicts some particular manifestations, like a law against lumber theft, the employment of child labor, the public system of education, or the philandering of family fathers. Marx's language hammers with a power reminiscent of the prophet who said of Israel: ". . . they that pant after the dust of the earth on the head of the poor, and turn aside the way of the meek . . . who turn judgment to wormwood, and leave off righteousness in the earth . . . that lie upon beds of ivory, and stretch themselves upon their couches, and eat the lambs out of the flock, and the calves out of the midst of the stall." But Amos' judgment was a true moral judgment, concerning concrete actions of concrete men in concrete circumstances, and generalizing only as he spoke of the multitude of wicked acts and attitudes. His alternative was the choice of good instead of evil: "Seek good, and not evil, that ye may live . . . . Let judgment run down as waters, and righteousness as a mighty stream." The evil he sees in Israel roots in men's hearts and could be avoided if men were converted to the Lord.

Marx's indictment condemns not this or that concrete choice or a pattern of evil actions but the entire historical condition of human existence. His judgment, strictly speaking, is not moral at all but rather ontological: all that which has gone under the name of reality appears to Marx as a nullity (*Nichtigkeit*), sheer inhumanity, a negation of essence, a gigantic deception. In this point Marx rejects existence in the same way in which the Gnostics and Manichees of old rejected, as an alien power hostile to man, the entire cosmos and everything that had been created. Once the reality of experience has been defined in this way, the problem of discerning moral qualities of human actions vanishes. By force of the overall definition, in the present society *all* laws are unjust, *all* consciousness is false, *all* relations must be corrupt, *all* institutions appear oppressive. Marx's "unmasking" consists in the reduction of every particular aspect of society to the overall formula of falsity. Marx's indictment has borrowed strength from the fact that a flaw indeed besets even the most noble human endeavor and self-interest lurks under every pretense of integrity. Reinhold Niebuhr has called this the universal "ideological taint" which is a permanent factor of human culture and which theologians comprehend through the concept of original sin. Because every man carries within himself a gnawing awareness of his own moral inadequacy, many of them fall easy prey to ideologies which center on the ubiquity and pervasiveness of evil, tieing all particular evils together in one comprehensive cause. To hurl an equally comprehensive "NO!" against this cause, other than oneself, appears as a patent solution of all moral difficulties.

Assuming the entire complex of human reality to be evil does not account for any reality of the good. This, the besetting difficulty of the Manichees, was sidestepped by Marx, who declared the prevailing universal evil a temporary condition. Good, while not possible now, would have existential reality some time later, so that good is related to human imperfection not as *higher* but rather as *later*. This is what Camus called "horizontal transcendence." Its most important implication lies in the fact that the "later" is seen as having some inchoation in the "now" and that men can be grouped together as inchoative who then partake in the later good's potency. In other words, the sole moral activity which Marx can see for man in the present is "to revolutionize the existing world, to attack practically the things one finds and to change them."[35] Marx's moral teaching thus consists in a simple polarization of "moral men and immoral society," (if one may be allowed to misplace Niebuhr's book title out of its context), the "moral men" being those who engage in the enterprise not of comprehending but of changing the world, by destroying "everything that exists," and their moral character being inferred merely from the negativity that is ascribed to the society at hand. The whole complex of moral judgment in Marx thus hinges not on a genuine discernment of actions and motives concrete that run counter to the good, but rather on Marx's inability or unwillingness to find in actual existence any kind of essential reality and his willful and fanciful construction of a reality apart from experience or memory.

THE LOST PAST

So far, we have concentrated on the axiological aspects of Marx's total critique. With the *German Ideology* began his attempt to combine the axiological with a teleological critique, this by constructing a course of historical causal necessity that would inexorably move through struggle and tribulations to the later actualization of the good which Marx had located exclusively in the future. On that showing, he himself would be dispensed from the need to arrange a practical plan for the "transsubstantiation" of the entire world.

Historical materialism, as summarized in the *Preface to the Critique of Political Economy* (but first sketched in the *German Ideology*) is widely regarded as the true core of Marx's thought. Behind this view lies the premise that he actually philosophized about history and seriously, with an open mind, inquired into the structure of civil society, a premise which we have come to deem unfounded. On the strength of that premise, however, it would appear as a solid achievement to have construed history as the interplay

[35] Marx, "Deutsche Ideologie," 351.

between developing human needs and evolving techniques for their satisfaction, thereby to have accounted for all recorded societies, their genesis and demise, and to have identified the forces of change irrespective of concrete human intentions. Even to many readers of Marx who refused to accept his revolutionary message, his "laws of history" seemed convincing as "laws" that could be "objectively" known, inasmuch as their causal necessity was not supposed to root in human consciousness, the freedom and unpredictability of which would hardly admit of any "laws." While some details of Marx's formulary have driven his systematizers to desperation, the whole bears a superficially plausible consistency which for many people suffices to establish history as a complete phenomenal datum, and that including the future. One would expect that in view of such "laws," each "phase" of history would enjoy the same reality as every other, each reflecting a given set of human needs and the techniques for their satisfaction, each valid in its time and place, and each acceptable and "valuable" as a necessary link in the chain of successive structures.

Actually, however, the past is not thus established in Marx's eyes. We have seen that he was unable to find that human labor had created anything like a human reality up to now. What characterized the past was "alienated society" and "animal existence," rather than human life. History in his sight is no continuum: a radical break occurs through the proletarian revolution which he "posits" as a coming, but all the same certain, event. After that revolution will arise human reality, something different in kind from anything that went before. Marx termed the developments up to that Revolution either "history," as in the *Communist Manifesto*, or "prehistory," as in the *Preface to the Critique of Political Economy*. At any rate, the reality index that he gave to the future applied not to the past, so that he seems to inhabit not a world of history but rather a world with the single dimension of the future. Because he put past and future into different categories of reality, we conclude that he cannot have taken his own historical materialism too seriously. Historical materialism operates with concepts of "phases" and "stages," with laws of change that obtain in perpetuity, whereas Marx's revolutionary doctrine radically divides history into "before" and "after," or "nonbeing" and "being."

There is no lack of evidence that Marx kept his historical materialism more in the foreground of his mind while being more fundamentally concerned with the problems of the metastatic revolution. In the *German Ideology*, for instance, he first insists that history is essentially the sequence of modes of production and that there is no such thing as a history of consciousness. A few pages later, however, he proclaims that "revolution is the driving force of history," which implies at least a history of revolutionary consciousness. In the *Communist Manifesto* he seems to wish to treat along parallel lines the rise of the bourgeoisie and that of the proletariat. His analysis of the bourgeoisie reads like a page from a textbook of historical materialism: the causes of its rise are new trade routes and markets, new techniques of production and a new type of property, while periodical political advances follow in the wake of the economic and technological pushes. As he then turns to the anticipated rise of the proletariat, Marx calls it a "similar movement." What he does describe, though, is a movement of a very dissimilar character. The proletariat, by his definition, is a class without property and for this reason cannot be economically motivated, as it is in its practice not attending to the requirements of its peculiar property. In Marx's own account, the proletariat appears to have a consciousness that is not economically determined but rather consists in the awareness of the proletariat's "historical mission" and thus arises not from the given historical situation but from "theory." The upward movement of the proletariat, as Marx describes it in the *Communist Manifesto,* stems not from the push of economic evolution but from the dialectic of a purely political struggle.

Furthermore, Marx treated the proletarian revolution not as one in a series of revolutions but rather as unique—totally unlike other revolutions. None of the others changed anything fundamentally in the conditions of society, each of them merely instituting a new set of masters, while the proletarian revolution brings about the "emancipation of mankind." In this sense, *Capital* is a work demonstrating the inevitability of that unique proletarian revolution. At the same time, it draws a picture of the "present-day society" as the nadir of inhumanity, unreality, and the negation of essence, so that in the present the entire past is represented in its negativity, and the destruction of the present amounts to a scrapping of the past as well. In *Capital,* the polarity of "before" and "after" is caught at the very point of the metastasis: ". . . the expropriators are expropriated." The "after" and its complete goodness are implied in the utter corruption of the present that is being negated.

Marx's total revolution appears to him as the genesis of essential humanity. Historical materialism has not helped to establish this result, but all the same has an indispensable function in the ideological structure. It takes the place of the former concept of Providence by first of all assuring man that there is a plan to history and then convincing him that a higher power will propel events toward the eventual happy conclusion. Unlike Providence, however, the "laws of history" need not be accepted by faith. One needs only to believe in Marx, who tells us that there are laws and that he knows them. The proletariat plays a role which in all respects must be called that of the savior of mankind. Nevertheless, this salvation in Marx's idea system has ceased to be a matter of faith and rather appears the object of positive certainty. The upward movement of the "gravediggers" of the bourgeoisie is presented to us as if it were a given fact; and the assertions that the proletariat is the "only really revolutionary class," the "class that bears the future in its hands" are supposedly derived from the analysis of phenomena given to observation. Another function of historical materialism is to furnish categories of thought to revolutionary strategy, as developed by Marx in his *Class Struggles in France* and *The Eighteenth Brumaire of Louis Bonaparte.* Again, it is obvious that Marx here does not take his own historical materialism as the revelation of truth, because he bends and stretches its concepts not only to fit the facts but also his preconception of the outcome of history.

All the same, revolutionary strategy now becomes subject to the strictures of time and social situations, it falls into categories of classes and subclasses arrayed on the vast battleground of society in shifting phalanxes, and its methods begin to respond to social analysis. Historical materialism enabled Marx to see the revolution as a long-term process, an enterprise of patient strategic maneuvers among powerful social obstructions which only time would gradually remove. It was historical materialism, then, that provided the elements of the ideologized "science" of revolutionary struggle which was eventually to be elaborated by Lenin. This "science," in turn, appears to the adepts as a *gnosis*, the possession of which guarantees the attainment of mankind's salvation by socialist power.

In Marx, the total critique of society attains the complexity that is typical for modern ideological movements. On the one hand, the axiological component is conceived as a sheer desirability, a free design of human fancy without responsibility to any insight into the constitution of being. In this sense, men assume the role as their own creators not merely through the objects they fashion for their sustenance, but even more for the kind of existence they venture to design for themselves in "bold" flights of the imagination. On the other hand, history is enlisted as the goddess who will translate men's dreams into future reality, so that history ceases to appear as the dimension of human mutability in which man lovingly appropriates the past and responsibly decides towards the future, but is rather a process in which a preknown future is brought into existence through inexorable causal necessities. Two types of irrationality combine into a whole in which the willfulness of the first seems corrected by the apparent objectivity of the second, and the meaninglessness of the second receives the inspiration of a supposed destiny from the first. Before essaying the task of finding rational alternatives to this kind of total critique, we must first trace its effect in the field of practical political action.

IV □ Totalitarian Activism

Lenin's basic experience was that of Marx having found the absolute truth; in this respect Lenin had his point of departure in Marx as Marx had it in Hegel.* In the ferment of revolutionary ideas among the Russian intelligentsia during the second half of the nineteenth century, Marx's message of a radically different world to emerge from the revolution of the proletariat struck Lenin as the answer to all questions, both Russian and generally human. His sober mind embraced the apparent realism of Marx's materialistic construction of history, while his pseudoreligious fervor embraced the vision of a total transformation of the world. With the grim consistency that was a personal character trait, Lenin committed himself to the cause of total destruction to which he assigned an ultimately creative role. Lenin took over all the essential elements of Marx's world view, not only without changing them but also with an attitude that precluded any further critical examination of this premise. The representative concepts may be briefly recalled.

REVOLUTION IN PERMANENCE

The "revolution in permanence,"[1] intended as a strategic formula, postulates a revolutionary movement that must never settle for any concrete achievement, never contemplate the end of change, never accept any gain as something to be lived with. The limitless change, the total or permanent revolution, has a corollary in the total critique of society, the negation of man's existence as given in experience. This negation begins with the radical critique

* The bulk of this chapter was published in *Review of Politics*, XXVI, 473–504. By permission of publisher.

[1] Marx, "Ansprache der Zentralbehörde an den Bund," in *Karl Marx, Friedrich Engels, Werke* (40 vols.; Berlin, 1958–68), VII, 254.

of religion, which Marx understands as representing the total rejection of the conditions of human life.[2] The active side of this radical, or total, critique of society is the "radical revolution" which, unlike the "partial revolution," will not "leave the pillars of the house standing." A practical revolution requires an effective social force. Marx specifies the requirements of this force with the concept "negative representative of society." The famous passage describing this entity, which is nothing and is to become everything, runs as follows:

> . . . a class in civil society which is not a class of civil society, an Estate which is the dissolution of all Estates, a sphere that has universal character because of its universal sufferings, that does not claim any particular right because no particular wrong but wrong in general is perpetrated against it, that cannot invoke any historical title but only the universal title of humanity . . . that, in one word, is the total loss of the human self and can win itself only through the total restoration of the human self.[3]

Having characterized his "negative representative" in abstract terms, Marx then pointed to a part of the empirical world and hailed it as the emancipator of mankind, "This dissolution of society as a particular Estate is the proletariat." Henceforth, Marx posited the axiom that the revolution of the proletariat is an historical fact, that the proletariat is the "really revolutionary class" which will not "leave the pillars of the house standing" and that its victory will emancipate, that is, transform human existence.

Lenin made no attempt to add anything further to the world view he received from Marx. From the very first, he considered Marx's positions on man, order, society, and history as definitive, something to be acted on but not to be critically reexamined. Lenin's significance lies in his systematic attention to the problems of activism based on Marx's premises. The title of Lenin's book on the party, *What Is To Be Done?* can stand as a symbol for all of Lenin's contribution to the Communist ideology. Marx had created the ideological attitudes toward man, society, and history.

[2] Marx, "Zur Kritik der Hegelschen Rechtsphilosophie," in *ibid.,* 379.
[3] *Ibid.,* 390.

Lenin created the patterns of organization, strategy, and tactics that presuppose the truth of Marx's views.

With the exception of his first book practically all of Lenin's writings are polemical.[4] In order to identify his thought, one has to study what he rejected as well as what he affirmed. Of the great polemics that studded Lenin's life, four have been chosen here as representative: (1) the polemic (1898–1903) against the Right-Socialist group called the "Economists," culminating in *What Is To Be Done?*; (2) the polemic (1904–1907) against the Mensheviks who then edited the exile newspaper *Iskra,* culminating in *Two Tactics*; (3) the polemic (1915–18) against the German Social-Democrat Karl Kautsky, culminating in *State and Revolution*; (4) the polemic (1919–22) against a group in the world Communist movement called the "Left Communists," culminating in *Left-Wing Communism.*[5] These polemics are chosen because they occurred at critical times when the party faced new problems and Lenin forced it to clarify its position. For this reason, Lenin's polemic against the Narodniki which justified his own acceptance of the Marxist gospel and his polemic against Neo-Kantianism (*Materialism and Empirio-Criticism*) are not included in this article. The four polemics under discussion between them cover the full range of Lenin's contribution to the ideology of total social critique.

ECONOMIC VS. POLITICAL STRUGGLE

The *Credo* was written in 1899 by E. D. Kuskova. Supposedly it represented the views of a group called the "Economists" who were Russian Marxists strongly influenced by the ideas of Eduard Bernstein. Lenin's attacks on these views are represented, among others, by his *Protest of Russian Social Democrats* and, above all, by *What Is To Be Done?*[6]

[4] Lenin, *The Development of Capitalism in Russia* (1899).

[5] Quotations from Lenin's writings in this chapter are the English text of the *Selected Works* (fourth ed.; 12 vols.; New York, 1943), except where no official English translation of a given passage is available. In these cases, quotations are from Lenin, *Sochineniia* (35 vols.; Moscow, 1952–57).

[6] The text of the *Credo* is found in Lenin, *Sochineniia,* IV, 153–56; Lenin's

The argument of the *Credo* was that in the West the bourgeoisie, struggling against the remnants of the medieval order, had won political liberty. Political freedom benefited the proletariat, for even bourgeois liberties enabled the workers to adopt political methods in the class struggle. Following the "line of least resistance," the workers thus entered the parliamentary arena with a political program envisaging either the capture of political power or the eventual collapse of the bourgeois order. As neither goal seemed to come nearer, the long uphill pull for a majority drained the workers' energy and caused them to lose heart. Bernstein therefore had demanded that in the West the maximalist goals of proletarian political action be replaced by gradualist objectives attainable within the existing social framework. Thus, implicitly, the bourgeois order was accepted as the basis for prolabor reforms and legislative collaboration with other progressive parties. From Bernstein's analysis of the situation in the West, the *Credo* drew certain conclusions for Russia. The bourgeoisie had not yet won political freedom in Russia and so political struggle there was impossible. For the Russian proletariat, economic rather than political struggle was the "line of least resistance." Russian workers should concentrate on wresting from their employers improvements in working conditions. The political struggle would have to be left in charge of the liberal bourgeoisie whom the workers should support until democracy had been won.

Lenin countered with the following arguments: The essence of Marxist socialism, as distinct from earlier nonpolitical socialist movements, is emphasis on the political struggle. This Marxist struggle is revolutionary, directed against the whole of contemporary society and to the seizure of total power by the proletariat. The political struggle requires a political party to join all partial and local discontents into a comprehensive rejection of the present order. The "acceptance" of the present order as the basis for reform is not revolutionary but liberal, bourgeois thinking. The workers must use reforms solely to advance their organized strength. All

---

"Protest of Russian Social Democrats" is published in the same volume. "What Is To Be Done?" can be read in English in Lenin, *Selected Works,* II.

discontents should be generalized, all kinds of opposition against the present order should be supported. Instead of attempting to reform existing society, the Marxist political struggle for the socialist society should pursue its ultimate goal by way of an intermediate minimal program. This minimal program should be the attainment of democracy. Once democracy is won, it will offer opportunities for the continuation of the proletarian political struggle with more effective means.

To clarify Lenin's arguments requires first a clarification of what he rejects. The "Economists" of the *Credo* thought in strictly developmental terms. History, an intelligible pattern of causation in their view, can be "scientifically" plotted and mapped. "Scientific" knowledge of history is knowledge of its successive phases. Principles of action follow from the ascertainment of one's own *locus* in the pattern, that is, of the here and now. The Economists thought that Marxists found themselves in a still unfolding capitalistic phase of history where the politically leading force was the bourgeoisie struggling "against the remnants of the medieval order." In the historical succession of class struggles the fight for democracy is the cause of the bourgeoisie par excellence. Unfolding capitalism and bourgeois democracy provide the setting which (for the time being) Marxists must accept and, to that extent, the principles of Marxist action are prescribed by the "rules of the game" of the bourgeois society.

Lenin, by contrast, derived the principles of action from the distant goal, the future socialist society. The strategy of the revolution is an unbroken struggle for the realization of the maximum, a struggle modified only by the necessity of directing one's forces towards intermediate objectives along the way. The fight for democracy, as one stage of this road, is therefore ultimately not the business of the bourgeoisie, but of the workers themselves, and is one of these intermediate objectives. Regardless of the developmental situation, the existing order must in no ways be "accepted" in guiding one's actions. The only acceptable criterion of action is the strategy of the revolutionary seizure of power by the proletariat.

A theory of action, as Aristotle taught, is rationally possible only if the means-ends correlation is not infinitely regressed. In other words, an ultimate end must be assumed if there is to be any systematic knowledge of right action. All theorizing on action thus depends on ontological foundations. Here Lenin as well as the *Credo* relied on Marx, but in different ways. The Economists focus their attention on the "laws of history," which they understand as material developments pushing mankind forward and upward, in well-marked developmental phases. Knowledge of right action follows from a survey of all of the phases through which history must run and the ascertainment of one's own place in this process, in terms of what phase has passed and which is to come. The peculiar emphasis on the Economists is on the causative factors of the forward movement. They would conceive action in terms of what it is that is pushing them at any particular moment of history. Thus they would not orient action toward a supreme end. History constructed as progressive material causation knows of efficient but not of final causes. The refusal of the Economists to orient their thinking to the ultimate end rendered them incapable of working out rational and enduring principles of action. All their precepts moved within the structure of the "given situation." Lenin called them, with some justification, "Opportunists." The Economists could "accept" bourgeois society as a passing phase from which they trusted history would deliver them in due time.

Lenin's theory of action differs in that it does conceive of a *summum bonum*: the ultimate and total victory of the proletariat. A characteristic feature of Lenin's writing is the often repeated emphasis on the "final goal."[7] His fundamental orientation toward the "final goal" enables him to formulate consistent principles of action which he contrasted with the "Opportunism" of his opponents. Aristotle insisted that only things eternal could define the meaning of things temporary. Lenin's "final goal," however, is entirely temporary, an end to be achieved in history by the organized and deliberate effort of people who "know" of history's final

[7] For representative examples, *cf.* Lenin, *Sochineniia,* IV, 191, 343.

stage. The characteristic structure of his theory of action is that it elevates a moment in history to the supreme good from which all human ends and, *a fortiori,* all means, derive their value. Lenin never gave attention to the problem of whether it is rationally possible to attribute that supreme rank to any moment in history or any of men's works. A theory of action ought to face such problems but Lenin had left them to Marx. In Marx's world the socialist society is the highest type and is born from the victorious proletarian revolution. Lenin accepted this as dogma and then turned to the corresponding theory of action. For him, all practical reason is oriented toward the revolutionary power of the proletariat.

Lenin may have been dogmatic and at fault in conceiving a historically immanent *summum bonum.* Nevertheless, his concept of a "final goal" is capable of creating principles of action for all times and situations prior to the goal's achievement. They resemble ethical principles in that they are not relative to temporary circumstances or situations. Kant's categorical imperative does not change with the phases of historical development, for it represents, as it were, a direct line from eternity to the human conscience. Lenin's imperative of political revolutionary action is similarly independent of the given historical environment, for it represents a direct line from the "final goal" to the human will. It holds good, as Lenin explicitly stated, in a bourgeois-democratic society, in a prebourgeois society, and in a prefeudal society. No matter where they find themselves, those who "know" of history's destiny are always subject to the duty of furthering the revolutionary power of the proletariat.

Lenin, of course, as a historical materialist, made the appropriate distinctions between the various "stages of advancement" of human society. He was fully prepared to change the content of revolutionary political action according to the society, capitalist, incipient bourgeois, or prebourgeois agrarian with which he had to deal. What never varies, however, is the imperative of political action beholden only to the "final goal" rather than to the requirements of whatever society one may happen to live in. The practical consequence was Lenin's demand for an "independent" political organization, "independent thinking," and an independent course of revolutionary political action. Here "independent" means: not derived from the rules of the game of the existing society but only from the requirements of the final goal. For Lenin an "independent" communist party and communist strategy was a revolutionary commandment not only in the phase of bourgeois democracy with its parties and freedom for political propaganda, but in any place where people with revolutionary "consciousness" can be found or educated. Lenin, had he had an opportunity, would no doubt have required a communist party even in a society of primitive communal property, for even there the "final goal" of history was the *summum bonum.*

PRESSURE "FROM BELOW" VS. ACTION "FROM ABOVE"

Lenin's polemic against the *Credo* had marked the shift of the Russian Social-Democratic Party to the principle of political struggle as socialist orthodoxy. It was upon the basis of this principle that he engaged in a new polemic against the editors of *Iskra.* That publication, after Lenin's departure from its staff, had become the organ of the Menshevik faction of the party. The polemic turned on the question of what the party could and should do in the revolutionary situation. Such a policy decision in turn hinged on an estimate of the possible accomplishments of a revolution in a country at Russia's stage of development.

Iskra's premise was that the Marxist pattern of successive revolutions marked the Revolution of 1905 as the struggle of the bourgeoisie for democracy. That phase of Russian history would not admit of any other social or political content, particularly not a proletarian-socialistic one. Consequently, the party of the proletariat should not try to play a leading role in the Revolution of 1905 and above all should not try to seize power. It should bring popular pressure to bear on the Liberals to whom the leading role had to be conceded in the present phase. To generate the appropriate "pressure from below," the Social-Democrats should also seek the widest possible diffusion of democratic powers.

The *Iskra* writers were willing to accept the acquisition of any democratic rights by landowners and capitalists, as long as all the people shared these rights. Its writers recommended that people everywhere form their own units of self-government in readiness for the day when they could exercise effective authority. The main thing was to broaden the effective formation and expression of popular will and to direct its influence so that the ruling classes would have to make concession after concession to the growing clamor of the people. On the basis of such increasing popular pressure, an effective Duma would "generate itself," that is, it would evolve strength independent of the government and grow into a genuine countervailing power.

This, the *Iskra* staff believed, was the "logic of the historical process" in Russia of 1905. The Social-Democratic leadership could conceivably do many things to abet the unfolding of this process. In particular the party would have to yield some leadership to "elements of spontaneous discontent." *Iskra's* appraisal of the historical situation and the party's role in it were epitomized in a number of slogans, the most important among which were "organization as process" and "action from below."

Lenin, in agreeing that the 1905 revolution was bourgeois-democratic, did not conclude that the bourgeoisie should therefore be conceded the leading role. The bourgeoisie, he argued, would never "complete" its own revolution. It was "treacherous" and would stop short of a democratization of Russia that might benefit the proletariat. Only a class that was "revolutionary to the end" because it aimed beyond democracy could "complete" the democratic revolution. A thoroughgoing democratic revolution could be accomplished only if the proletariat assumed political leadership even in the bourgeois phase of history.

The single concession to the bourgeois character of this historical phase would be in the program the proletariat sought to realize. This would have to be a program restricted to the objectives of a "bourgeois revolution" and well short of a full-fledged socialization. Lenin thus arrived at the distinction between a "minimum program" to apply to the first phase of proletarian power and a "maximum program" to be enacted later when proletarian strength had increased. In the bourgeois phase of history the party could come to power only with the help of petty-bourgeois allies, particularly the peasantry. These would no longer be needed as proletarian strength was increased by "action from above."

Lenin's main slogans were what he called the "Troika": armed insurrection, a revolutionary army, and a provisional revolutionary government. For the last, Lenin coined the phrase "the revolutionary democratic dictatorship of proletariat and peasantry." The Social-Democratic Party would first work for a revolutionary government with the peasantry as its main ally and support; later, having strengthened its own position, it would turn against its former ally "as an enemy" and proceed to establish a purely socialistic dictatorship. "Continuous revolution" is what Lenin called this succession of strategic upheavals. To the Iskraist concept of "process" he opposed that of "organization," to the principle of "pressure from below," that of "revolutionary action from above," to the "pressure on the Liberals" the "armed insurrection," to the expectation of a formal liberal democracy the demand for a "revolutionary democratic dictatorship."

What was the issue? Since 1903, there had been considerable agreement concerning the emphasis on political action. Both sides also were disposed to gauge action by a "correct" understanding of the phases of history, as defined by the ascendancy of a given class. Both agreed that the present phase in Russia was that of bourgeois ascendancy and that the advance to socialism must be made through a period of bourgeois political institutions. The disagreement centered in a new fear that had arisen in Marxist minds: the threat of a Restoration. If the situation was mismanaged, would not the course of history take the wrong turn and, instead of progressing toward socialism, revert to absolutism? The Iskraists predicted such an outcome if the party of the proletariat attempted to push itself into the leading role during the bourgeois-democratic phase of history. Lenin too feared a Restoration, but assumed that it would occur only if the party did not take the lead in the phase of bourgeois democracy. The question then hinged on the estimate of which of the party's alternative policies would promote revolution and which restoration. This was indeed a matter of the gravest importance. For the historical materialist, Restoration is nothing less than the equivalent of antimatter, a failure of the "necessary" course of history, the worst fall from being one can envisage. Once the danger of Restoration was envisaged the choice of evils was between premature socialist leadership and trailing in the wake of developments.

The Iskraists considered political phenomena secondary and factors of social development primary. The factors of social development must be allowed to operate in their own way and under democratic freedom would inevitably produce increasing political strength behind the demand for socialism. Political power, in turn, could not be expected to produce the social forces that were its foundation. If social forces were allowed to be reflected in political power, the proletarian influence would eventually become irresistible. Representative democracy, however, could be won only if the bourgeoisie did not take fright before a broad proletarian solidarity had a chance to develop.

Lenin, by contrast, was convinced that the mere spontaneous development of social forces would arrest the forward motion of the Revolution. The bourgeoisie, even though its peculiar form of government supposedly was democracy, could not be expected to institute consistent democracy, for fear that the latter might favor the proletariat. The proletariat, in turn, was liable to succumb to the temptations of bourgeois "harmony" and "reforms," unless directed to more radical revolutionary action. No kind of "process," then, could furnish reliable guidance for socialist conduct. Neither the organization nor the tactics chosen by the party must in any way be based on the assumption that "processes" will do part of the work. Salvation was only in deliberately initiated, organized, and actively pursued armed insurrection. The party ought to mobilize the masses into a revolutionary army in order to keep all developments fluid, to remain consistently ahead of the evolving social forces, and to prevent the worst development of all, accommodation to the existing social order. Lenin condemned as, in effect, reactionary any course that failed to go beyond the "framework of an orderly bourgeois society."[8]

For Lenin, the struggle as such was the only reliable pattern. Any acceptance of "order" or temporary accommodation to things as they are was a betrayal of the revolution and of the ultimate truth. The struggle itself can remain real only by constantly renewed hostility. It does not require particular forms, either legal or illegal, so long as the will to destroy is manifested in some active way. A revolutionary force can have its being only in ceaseless conflict with the existing order, and only a revolutionary force can carry history forward to the "final end." Since true human order is not possible in the present class-divided situation, the reality of human existence is vested in that social force which can never be induced to give up the struggle. Any failure to keep moving, any reconciliation with the forces and institutions of the present amount to a betrayal of true being. In this sense, to resign one's revolutionary activism to the "processes of development" is the way to lose oneself in nonbeing and the way to stay in being is to keep the struggle alive in open militancy.

Lenin as a Marxist believed that the "bourgeois-democratic" revolution necessarily had to precede the proletarian one. Lenin's "new slogan," however, postulated that even the "bourgeois-democratic" phase of history be initiated and dominated by a revolutionary proletariat allied with the peasantry, that is, the classes which together were assumed to form the vast majority. Organized as a revolutionary army, this majority would set up a revolutionary government dominated by the proletariat. Lenin demanded that through the phase of "bourgeois democracy" this government should develop "democracy" by "action from above." It would undertake a sweeping land reform, claiming all land as property of the nation and turning over its use partly to state farms and partly to poor peasants. The workers were to be given the eight-hour day,

[8] Lenin, *Sochineniia,* X, 137.

and other democratic demands should be satisfied. This government of the people and for the people, however, was not to be a formal democracy but a dictatorship, "rule based on force." Lenin's insistence on this point is most revealing. At the Third Party Congress Lenin defined dictatorship as "the organization not of 'order,' but the organization of war."[9] He thought of society as "war" even when the "overwhelming majority" of the people are the rulers. Lenin could conceive of no elements of "order" even in a society in which the people, having driven away their oppressors, are no longer subject to alien wills. The only explanation to make sense of Lenin's position is that he is here dealing with the bourgeois-democratic period in which, by definition, there can as yet be no socialism. In other words, the concept of "order" is out of place anywhere except in a fully socialist society. Any other society, on Lenin's showing, represents not "order" but rather "war."

The concept "democratic dictatorship of proletariat and peasantry" also illuminates Lenin's view of the successive "phases" of history. For the Mensheviks, each of these phases constituted a temporarily stable social system with its peculiar principles of order that would prevail until its time had run out and the next phase ensued. In this view, history is a succession of societies, each orderly and real at a certain stage of human development. Lenin accepted the law of "successive phases," but he allowed only to the phase of socialism the concept of "order."

History subdivides not into successive worlds of social order but into successive stages of revolution.[10] The revolution is the continuum, the ongoing reality that makes a concept of history possible. Its phases are divided from each other by the predominance of certain classes for a limited period. The revolution, always the same, is the business of the proletariat, the "only really revolutionary class." In each of the successive phases, a peculiar strategic

[9] *Ibid.*, VIII, 353.

[10] "When the democratic bourgeoisie or petty bourgeoisie has moved a step higher, when not only the revolution but the full victory of the revolution has become a fact, then we shall 'replace' . . . the slogan of democratic dictatorship with the slogan of the socialistic dictatorship of the proletariat, i. e., the complete socialist transformation." "The Two Tactics," in Lenin, *Sochineniia,* IX, 109.

situation confronts the revolutionary forces, so that to every phase corresponds a temporary revolutionary program. In the "bourgeois-democratic" phase, the proletariat is allied to the peasantry, a class with bourgeois characteristics, and the revolutionary strategy envisages a "democratic dictatorship."

Lenin did not at this time extend the logic of this idea any further, but one can readily see that it could be applied to the most varied situations. If in the "bourgeois phase" the proletariat attaches to itself a bourgeois element and together with it sets up a dictatorship with a "bourgeois" strategic objective, then in a pre-bourgeois "phase" the proletariat could combine with some pre-bourgeois element (for instance, the national element of colonial peoples) and together with it set up a dictatorship with a pre-bourgeois program, always, however, under Communist guidance and pursuing the ultimate cause of Communists. In 1905 and 1917 Lenin called for a "minimum program," insisting that the "maximum program" be left for a later time. The minimum program is nothing but the phase of the continuing revolution strategically indicated in the given phase of history. History, both past and coming, is thus nothing but a series of successive strategies, each on its level of social development, each confined in its objectives to what is then attainable, all of them nothing but parts of the one great revolution moving toward history's "final goal."

DEMOCRACY VS. DICTATORSHIP

Lenin considered Kautsky to be the leading Marxist theoretician. For many years, Lenin held up Kautsky's views to the Russian "Opportunists" as model revolutionary Marxism. After the outbreak of the World War, however, Lenin began to attack Kautsky. The immediate object of the quarrel was the war, behind which loomed the more basic issue of the appraisal of imperialism and, as a consequence, one's attitude toward national self-defense. Imperialism is capitalism, Lenin held, and war is its typical product. He was profoundly disillusioned with the parties of the Second International which had rallied to the support of their respective countries on the basis of a distinction between international right and wrong, aggression and defense. Kautsky's interpretation of imperialism as nothing but a passing phase in the great powers' foreign policies had left the road open for a case in favor of national self-defense. Lenin, accusing Kautsky of treason, insisted that imperialism was the very essence of capitalism in its last stage, and war the inevitable product of that system's inherent contradictions. The distinction between right and wrong, or aggression and defense, was immaterial, as was also the winning or losing of the war.

This first phase of Lenin's polemic against Kautsky carried over into the second which concerned the character of the Soviet regime. Kautsky's criticism of Soviet rule was first published in his pamphlet "The Dictatorship of the Proletariat."[11] Lenin's counterattack is represented by his *State and Revolution* and *The Proletarian Revolution and the Renegade Kautsky*.[12] Kautsky argued that socialism is not an end in itself; the end is the "elimination of every kind of exploitation and oppression, whether of a class, a party, a sex, or a race."[13] Socialism is a means to this end and, necessarily, so is democracy. Socialism can be realized only by a proletariat forming a majority of the people and with the necessary will, numbers, and political maturity. Democracy is the best setting for conducting the struggle before the proletariat's rise to power and afterwards is the strongest basis of proletarian rule.

In a democratic environment, the revolution of the proletariat would not have to take on the violent forms characteristic of the bourgeois (the French) revolution. A period of proletarian dictatorship would be necessary, but this state of emergency would have to pass quickly into a permanent democratic government. In power the proletariat would require democracy above all because the modern bureaucratic state machinery has to be put under popular control if it is not to alienate itself from society. The maintenance of democracy required rigorous government impartiality

[11] Kautsky, *Die Diktatur des Proletariats* (3rd ed.; Vienna, 1918).
[12] Lenin, *Selected Works,* VII.
[13] Kautsky, *Die Diktatur des Proletariats,* 4.

and equality of basic rights, for any exceptional privilege for a class or group, even the proletariat, would necessarily lead to dictatorship, which under modern conditions would become some kind of Bonapartism. Similarly, to introduce socialism by forceful action from above instead of by democratic action of the majority of the people must issue in Bonapartist dictatorship rather than the hoped for freedom. On these grounds, Kautsky deplored the use of soviets (worker-peasant councils) as the basis for the Russian government. The soviets, he said, are admirable partisan combat organizations and as such invaluable in the struggle for power. Once power is attained, however, they are too undemocratic and arbitrary to serve as the basis for a new political order. Only full representation of the entire people, as achieved through a Constituent Assembly, could provide a sound political foundation and bring the revolution to its full fruition.

Lenin's counterarguments are conceptually confused, perhaps even deliberately muddled. This much emerges clearly: the real issue is not democracy (majority *vs.* minority) but class struggle (exploiters *vs.* exploited.) Formal democracy is merely a bourgeois window dressing for bourgeois rule that is actually arbitrary and dictatorial. Moreover, as the state is everywhere an instrument of violence practiced by one class against another, it is futile to expect a peaceful "development" from bourgeois power to proletarian majority rule. History makes its major changes not by "development" but by "leaps," and such a revolution is violent in its very essence. Violence is characteristic not merely for a brief emergency but for the indefinite period intervening between capitalism and socialism. During this period the proletariat is continuously threatened by its enemies who, after the proletarian seizure of power, become more dangerous than they had been. The success of the revolution therefore requires that the proletariat organize its rule as a ruthless struggle to be continued until all its enemies are eliminated and a return to exploitation is no longer possible.

When Lenin proceeded to define the state in the "period of transition," he used vague and contradictory concepts that make it difficult to clarify his meaning. Lenin of course attempted to reconcile his proletarian dictatorship with the "sacred" language of the Communist classics, particularly with Marx's praise of the democratic Paris Commune of 1871 and Engels' statement that after the revolution the state will "wither away." As Lenin's attempt is unsuccessful, here one can only repeat the contradictory concepts as he used them: the proletariat cannot and must not "abolish" the state but rather use it in the period of transition from capitalism to socialism. At the same time, the proletariat cannot simply take over the bourgeois state which must be "smashed." The new state differs from the old in that it is a state of the masses and for the masses. Yet, in the period of "transition" the state cannot be anything else but the dictatorship of the proletariat. Dictatorship is power based on force and unlimited by law, the opposite of democracy, liberty, equality, and civil rights.[14] But Lenin also defines the dictatorship of the proletariat as the "most democratic" regime of human history; it is democratic, not for the former ruling classes but for the proletarians and poor peasants and so for the majority of the people. Although democratic, the government of the new regime is not to be derived from parliamentary processes. Rather, it is conceived as a "state based on the subordination of the minority under the majority," with the emphasis not on rights but on "organization for systematic violence by one class against another."[15] The new state is to be essentially control, force, power. As long as its control remains in the hands of the revolutionary class, Lenin is "fully and unreservedly in favor of a strong state power and centralism."[16] At the same time he insists that the state of the proletariat really will be "no longer a state in the true sense of the term,"[17] but rather a state that already has begun to wither away.

Not "abolished" but rather "smashed," "dictatorial" but also "democratic," a "strong state" but no longer "really a state"—these

[14] For one of Lenin's clear statements of this point, see Lenin, *Selected Works,* VII, 144.

[15] *Ibid.*, 75.

[16] *Ibid.*, VI, 277.

[17] *Ibid.*, 74.

are Lenin's contradictory definitions. Marx's and Engels' "sacred" language is grafted onto concepts of a quite different meaning. The result is a doctrine of the proletarian state that consists of the manipulation of paradoxical slogans rather than of instructive concepts. Lenin's handling of this problem left a legacy of confusion between the revolution's promise of freedom and its resolve to amass power in order to defeat its enemies. Lenin's own ideas are nowhere stated as such. Still, it may be surmised that, as he did not succeed in reconciling the classic formulae with his notions, everything that is not Marx and Engels represents his own position. Lenin then stands for a "revolutionary government" in the Jacobin sense, a regime of force unlimited by law and rights, and ruthless class struggle continued for a period of indefinite duration.

In this debate Lenin and Kautsky came to grips with a problem to which Marxists had given very little attention. Marxist thinking had stopped, as it were, at the terminal point of the revolutionary seizure of power and the "expropriation of the expropriators." Now a Marxist party had obtained power in a great country, and the problem was how to organize and use its authority, over an indefinite period of time. Lenin and Kautsky approached this problem with certain shared premises. Both agreed that socialism must be the eventual result of a proletarian revolution and that the state must be used during the period of transition. At issue was the constitution and operation of the state under new social conditions. On whom or what would the government of this state rely? How should political power be constituted? On what historical developments could one count? What values was the new state to represent? What principles ought it to obey?

Kautsky pleaded for democracy. That in itself tells us very little. It is more important that Kautsky considered democracy a means coequal with socialism for the end of human freedom, which, in Kautsky's view, required a political as well as an economic order. A free political order meant to him that each individual's reason is allowed to have an unhampered and formally equal part in common affairs. The common content or common orientation of individual minds induced by the common economic existence of men makes the political unity. Kautsky could see only two alternative systems for large-scale industry: capitalism or socialism. Property owners and their followers are existentially wedded to the former system; propertyless wage earners are just as naturally interested in the latter. The inherent reasonableness of socialism will in time make socialists of a growing number of people regardless of their economic position. Eventually, socialists will constitute the vast majority of the voters. Where the government is derived from universal suffrage, a political consensus for socialism constitutes a real force by which political control can be won and on which a new public order can be founded. The proletariat will acquire the necessary political maturity and comprehension of modern social problems as it participates in political decisions.

Kautsky put his trust in the politically mature individual mind. In his thinking the community of reason alone furnished a durable basis for political authority. Guarantees of free thought and free vote are the cornerstone of a nonoppressive political order. His confident expectation of a majority embracing socialism and of the political educational and maturing effect of popular participation in politics enabled him to have faith in free individual reasoning and to protect each individual's political will by a rigorous equality of rights from which not even capitalists, landowners, and labor dissenters, would be excluded. The people's reasoning is not only ultimately wise but also powerful enough to support the new political regime without need for extended compulsion. A revolutionary regime not subordinated to this source of authority will become a power machine alienated from the people and the common good. If a proletarian regime has to maintain itself by dictatorial methods, conditions are not yet ripe for the revolution. A premature attempt to realize socialism by force must lead to the loss of the revolutionary objective and the rule of the sword.

Lenin found these assumptions unacceptable: the reason of the proletariat would not tend to embrace socialism. In *What Is To Be Done?* Lenin had noted that the proletariat by itself was capable only of "trade-union consciousness," that is, of the intent to improve its position within the existing order. For Lenin such bread-and-butter thinking was incompatible with "revolutionary consciousness," with the will to destroy the present system in order to replace it by a wholly new society. He could not accept Kautsky's reprimand that the Soviets had "arbitrarily" excluded not only capitalists but other proletarian parties of various socialist persuasions. In Lenin's view there was no other socialist party besides his own; all others had been convicted by him of "opportunism," "petty-bourgeois vacillation," and "liberalism"—of lack of revolutionary consistency. On this showing, other proletarian parties were objectively servants of the bourgeoisie and traitors to the Revolution—an epithet which Lenin applied to Kautsky himself. Lenin, moreover, assumed that the proletariat would constitute a majority only in combination with the peasants who, subject as they were to "petty-bourgeois vacillations," would not be "consistently revolutionary."

The forces committed to socialism would be a minority for an indefinite period, not because conditions for a revolution had not matured but because by the very nature of things only a select few and not the masses could be expected to have "theory"—that is, the vision for the "final end."

For the remedy of present deficiencies Lenin did not put his trust in "developments." Indeed, the inevitable changes would occur as "leaps," convulsions, revolutions, rather than as "developments."

Lenin made positive distrust of common reason the basis of his thought. Except for those revolutionary few, capable of "independent thinking," the habits of thought of most people were still entirely under the influence of the bourgeois world. Its habits and concepts persisted even after the overthrow of the ruling class. The former rulers had their main residual strength in the realm of public reason. Even without their lands and factories, they still towered over the proletariat by virtue of education, knowledge, skills, and connections. Most proletarians, even many Communists, if not constantly controlled and corrected, would fall into the reasoning patterns of the former order. Political trust in free individual reason therefore was tantamount to capitulation to the bourgeoisie. A state based on equal rights, universal suffrage, and proportional representation would sell out the revolution to the class enemy. Lenin went even further. To assume the absence of a community of reason was his touchstone of correct revolutionary attitude. The "consistently revolutionary" are conscious of *not* sharing premises, convictions, and principles with the majority of the people. The Communist, oriented wholly by his knowledge of the "final end," has nothing in common with those who want merely to live well in the present. The party of the Revolution must proceed on the assumption that it is surrounded by either bitter enemies or false and unreliable friends.

A political order is association oriented towards a common good. According to Aristotle it differs from economic or other associations in that the political common good pertains to the power of human reason to judge actions by standards of right and wrong and to conceive of all life in terms of a meaningful whole. A political community is thus a "world," representing the order of all being of which man knows himself as a part, and the moral judgment separating good from evil. In both respects, it constitutes a community of reason in which individual minds participate. Hence a political order creates trust, friendship, peace to the extent to which there is individual awareness of shared notions of being and shared standards of conduct.

Kautsky succeeded in conceiving of such a political order and Lenin did not. Kautsky did envisage that the Revolution would culminate in a regime founded on the community of reason and devoted to justice, in which the shared notion of the common good would unite people in trust, friendship, and peace. Lenin, addressing himself to the same problem, had the concept not of a political order but of battle order, an association mainly for the elimination of enemy forces. Lenin rejected the premises as well as the fruits of a political order. In place of the community of reason, he assumed ubiquitous danger, suspicion, mutual *animus* to destroy or be destroyed. Instead of peace and friendship, he looked for victory. Dictatorship as a principle of government rather than a passing emergency condition is, as Lenin himself had stated, the "organization of war," an arrangement benefiting a world of perennial hostility.

Lenin's rejection of political order for the concept of battle order also barred him from access to the problem of freedom. Kautsky, however, was able to theorize about human freedom in the change-over from an old to a new society. Lenin could only manage to assert that somehow freedom would result from total victory, the "systematic practice of violence" would eventually issue in harmony, and the consistent fight against external and internal enemies would eliminate all conflicts between the rulers and the ruled. While Kautsky could show that consensus is the basis of nonoppressive power, Lenin had to claim that persuasion was compatible with a dictatorial denial of freedom, and the "force unlimited by law" could inspire trust as well as create the virtues of the perfect socialist man.

Lenin's rejection of the very idea of political order followed necessarily from his appraisal of extant realities. Any political order links transcendent elements with that which exists here and now. Kautsky conceived of a future political order because there were elements in the present society which he was willing to consider real and reliable. Existentially he based his political structure on the proletariat, the developmental tendencies of the time, and the popular appeal of socialism. Because he could relate the transcendence of reason to these existential realities, he succeeded in constructing political principles. Lenin discarded the proletariat as a reliable social force, distrusted "developments," and discounted the efficacy of the popular appeal of socialism. He saw only two realities: the organized force of the Communist "Vanguard" and the power of the bourgeoisie. There will be order in the future society but the transcendent principle of order is not represented by any existential factor in present society. At present, all is chaos, or alienation, or comprehensive hostility. The principle of order thus is now entirely confined to the mind of those who have knowledge of the future society. If order is real in the sense that chaos is unreal, then nothing outside of the small band of fighters for the future now can have title to reality.

Lenin was the Solon of a society that fancied itself a-borning. Although he presided over a new government, he did not give laws to that society but left it with a void. Not that he did not try; but instead of creating a political order, he set up a mobilization scheme for warfare without the end of peace. Consequently, the only order the new society can claim is the economic one of large-scale production. Instead of guiding future generations by a new political doctrine, Lenin merely devised rules for the management of perennial conflict. Power, strength, irreconcilability, discipline, ruthlessness: these concepts are well anchored in Lenin's teaching, but peace, community, friendship, justice, forbearance have no home in the world in which he dwelt.

"MERE" NEGATION VS. NEGATION IN COEXISTENCE

The last great polemic of Lenin's life was directed against Left Communists (not to be confused with Trotskyists). The campaign was conducted through a number of engagements from 1918 to 1922. There were Left Communists in Germany, England, Italy, Holland, and other European countries whom Lenin identified by their pamphlets and articles. In Russia, Left-Wing Communism was represented by the periodical *Kommunist* and the Left Social-Revolutionary publication *Znamya Truda*. Lenin's arguments are strikingly presented in *The Immediate Tasks of the Soviet Government* and *Left-Wing Communism, An Infantile Disorder*.[18]

The Left Communists fully accepted Lenin's teachings about the irreconcilable class conflict, the total negation of existing society, and the "consistent" revolutionary struggle. The Bolshevik victory in Russia had given them the impression that "imperialism was finished" even in the West, that powerful revolutionary forces could be mobilized by a call for the final battle, and that the bourgeois institutions could now be brushed aside as no longer of any

[18] Lenin, *Sochineniia,* XXVII and XXXI; Lenin, *Selected Works,* VII and X.

consequence. They demanded above all a policy of "no compromise" with the bourgeoisie. This led them to criticize, in the name of Lenin's own teachings, the policy of the new Russian government, particularly the Treaty of Brest-Litovsk, the establishment of "State Capitalism," and the payment of high salaries to specialists in industry. They demanded of Russia an "active foreign policy," the democratic management of industry by the workers rather than by professional managers, the investment of ruling power in the proletariat as a class rather than in the Communist Party. In Western Europe, they rejected any participation in bourgeois parliaments, in trade unions, and other institutions of the bourgeois regime.

Lenin scorned the "revolutionary phrase" of the Left Communists as petty-bourgeois revolutionary emotionalism. The period of transition, he said, is long and characterized by the simultaneous existence of capitalist and socialist institutions and forces. The proletariat is not yet strong enough to sweep away the structure of the old society, not even in Russia. In fact, the proletarian regime in Russia is in danger of being swept away by the "elementary force" of the small producers. In a long drawn-out struggle of this kind, "compromises and maneuvers" are inevitable, requiring coexistence with bourgeois institutions and the use of them. Such compromises would be antirevolutionary only if the political strength of the proletariat is thereby impaired. As for Russia, the Treaty of Brest-Litovsk, for instance, was imperative as a measure of national self-defense of the Soviet power. The offensive against capitalism in Russia had to be stopped temporarily in the interest of Soviet power so that it could gather strength for new advances. State capitalism and highly paid industrial specialists will protect the Soviet power from the dangerous force of the small proprietors. At the same time, large-scale industry is the best preparation for socialism. The unions, whose "reactionary tendencies" Lenin acknowledged, can and must be used to mobilize and control the workers. Worker management is childish: the strictest labor discipline must be imposed by plant managers with dictatorial powers, since democratic management would spell chaos and the political defeat of "Soviet might." As for the West, Lenin warned that parliaments and other bourgeois institutions would not simply disappear just because, historically speaking, their death knell had sounded. Communists must therefore work in these institutions, participate in parliaments, in unions, and in England's two-party system. The aim of their participation should be to discredit the particular institutions as well as the entire bourgeois system and to promote the growth of revolutionary strength.

Lenin thus attacked some disciples who had learned the master's lesson too well. In fighting the Economists and the Mensheviks Lenin had stressed that to accept the bourgeois framework is to betray the revolution and to serve the cause of reaction. This had become the Left Communists' guiding principle. They demanded that a "revolutionary army" be uncontaminated by any contact with bourgeois institutions and that revolutionary action be publicly divorced from every trace of community with bourgeois ways. In so urging apartheid from the bourgeois order the Left Communists trusted in two things: the revolutionary momentum of their time which had manifestly brought "imperialism" to the end of its tether; and the purity of revolutionary spirit which could alone be expected to carry history's death sentence on capitalism to the point of actual execution. The time was ripe: only revolutionary action in a pure and wholly antibourgeois spirit could bring success. This premise prompted the Left Communists to call for "unlimited use of freedom by the workers," as well as for a policy of severely pure proletarian principle in the post-revolutionary Russia. In all this, the Left Communists evidently felt that proletarians are men endowed with the power of truth by their proletarian existence. Proletarians are the bearers of a new spirit which they must make manifest as the crumbling time permits it. The "correct" revolutionary line, then, would call for giving the workers free rein and control in Russia and separate organizations and institutions in the West.

In rejecting this idea as a "revolutionary phrase," Lenin seemed to imply that he believed neither in the proletariat nor in the power of the spirit. But Lenin was far from discounting spiritual factors in history. In his view, however, the spirit was then doing battle for the "ideological resistance" of capitalism.[19] The "traditions of the old society," the "force of habit" of millions and tens of millions is a "very terrible force." The spirit of this majority is strong but hostile. Only the infinitesimally small "Vanguard" is detached in its thinking, "independent," shaped entirely by the new society, and thus "consistently revolutionary." The guarantee of its purity, moreover, is not any proletarian existence but the correctness of socialist theory which in turn requires constant critical vigilance of the leaders. But purity of revolutionary intent will not permit this Vanguard to prevail, in spite of the decrees of history, if the party does not attach to itself the immense power of noncommunist masses. These masses are not to be won, as the Vanguard is, by the explanation of the world in the light of Communist ideas.[20] Psychologically they must be maneuvered into "battle positions" that permit further advances of the Communist forces. Hostile elements must be confused, vacillating ones made firm in their support of the party.

The objective is not mass demonstration of revolutionary purity, but mass "support for Party leadership" based on mass persuasion that the Vanguard's strategy and tactics have been "correct." This necessity of mobilizing large masses without the appeal of Communist principles requires that the party coexist with institutions and traditions of the bourgeois order that still have mass appeal —parliaments, small property, and trade unions. Lenin's concept of coexistence acknowledged the futility of violence in dealing with the "terrible force of habit," but it is not a concept of peaceful relationship. It aims to "vanquish" millions and millions and their "demoralizing activity,"[21] to reduce a political idea to absurdity while ostensibly defending it,"[22] to "discredit and expel" "undesirable leaders."[23] The strategic search for mass support must be car-

[19] Lenin, *Sochineniia,* XXXXI, 345.
[20] Lenin, *Selected Works,* X, 84, 137.
[21] *Ibid.*, 61, 84.
[22] *Ibid.*, 103.
[23] *Ibid.*, 92.

ried on "wherever the masses are found."[24] If this is on the ground of capitalism, then Communists must adjust themselves to that terrain rather than insist on their own battleground.

Only in one respect did Lenin waive his precept of winning the masses on their own terms: the strictest discipline of labor is imperative if the Communists are to prevail. This, Lenin fully knew, is neither popular nor a Russian habit. It was the fundamental new demand his regime made of the masses. One-man dictatorship of the plant manager is the local manifestation of the dictatorship of the proletariat. Neither one nor the other can be replaced by democracy, the order peculiar to the bourgeoisie.[25] Here, then, we have one of the few, if not the only, feature that seems to belong wholly to the new society without any strategic "compromise" with bourgeois habits. The characteristic condition of the period of transition is that there are as yet "no bricks with which to build socialism,"[26] but this much can be glimpsed of the future "realm of freedom": its order consists in the strictest control of work in large-scale industries.

The Left Communists agreed with Lenin that the prevailing system is no order, no community, no source of obligation. In the sense in which chaos is unreal and order real, the bourgeois regime is wholly unreal and reality is found only in the future society of the proletariat. But as the proletariat had achieved cohesion sufficient to wrest control from the bourgeois rulers, how should it act? Revolution means active total negation of the present system. What kind of conduct does total negation of the present require of proletarians? The Left Communists, in urging that the old ways be rejected and the new ways be made manifest in our actions, recall something like St. Paul's instructions to the early Christians: now that you know you have been redeemed, walk as children of God, do away with your former life, reflect in every action the spirit of salvation, because the old law has been overcome and the new freedom is here. The Left Communists similarly felt that knowledge of the presence of the new reality called for new behav-

[24] *Ibid.*, 94.
[25] Lenin, *Sochineniia,* XXVIII, 410.
[26] *Ibid.*, XXVII, 123.

ior, a manifestation of the order that was irrupting into the prevailing chaos.

Did Lenin, in urging on Communists compromise with bourgeois institutional patterns, thereby deny his own thesis of that system's unreality? When Lenin chided the Left Communists as counsellors of chaos, did he not vindicate the attribute of order for bourgeois patterns, even if only partially and conditionally? If this had been in Lenin's mind, he would have taught his disciples to work within bourgeois institutions in good faith, awaiting the eventual end of the bourgeois society. Actually, what Lenin demanded was that Communists use bourgeois institutions without keeping faith with them, that they participate solely with the intent of destruction, and that they obtain the institutions' power but deny their order. If Lenin acknowledged any reality in the bourgeois system, it was but the reality of power, the ability to sway and direct masses of people. Bourgeois power, according to Lenin, is still unbroken, all the stronger because of its increased resistance following the revolution's victory in Russia. The relevant evidence is that the masses are not yet in "battle positions" that would allow the Communists to advance further. The Communist offensive, therefore, had to be halted because it had gone as far as the present equation of forces would permit. If the party must then enter into a kind of "peace" with the bourgeoisie, the peace did not involve a reconciliation of wills: it was only a "breathing spell," a means to "gather further strength."[27]

Lenin, then, did not ignore the postrevolutionary presence of the realm of freedom in asserting the superiority of bourgeois power and in rejecting the Left Communist demand for conduct in accord with the new socialist order. Communist power provided for the future "true order" a *pied-à-terre* in the present. The Communist Vanguard is the future's spearhead into the actuality of bourgeois power, but it is real only inasmuch as it, too, is power. An essential difference between the two is that the Vanguard's power carries the promise of eventual order and is, therefore, essentially justified.

[27] *Ibid.*, 82, 90.

Bourgeois power, representing chaos, is not. Future order gives to the Vanguard the title of true authority but power requirements alone govern the proper line of revolutionary conduct. The task, then, remains that of developing advantageous "battle positions," of recruiting masses for the infantry of the class struggle, of outmaneuvering an enemy infinitely superior in strength.

Not a principle of pure "proletarian" conduct but the success of Communist power is the present manifestation of future reality. In this sense Lenin calls on workers and peasants to hold Communist power "sacred."[28] Among all the powers that be, that of Communists alone is hallowed. In the same sense, Lenin insists that Communist power cannot and never will be shared.[29] There is, for example, no sharing of power in Lenin's compromises with bourgeois institutions, for he precluded any merging of Communist with bourgeois power in a community of purpose. The idea is rather to strengthen Communist capabilities for the further pursuit of their hostile intent. Thus Lenin's recipe is: power secured, everything secured. No amount of borrowing from the bourgeois order can be detrimental to the revolution as long as Soviet state power exists and continues to wax stronger. The party in command of the state, supported by increasing masses, disposing of means and methods of compulsion: this is the future's stronghold in the present world. This is the key position that alone admits of a genuine transformation, as the example of Peter the Great demonstrates.[30] The only possible form of this power is dictatorship, the uninhibited and unrestricted use of force within the limits of the prevailing equation of opposed forces. The advent of the future true society then is expected as the result of a continuous increase of political strength wielded by the party through the Soviet state. The measure of its growth would be the progressive suppression of resisting elements, mobilization of larger masses for the party's support, and the territorial expansion of the party's monopoly of force. The requirements of naked power rather than the spirit of socialist

[28] *Ibid.*, 398.
[29] *Ibid.*, 313.
[30] *Ibid.*, 306, 307.

order: that was Lenin's choice when he rejected the Left Communists. In Communist regimes, it is now habitual to offer public thanks to "the Party and the Government," much as other peoples offer thanks to God, for all good things in life.

The order of human existence has always been a problem of relating human arrangements and actions to the structure of something that *is*—to a realm of being experienced as independent of human willing and doing. Without going into the question of which of these are sound theories and which ideologies, one may mention here the transcendent realm of being, the natural law, the realm of physical nature, the structure of changes in time, the pattern of economic causation, the laws of biological heredity as examples of realities objectively given to the human mind, realities to which men have in the quest of order related their own wills and judgments. In the course of his various polemics Lenin rejected all ideas of any reality which, if accepted as such, would bestow a semblance of order on the present-day society. He radically denied any possibility of order apart from the socialism of the future. In the chaos of the present, only the foundation of power preparatory of the future can be considered an island of order, and only for those whose intellectual eyes can behold the distant future's gleam. This reduced the extant representation of future reality to the Communist power, the power that was in Lenin's own hands. Whether Lenin was or was not aware of what he was doing, the fact remains that through this concept he removed the difference and tension between the human will that is to be ordered and the objective reality in the light of which order is conceived. It is as if Aquinas had said, "The measure of human actions is the Natural Law, and the sole actualization of the Natural Law that is possible is by my will"; or as if Plato had said, "God is the measure, but God exists only through my creation." That realm of being which is assumed to be fundamental is identified with the will or, in Lenin's case, the power of the subject. Lenin saw a future realm of true being as the measure of human actions, but he implied, in his argument against the Left Communists, that there would be no such realm of true being except for his, Lenin's, strategic success. Thus Communist strategy is seen not merely as creating order in human existence, but as creating the very reality which is the measure and model of human order. He thus lost the possibility of measuring and judging his own power. There is nothing left against or by which to judge and measure. Objective reality is the socialist future, and that future is wholly contained in Lenin's present strategic capabilities.

But no—one remnant of objective measurement is left: the enemy's power circumscribing that of the Communists. Whatever strength the bourgeoisie can mobilize does not have the character of order, since it represents no real being, but it does set objective bounds to what the Communists can do. Thus a curious mutation brings Lenin around to attribute to the bourgeoisie some of the same kind of reality that he claims for his side. As a result of the hypostatization of Communist power as the present embodiment of all real being, he has to concede to the antithesis of that power a similar status.

TOTALITARIAN ETHICS

Lenin was a Marxist fundamentalist, for fundamentalism is by no means confined to Christian sects. It is a general tendency to order human life through symbols of reality which are mistaken for reality itself, a tendency that spreads as mature civilizations accumulate a heritage of concepts which people begin to take for granted. Human order is in the last analysis possible only as men are aware of participating in realms of being that transcend human purposes. Such awareness feeds on continuous experiences of these realms of being as objectively given realities. In the progress of civilization, layer upon layer of concepts are piled up, testimonies to successive experiences of reality and attempts to symbolize them. The richness of this possession eventually tempts people to look upon the conceptualizations no longer as helps toward the experience of participation but as the realities themselves. Victims of advanced education, people then look for truth in the interpretation of formulas coined by others. Fundamentalism thus leads to social order based on derivation rather than participation. Its core is an ideological faith that the inherent logic of concepts can contain the measure of right living.

Lenin concentrated his entire effort on extracting the last logical derivation from the thoughts of Marx rather than on understanding reality in itself. Marx had called the present system one of "alienation," in which no relation reflected man's true nature and no authority man's true good. As for a "true" society, Marx had asserted that it would come into existence only when private property no longer dominated human labor. For Lenin, these two concepts had turned into fixed ideas decreeing that no order could be found in present-day society and that no value could be considered real except as pertaining to the socialism of the future. Instead of attempting to experience for himself what Marx sought to convey through the symbol of "alienation," Lenin spelled out the implications of Marx's dogmas in political action. Nor were his opponents, the Mensheviks, less fundamentalist; they differed from Lenin merely in deriving their principles from different concepts of Marx. For the Mensheviks the "laws" of historical development, the succession of historical "phases," were the gospel truth, the point at which an intelligent man would begin to draw his practical conclusions.

Between Lenin and the Mensheviks, two Marxist fundamentalisms were in conflict, each fastening to certain formulations of the master's and spinning out their logic in rules of action. Where Lenin took as literal truth the axiological elements of Marx's thought, the Mensheviks clung to Marx's teleological formulations. Lenin scored many polemical victories precisely by convicting his opponents of knowing the letter of Marx and of being unable to think with his sense of reality. Unfortunately, none of his opponents was capable enough to convict Lenin of the same sin, although all of Lenin's thought was derived from a wholly literal acceptance of Marx's damning verdict on the present and hopeful praise of the future society, so that all of Lenin's judgments of the surrounding world were in the nature of foregoing conclusions.

Lenin's problem was to find a principled answer to the question "What is to be done?" The dogmatic basis of his answer was Marx's total critique of present-day society coupled with total endorsement of a future socialist order. Thus all intermediary ends were to be judged by their instrumental relation to the future socialism as the "final end." Lenin felt that "revolutionary theory" constituted a rational theory of action providing reliable principles for all situations. He was always scornful of his opponents for their "unprincipled" ways of drifting with events.

Lenin was primarily bent on a total denial that in the present-day world *anything* can be treated as real or a bit of order. His dogmatic principle, "derived" from Marx, was that the present is wholly dominated by the powers of darkness. The false spirit of the bourgeoisie engulfed it on all sides. Reliance on *any* element within the present system is therefore an opening for the corrupting power of bourgeois ideology. Nothing was to be trusted or accepted apart from the embattled force of the Communist Party.

Lenin's position, however, had a result which he may not have desired. It destroyed any certain causal connection between present social factors and the future socialist reality. Lenin refused to rely on any factor other than class war. The fortunes of war are unpredictable; success is possible but so is defeat. An army fighting against bourgeois power and with its mind on future socialism cannot be said to represent that future in the sense of a necessary series of causes and effects. It is the future's representative only through its intent. Curiously enough, this is precisely the idea for which Marx and Engels assailed the utopian socialists. As Lenin eliminated all conceivable causal necessities linking the present with the future, the highest good was deprived of any present basis and receded into the rank of mere future possibilities. As far as present action was concerned, its sole content then became the Communist struggle as such. Party strategy came to be identified with the supreme good to which all intermediary ends must defer, and party interest was elevated to Lenin's criterion of right action.

"Is there such a thing as Communist ethics? Is there such a thing as Communist morality?" he asked rhetorically in 1920, and answered his own question:

> We say that our morality is entirely subordinated to the interests of the class struggle of the proletariat. Our morality is deduced from the class struggle of the proletariat.
>
> . . . .
>
> We say: Morality is that which serves to destroy the old exploiting society and to unite all toilers around the proletariat, which is creating a new Communist society.[31]

This passage should be read together with that in which Lenin, in 1905, laid down the principle of *partiinost'*, subordination to party interests, for all literary activities.[32] Lenin's principle of rational action thus amounts to the elevation of the party's strategic requirements to the rank of the good that ultimately governs all other ends. Not merely has Lenin completely relativized all ethical values to the service of the party but the governing principle itself, the party interest, is one that is relative to the changing strategic situation. Blind, total subjection to the party thus remains the only straw to which the practical reason of Communists can cling.

The radical relativization of principles of action, Lenin's final product, extended into the notions of "phases" and "stages," the segments of time cardinal to any Marxist analysis. The concept of "transition" was given unlimited extension backward and forward. Transition is a most important concept in any doctrine operating with successive "phases," "ages," or "social orders." The identification of any society as a phase or age presupposes a certain stability, an order which for a period of time remains by and large the same. Presumably the next succeeding phase or age or society would also endure in stability. In between, there is a process of change that is more abrupt, more radical than any change that occurs within the framework of a phase or age. Whether this transition is of an evo-

[31] Lenin, *Selected Works,* IX, 475, 477.
[32] Lenin, *Sochineniia,* X, 26.

lutionary or revolutionary character or whether it happens through a process or deliberate action is beside the point. What matters is that it is exceptional in every way. All relations are upset, violence plays a key role, and men live with their eyes either on the past or on the future but not on the shapeless present. In this sense, Marx characterized the "period of transition from capitalism to socialism" as one of "despotic inroads," in which government could be nothing else but the "dictatorship of the proletariat."[33]

Lenin viewed the concept of transition as involving lawless force and conflict rather than orderly government. He extended the concept both backward and forward into something of indefinite duration. The "period of transition" characterized by the "dictatorship of the proletariat" would begin, according to Marx, when capitalism collapsed and socialism was about to take its place. Lenin, however, postulated a proletarian-dominated "revolutionary dictatorship" an entire phase earlier, at the time when the feudal order collapsed and the bourgeois one was about to take its place. Not content with that, he even hinted that a proletarian-dominated dictatorship was possible in prebourgeois "phases" of social development. The Communist subdivision of historical time acknowledges primitive society, slave-holding society, feudal society, bourgeois society, socialist society. The proletarian-dominated transition was supposed to occur between the last two of these phases. By extending the principle of a transitional type of regime backward into all previous "phases" of society, Lenin imparted to all of them the character of "transitional" phases. He did the same to socialism. By assuming that even after the proletarian seizure of power classes would remain for an indefinite time to come, that the class struggle would continue with increased intensity, and by his refusal to contemplate anything like a normalizing of government in the socialist society, he stamped that period, too, as one of indefinite "transition." It is significant that since his death, a proliferation of "phases of transition" has been characteristic of the Soviet regime. There

[33] Marx, "Critique of the Gotha Programme," in *Karl Marx and Frederick Engels, Selected Works in Two Volumes* (Moscow, 1955), II, 32. *Cf.* "Manifesto of the Communist Party," in *ibid.*, I, 53.

have been the "transition from capitalism to the construction of socialism," the "transition from the construction of socialism to socialism," the "transition from socialism to the construction of communism," and further transitions to a "first phase" of communism and "mature communism" are envisaged. The period of transition has thus been gradually converted into "life as transition." All previous and present history is seen as a prolonged phase of preparation for something which in its final perfection recedes further and further into the future.

Lenin's attempt to construct an ethic based on the radical negation of the present world has resulted in the most complete dissolution of rational criteria for action in the present. His failure to elaborate a political theory for Communist regimes has left a fatal void. Stalin and Khrushchev made strenuous efforts to fill the gap but, not daring to set aside Lenin's basic reasoning, did not succeed.[34] Lenin's followers have not been able to create a semblance of genuine order for the peoples under their rule. They have wielded the sword of authority, not as servants of reason, but as restless and peaceless whips pursuing ever receding "goals."

[34] Stalin, *Marxism and Linguistics* (New York, 1951) and Stalin, *Problems of Socialism in the USSR* (New York, 1952); "Programme of the Communist Party of the Soviet Union," in J. F. Triska, *Soviet Communism: Programs and Rules* (San Francisco, 1962).

V □ Past, Future, and Present

THE IDEOLOGIST'S "FALSE CONSCIOUSNESS"

Lenin, alone of all ideological activists, worked out definite principles of practice, conceived in the strict logic of the total critique of society. True, Babeuf also left detailed instructions for the conspirators he directed, Hitler wrote *Mein Kampf,* and Mussolini lectured the public on what a proper Fascist life would be like. Lenin differed from them and from his fellow Marxists in the strictness of his adherence to the premise of total critique and in his razor-sharp distinctions between practices compatible and incompatible with that premise. He demonstrated that the characteristic inability of the ideological activist to attain any kind of order or to settle down to any kind of peace is endemic to a peculiar state of consciousness —that is, to a peculiar set of ideas concerning reality, man, and society. We can accept Lenin as representative of ideological activism in general, inasmuch as the pattern of practice recorded for such ideological movements as the Taborite Hussites, Thomas Müntzer's followers, the Anabaptists under Jan van Leyden, the Ranters in England, shows striking similarities with Lenin's prescriptions. Camus, in *The Rebel,* has worked out the corresponding similarities between the terror regime of the French Revolution and communism. Ideological activism in practice adopts "the organization not of order, but of war," sets up regimes "based on force and unlimited by law," and considers itself committed to a "protracted" and "irreconcilable" struggle as the road to the ultimate fulfillment of man's destiny.

We have come to designate this type of political practice, stemming from the total critique of society, as totalitarianism. Hitherto, the attempts to define totalitarianism in structural terms of political power have remained unsatisfactory: they enable us neither to make significant distinctions nor to take pertinent action; and they usually include in totalitarianism other phenomena which share neither the destructiveness nor the aggressiveness nor the viciousness of totalitarianism. Totalitarianism cannot be comprehended either as a mere quantitative expansion of governmental or executive competences or as a mere rebellion against a social class or political system and its representatives. The quality that we designate by the word "total" applies to totalitarian movements not because they invade what had until then been a "private" sphere of action, but because they aim beyond mere structural change at the denial and destruction of ontological foundations of order. A totalitarian movement acts in a society as a dissolvent of the *xynon* (Heraclitus), the common awareness of the bonds between political order and the nature of being. Where and insofar as the totalitarian attack is crowned by success, it destroys not merely institutions and powerholders but the transpositive guidance of laws, as well as the order by which families and individual persons live. Victims of totalitarianism find themselves reduced to a condition of spiritual, moral, and intellectual nakedness and emptiness which is the ultimate meaning of their physical punishment. In most of these cases, the victim himself gives intellectual assent to at least part of the persuasion that thus annihilates him by depriving him of the consciousness of his place in the order of being. This fact indicates that totalitarianism would not be possible in practice if it were not for a long period of intellectual erosion preceding the advent of the activists.

Ideological activism, then, presupposes certain intellectual and spiritual movements which can be seen as two, going in opposite directions. Ontologically, the first of these movements denies reality to the given world of experience and proclaims the reality of a phantasmal realm; praxiologically, the second movement pulls norms pertaining to the phantasmal realm and its present unreality into the world of experience and orients activities by them. To come back to the first movement: the reality of the given world of experience can be denied either axiologically or teleologically. The axiological denial radically opposes goodness to the historical world by envisaging a good wholly alien to both past and present society, as well as a given society wholly alien to goodness, so that man's historical existence is seen as essentially separated from his true reality. The teleological denial contracts meaningful time wholly into the future, withholding the attributes of reality from both past and present, so that neither past nor present is embraced as "ours," but the future alone is. Regarding the second movement, one again may distinguish an axiological from a teleological transformation of practice. Axiologically speaking, political practice is changed from "acting" to "making" in the sense of Aristotle's *Nicomachean Ethics,* book 6—that is, from rational choice confronting "things that are, or come into being, by necessity, or things that do so in accordance with nature" and which have "their origins in themselves," to the "contriving or considering how something may come into being which is neither capable of being or not being, and whose origin is in the maker and not in things made." In less technical language this means that Aristotle's rational man considers politics a matter of action within a world which he knows not to have made himself; whereas the totalitarian activist fancies himself engaged in making a world that so far has not had any being. Teleologically speaking, political practice is switched from the time dimension of the present—the contemporaneity of one's fellow-beings—to the dimension of the "period of transition" in which all actions lose their character of choices and take on that of the making of a preknown future. From the point of view of the "makers" of that future, the present is something to be removed, so that ideological activists are inescapably engaged in "protracted struggle," because they experience the conflict between the present world which "has come to be either of necessity, or in accordance with nature" and the phantasmal future "whose origin is in the maker" and which is capable of "either being or not being."

IDEOLOGY AND ITS OPPOSITE

In contemporary language, we call this type of thought, and the corresponding practices, "ideological" or "gnostic." The term "ideological" refers to the subordination of contemplative theory to the *libido dominandi*, which manifests itself in the building of closed systems around dogmatically willed "positions," in reductionism of both scope and materials of analysis, and in the determination to substitute an intellectually fabricated "Second Reality" for the reality given to man. "Gnostic" is a word based on the structural similarity between the Gnostic religions of the first three centuries of our era with modern ideologies. This similarity is found in metaphysical discontent, the attribution of evil to the environing world rather than to the human heart, belief in the possibility of salvation from the evil world as a whole, certainty that salvation is to be wrought by human action, and the acceptance of ideological "knowledge" of the methods of total change as the message of salvation for mankind.[1] The types of total critique of society which we have here reviewed differ, then, from what Camus calls "rebellion," the determined "No" to some kind of treatment, condition, or institution, spoken in the name of the good of which all men are aware in their existence. By contrast, the total critique of the ideologists assails society but actually aims at God, the cosmos, morality, and reason. In that respect the modern ideologists display an ontophobia similar to that of the ancient Gnostics. Their total critique is neither practical, nor merely social, nor moral in its roots. This explains why their hostility is not the function of any concrete grievance or aspiration and why their struggle is a limitless condition rather than a limited action.

Unfortunately there is not yet any language to identify the opposite of the thoughts and movements of total destruction. The word "philo-sophical," sometimes heard as the antonym of "ideological," is adequate as far as it goes, because it connotes theory, contemplation born of the love of truth rather than of the will to power. The term, however, is confined to the *noesis* of the Platonic-Aristotelian type and thus leaves out thoughts and attitudes about

[1] For an analysis of the experience underlying the Gnostic deprecation of being, *cf*, Hans Jonas, *The Gnostic Religion* (2nd ed.; Boston) and Eric Voegelin, *Science, Politics, and Gnosticism* (Chicago, 1968).

reality that are shaped by the myth and which likewise must be considered the opposite of ideology. Furthermore, a word is lacking to designate the opposite of "gnostic," with its assertion of the positivity of evil and the negativity of good, its espousal of alienation, and its antinomianism. It would seem that the term "philo-ontic" comes close to capturing the quality that is the obverse of "gnostic" and also might be applicable to the mythical symbolization of reality. One could then contrast "ideological" or "gnostic" thoughts, practices, and movements to "philo-sophic" and "philo-ontic" thoughts and actions, and one might wonder whether, opposite the ideological and gnostic total critiques of society there would not be a philo-ontic variety of total critique.

THE QUEST FOR LIMITS

Camus, one of the few who clearly recognized modern totalitarianism as "metaphysical revolution"—the presumptiousness of men usurping the role of God in history—called in response for a "philosophy of limits." He did little beyond setting up this concept as a *desideratum*, as an early death deprived him of the chance to clarify his idea. The last chapter of his *L'homme révolté* contains some very few hints about how he would have proceeded. "Each tells the other that he is not God, . . . a limit, under the sun, shall curb them all." Camus quotes approvingly the remark of "the future Communard" Tolain, "Human beings emancipate themselves only on the basis of natural groups." Camus ends with the confident statement: "There does exist for man, therefore, a way of acting and thinking which is possible on the level of moderation to which he belongs. . . . Politics is not religion." For Camus, this way of acting and thinking consists in rebellion, a negative affirmation in which he sees the establishment of a common human dignity. Like Camus' book, this study has so far yielded insights that sum up to no more than a fundamental condemnation of the type of total critique that leads to ideological activism. One cannot leave things at this point, though. The condemnation of totalitarian ideology and activism must not be allowed to include, even by implication, a condemnation of all criticism of society, not even all total critique, even if one does not go so far as Camus in reducing all meaningful political activity to rebellion. Such distinctions do precisely constitute a consciousness of "limits." A mere desire for "limits," however, will not produce such consciousness. The sense for limits was lost as a result of the destruction of the bond between political order and the order of being. Even the existentialist Camus pleads for "nature" against "history." He berates Europe which "no longer loves life," and ties himself to "the earth," "our first and last love." The development of "limits" requires a restoration of the sense of realities on which all sound political order rests.

In the following chapters we shall pursue this goal through work on three problems selected for their pertinence to the negative studies of total critique in the first three chapters. A recurrent trait of those ideological total critiques was the destruction of the past. This suggests an attempt to elucidate the relation of the past to any possibility of political order, an attempt here undertaken through a concrete though representative example—Israel. Another aspect of total critique was the resort to an ethics and a conception of good abstracted from any given society and particularly one's own society. This seems to call for a chapter on "the ethics of existence," meaning political existence in time and space. The final chapter addresses itself to the problem of a reasoned distinction between a critique, even total critique, of society within "the limit" and the limitless and totally destructive critiques treated in the first three chapters. Together, these three do not pretend to a comprehensive "philosophy of limits" but are meant to be a first move in that direction.

THE PUBLIC PAST

The past of a society constitutes a problem inasmuch as a society is not a subject equipped by nature with memory. A public past, therefore, is a problem *sui generis* differing from that of a personal past. An individual person, being a natural substance, grows up through various stages of childhood, adolescence, and adulthood, passing through many different situations, all the while knowing himself and being known as the same person. He can remember these stages as his own and others have seen him change while remaining the same person. Thus, the salient fact of his personality is precisely the experience of identity through and in spite of change. An individual, as a person, experiences his identity through memory of his past. A society has not been constituted by nature to assimilate the past through memory and indeed has not even been constituted as a natural physiobiological entity. How can one then speak of society's past? To be sure, a multitude of actions, events, relations attributed to a multitude of individuals are known by many persons, but this knowledge cannot prima facie be regarded as identical with a public past. These actions and events at the time of their occurrence could not possibly be known to all members of a society, and even less can one assume that everybody carries them in his memory. Even if, *per impossibile*, they could all have been recorded, what or who could look at this flood of happenings and experience in them a continuous identity? Actions and events, the *res gestae* as such, do not amount to a past; they are, indeed, "happenings" in the sense in which a modern fad presents them at parties, occurrences empty of meaning, not memorable, and therefore symptoms of nonbeing.

Insofar as one can attribute a past to a society, it appears as if that which one regards as a present unity of action has endured in time through different situations and events; in other words, a society is being considered an identity similar to that of a person. One can go further, however: because a society is not a natural substance; because there is not a body surrounded by a "sack of skin" which one can touch and see and whose changes one can observe with one's eyes, whose actions are performed by organs of that tangible body; because a society, then, is lacking this tangible phenomenon testifying to identity, the past alone is what could give identity to a society. As we have seen, this is an identity resembling that of the human person. Society is indeed "man, writ large." As a past is not attributable to a natural entity, it must be created and cultivated, and its maintenance is necessarily one of the most important activities in the founding and managing of a society. To begin with, the identification of many with a mythical common ancestor appears as the sole possibility of establishing a society in which not the blood ties but rather the ties of a common past constitute the public identity. Professor Voegelin has treated of a number of known creations of a past which engendered a society, chiefly Homer's appropriation of the Achaean *res gestae* to the Hellenes, as their supposed past,[2] and the somewhat different but yet relevant case of the merging of sundry local Mesopotamian dynasties into a dynastic past of the newly established empire of Sumer and Akkad.[3] Voegelin called this process *historiogenesis.* It is an appropriate term, but I should like to consider also the alternative *historiopoeism*—history making.

Underlying the public past is the cognition of each individual self through the awareness of the past. Consciousness of self emerges in and through the consciousness of objects and experiences.[4] Only after having perceived does one become aware of the self as perceiving; only after an experience has occurred does attention focus on the subject of the experience. From the past lights occasionally flare up, apart from any purposeful or normative thought; something that at the time was rejected now stands revealed as a landmark; something which the will classified at its time in one way now shows itself in a completely different light. Present contemplation thus is "returned past" and only what is past can return, only that is past which has returned.[5] In this way the past moves us to present being, to experiences of remorse, contrition, elation, or joy. Confronted with the unwilled and un-

[2] Voegelin, *The World of the Polis* (Baton Rouge, 1957), 67–110.

[3] Voegelin, *Anamnesis: Zur Theorie der Geschichte und Politik* (Munich, 1966), 87.

[4] A. A. Bowman, *A Sacramental Universe*, ed. J. W. Scott (Princeton and London, 1939).

[5] Heimito von Doderer, *Tangenten* (Munich, 1964), 88.

planned return of the past, we experience the I to whom all this happened and who, enduring in the stream of time, proves his being. Our identity is more than physical *gestalt*, just as the past, which on return evokes this consciousness of self, is not a collection of facts. We do not remember every step our feet have taken but we may remember a certain walk. We cannot recall every word that escaped our lips, but some of them return to haunt us as either bitter or fond memories. Leaving psychopathic cases aside, however, whatever wells up again in memory has at some time happened; we do not invent it, even though the meaning of what has happened may appear changed upon its return in memory.

The process of coming-to-be of conscious self in the awareness of past events does not occur in isolation. To begin with, the members of our family are interwoven into the same events and developments which we remember, and their presence in our lives constitutes a continuously modifying factor. What happens to us also happens to them, and their history is necessarily ours; we would not be the selves we are without them. Thus one's self is at least partially shared with a group. There is such a thing as a family history which is an inescapable dimension of each individual person's own past, and each individual's history constitutes an element modifying that of all other family members. One wonders at this point whether Aristotle, in characterizing the family primarily as an association for daily sustenance, did not unduly slight the importance of the family or village for the constitution of a common history of human selves. Friendship, too, is capable of engendering a common history in which the friends are involved individually as well as collectively. Enough has been said to make the point that individual man does not have the past wholly to himself; each person experiences himself as an identity together with other selves, so that the consciousness of his self involves partially the awareness of the consciousness of other selves. The past is both social and personal.

Aristotle's list of associations evolving toward the polis includes man-wife, family, village, but not business partnerships, athletic teams, or crews of sailors. He obviously included under "associations" only such groupings as set the stage for human personality by the intertwinement of the past of individual selves. The polis, the highest step in this series, differs from the others in that the intimate sharing of events and experiences between person and person is absent. The polis, and every political community in Aristotle's sense, is characterized by the public (i.e., impersonal) character of the social bond which comes, among other factors, from the size of the association which precludes the mutual sharing of personal pasts. In the impersonal public atmosphere of the political association, the common good is no longer personally but publicly defined as justice. Hence, the past must also be a public past that no longer can be discerned in the intertwining of individual pasts.

We know that every society on record has had a public past; in some cases we know how these historical pasts were generated. A society is a kind of common selfhood shared by a multitude of people. The experience of an individual self occurs in and through the experience of the past. Inasmuch as man for the fullness of his life requires a society, more particularly a political association, he requires also a public past. A public past is not simply given as a result of *res gestae* of a number of persons. Above all, there is no public past when a society is young. Later, it may fashion for itself a past from memorable actions of certain great rulers, certain victories, a heroic last stand, a creative achievement, an inspired teacher. But such events cannot be made to order. What does a public past embrace where there is a dearth of memorable deeds? Even where a record of *res gestae* of rulers, leaders, soldiers, teachers is available, it does not automatically constitute a public past. The identity of a society in terms of its public past constitutes a problem similar to that of a person's identity through the experience of his past.

The consciousness of one's self arises from the awareness of something else, from our experience of the self engaged in perception. In memory, past apperceptions become present, Bowman has spoken of the "objectification" of the past. It would be more appropriate to speak of a *praesentification* of the past as it wells up from the death of oblivion to stand before us. What is praesentified, however, is not a matter of indifference or strangeness, it is something that we have done or that was done to us, something we experienced or thought, something we hoped or feared, loved or hated. And this praesentification of something that is utterly gone by now has the power to move us deeply, to release emotions, force our minds to conclusions, excite our will. We cannot say that we deliberately select what we choose to remember. We cannot control what returns to the here and now. Memory has a power of its own that will not be denied—a fact on which all psychoanalysis is built. Thus we do not recall only aspects of the past which we deem paradigmatic or normative. On the contrary, that which returns from the past with power to force itself on our attention and to move us toward the future becomes thereby paradigmatic or normative. The past is not made by our preferences or intentions. Rather, in the return of the past something uncovers itself to us. And in the reflection prompted by what returns, we go through a process of discovery that is in a sense a revelation of our self. The return of the past poses the problem of the truth, the real truth of what has happened. As we wrestle with the truth of the past and thus with the truth about ourselves, we confront the problem that is usually called the meaning of life. The process itself, so little subject to deliberate control, and the impulses coming from the "returned past" prompt us to reflect on the order that makes itself felt in all this. At this point of wonder, the mind responds by producing a comprehending symbol, somthing like a perceptible reality by means of which we can understand what has happened and is happening and to what it all adds up to. Most commonly this symbol created by the mind is a variety of the myth.

Our problem, however, is not the personal past but the public past, the latter pertaining to an entity that is not equipped with personal memory. All that we have said of the "return" of the past, the revelation of self, the impulse to speculate on the wider reality of which we become aware in the process does not apply to a society, because it all hinges on the powers of subjective memory. All the same, man requires also a public past. Does it follow, then, that a society's past is arbitrarily fabricated and that it has nothing to say to that sense of discovery which in the case of a person accompanies the return of the past? Are a public past and a personal past different in kind rather than in degree? Socrates, for one, would disagree with this, as he proceeded to explore the order of the human soul though an examination of the processes of public order. Instead of simply deferring to his authority, however, let us analyze a particular empirical instance of the generation of a public past, a past acquired when a society attained unified existence. The example to which I should like to turn is that of Israel.

ISRAEL AND ITS PAST

Israel attained full political development when David, then king of Judah with his capital at the southern Hebron, was also made king of Israel, the northern political entity that had previously taken shape through the elevation of its charismatic leader Saul to kingship. Subsequently, David conquered Jerusalem, a Canaanite stronghold located in the corridor between Judah and Israel, which thus became "David's city"—that is, a kind of royal district similar in function to the District of Columbia. Thus, the transfer of the Ark to that place put Israel's cult under the auspices of the "united kingdom" and the priesthood under royal authority. During the reign of David, or his son Solomon, probably, began the literary composition of the Hexateuch, the official history of Israel, in a work which scholars call J, or the Yahwist. The Hexateuch pulled together the various strands of a tradition connected with the cult of Yahweh, a cult that was common to Judah and Israel. The Hexateuch contains a narrative, interspersed with statements of the law, in which is established the identity of Israel from the present (the time of David) through the past settlement of Canaan, the preceding migration, the events at Sinai, the Exodus, back to the patriarchs to whom Yahweh's promises were made, all this capped off with the aetiology of primeval history. The function of this public past can be seen in the formulary which Gerhard von Rad[6] has identified as a brief *credo* (Deut. 26:5ff.).

> My father was a wandering Aramaean. He went down into Egypt to find refuge there, few in numbers; but there he became a nation, great, mighty, and strong. The Egyptians ill-treated us, they gave us no peace and inflicted harsh slavery on us. But we called on Yahweh the God of our fathers. Yahweh heard our voice and saw our misery, our toil and our oppression; and Yahweh brought us out of Egypt with mighty hand and outstretched arm, with great terror, and with signs and wonders. He brought us here and gave us this land, a land where milk and honey flow.[7]

What we find here combined are two original strands of the traditionally "remembered past": the "bringing out of Egypt" and the "bringing into Canaan." Another strand consists of the patriarchal stories and the promise of the Lord to the effect that (a) Abraham will become a great nation, (b) Yahweh will give the land of Canaan to his progeny, (c) in Abraham all people will be blessed. Furthermore, there is the "Sinai tradition," telling not of God "bringing out," but rather of God "coming down"—that is, the tradition of God's self-revelation and the people's self-subjection to Him and His will. Finally, there is the strand of primeval history, including an account of the Creation, the story of Cain and Abel, the flood and Noah, the tower of Babel, and some relevant genealogies plus assorted minor themes. Martin Noth has singled out yet another strand, the wanderings in the desert, but admits that this tradition cannot stand on its own feet and depends on both the Exodus and the Settlement traditions.[8]

There is wide agreement that it was not the literary author of the Yahwist document who fused all these strands into a single narrative. The fusion, rather, had occurred beforehand. What the Yahwist seems to have done is to detach these traditions from the particular sanctuaries with which they were of old connected—

[6] Gerhard von Rad, *The Problem of the Hexateuch,* tr. W. T. Dicken (New York, 1966).

[7] All scriptural quotations are taken from the *Jerusalem Bible*, ed. Alexander Jones (New York, 1966).

[8] Martin Noth, *Überlieferungsgeschichte des Pentateuch* (Stuttgart, 1948).

that is, from the cults of Gilgal, or Shechem, or Mamre, or Beersheba. In doing so, he "historized" the tradition, separating it from local cultic interests and converting it into something more of a common history which embraced not merely Israel but also other peoples and the world as a whole. It may very well be, as Alt says, that the impetus to this historization came from David's conquering unification of the whole of Palestine.[9] Prior to this, Yahweh's promise of the land had obviously remained only partially fulfilled, as attested by Joshua, 13–19, so that it was the extension of the king's jurisdiction to what hitherto had remained unconquered that enabled Israel to look back on the whole as a completed story. In any case, the problem of Israel's "remembered past" arises not for the Yahwist document but rather for the period before the monarchy.

The problem is posed by the undeniable fact that before the settlement in Canaan there was no "Israel," a whole composed of twelve tribes. The campaigns reported in Joshua, 1–12, obviously are the enterprises of some clans or tribes who settled in central Palestine in what later became the territory of Ephraim, Manasseh, and Benjamin (the so-called Rachel tribes). It is not clear how many of the tribes existed as such before the settlement. Judah in particular is surrounded by all kinds of doubts in that respect. At any rate, the people as a whole acquired an identity only in connection with the land occupied. In all probability, the convocation at Shechem reported in Joshua, 24, is the foundation act of an amphictyony of tribes and clans that formed around a common sanctuary at Shechem.[10] This impression is confirmed by the sagas of the book of Judges which report of heroes and heroic deeds, each linked to a particular tribe. We have, then, either tribes or clans taking land in Palestine and proceeding to form an amphic-

[9] Albrecht Alt, *Kleine Schriften zur Geschichte des Volkes Israel* (3 vols.; Munich, 1959).

[10] Roland de Vaux rightly reminds us that the Twelve Tribes, unlike the Greek amphictyonies, were held together by their common acknowledgment of Yahweh rather than by a political ruling body. De Vaux, *Ancient Israel* (2 vols.; New York, Toledo, 1965).

tyony on the basis of a cult, the substance of which is a "remembered past," remembered as the past of twelve tribes which together form a unit called "Israel." What was accepted as a common or public past could not have been the memory of the twelve tribes as a whole or of some tribes in particular. In what sense, then, can one speak here of a "remembered past"? How and why would anybody acknowledge a past that was neither his own, nor that of his family or his tribe, and yet claimed to be an object of memory?

What is the hard core of the "remembered past," that which is left after all the later accretions and embellishments have been peeled off as far as possible? In terms of something like a historical record, there can be no question. Throughout the Old Testament there reappears with ubiquitous insistence the identification of Yahweh as "your God, I who brought you here from Egypt (Ps. 81:10)"; and the corresponding identification of Israel: "Once we were Pharaoh's slaves in Egypt, and Yahweh brought us out of Egypt by his mighty hand (Deut. 6:21)." Von Rad links the deliverance from Egypt to the Settlement tradition which he distinguishes from the wholly separate "Sinai tradition." He explains the Settlement tradition in terms of the need of the new proprietors for a valid title to the land; and he drives his point home by identifying the Settlement tradition with the cult of Gilgal, the place at which Joshua apportioned the land to the various tribes. This explanation seems plausible enough and might be extended to include the divine promise to Abraham, part of which was indeed the possession of Canaan. The explanation, however, cannot possibly account for the memory of the "bringing out of Egypt" and of delivery from affliction because this story has no necessary logical connection with the "bringing into Canaan" and a divinely assisted conquest. The Exodus episode makes no contribution whatsoever to the legitimation of Israel's land occupancy. The Exodus story, indeed, is not logically related to anything else. No other event can be classified as its anticipation and the episode itself does not lead to anything. The Sinai experience stands on its own feet apart from the Exodus and even apart from any historical narrative. Unexpected, singular and reported with all the curious quirks of reality, the deliverance from Pharaoh stands out from all the rest, unaccountable unless it really happened. It bears all the marks of a factual occurrence, and biblical scholarship seems generally to assume that an actual event alone can account for the Scriptural insistence on the tale.

At this point a number of other problems arise. The Settlement tradition does indeed always include the Exodus as part of a public cult centering on a "remembered past." Even the Settlement story itself imitates the pattern of the Exodus tale, for example, the stopping of the waters of Jordan in Joshua, 3. If Exodus ever was a separate tradition, then the fusing between it and the Settlement tradition must have occurred very early. Why should there have been such a fusion? We know that the groups who campaigned in the Settlement were neither individually nor collectively identical with those who escaped from Egypt. Some scholars suggest that the escapees from Egypt consisted of clans or a clan, elements of whom were later adopted into the clans that invaded Canaan. Others assume a possible ethnic affinity. In either case we must conclude that the Settlement tradition included the report of events which happened not to the settling clans or tribes but to other persons, in another country, at another time, and in an unrelated context. Why should the groups invading Canaan in the thirteenth century B.C. remember an event that had befallen neither them nor their kinfolk, and why should they remember it in the context of the Settlement? Why would the invasion of a few tribes into Canaan be represented as an action of "all of Israel"? Why should the deliverance from Egypt be reported as having occurred to "Israel"? And why should this kind of "remembered past" have the power to forge a unity that later could produce a king and subsequently impose on the ruler of a Jebusite city the full authority of its tradition?

Such questions have their parallel with regard to the group that left Egypt in the reign of Rameses II. We must assume that they actually were in bondage and compelled to perform forced labor, that they escaped into the desert, were pursued and somehow delivered from their pursuers. What is puzzling is why such an event should be inordinately memorable. It cannot have been the first time that parts of Egypt's forced labor subjects fled nor the first time that a group of such fugitives made good their escape in the face of military pursuit. Out of many similar occurrences, however, this particular one must have stood out as totally different in kind. The record tells us about the differentiating quality: the escape and the deliverance were experienced as a theophany. We need not ask what brought this experience about. An experience is one of the rock-bottom realities of human existence that admits critical examination only with respect to its substance rather than its facticity. The fact is that the escapees from Egypt, when they finally stood in safety and freedom, experienced their deliverance as an act of God, an irruption of divine might into time and the affairs of men. It is probable that the experience was had by one among them, their leader, or a prophet, or one who through the experience became a prophet; and it matters little whether he was Moses or someone later identified with a Moses who belonged to a different place and period, as Noth suggests.

A "SINGLE EVENT" THEOPHANY

In order to appreciate the quality of this particular theophany one should remind oneself that to the peoples of the second millennium B.C. the sacred was something that one could not intentionally produce but could only discover or invoke, and that for them the discovery of the sacred was a matter of being or not-being. For in their eyes the sacred was that which eminently *is* or manifested that which eminently is, and the profane was that which had no part in the ultimate reality.[11] It would not be necessary to insert such a remark had it not been for the attempt of G. E. Mendenhall to interpret the Settlement as a movement of self-liberation, on the analogy of the French Revolution and nineteenth century progressivism.[12]

[11] On the sacred and the profane, *cf.* Mircea Eliade, *Patterns in Comparative Religion*, tr. Rosemary Sheed (Cleveland, 1963).

[12] G. E. Mendenhall, *Law and Covenant in Israel and the Ancient Near East* (Pittsburgh, 1955).

The theophany of the Exodus was remarkable particularly because it was experienced in the Egyptian-Mesopotamian world of the second millennium B.C. which knew only of nature hierophanies or theophanies. The kingdoms of this world were founded on cosmological symbolism, which in our historical retrospection has come to be called "the myth." The myth stems from the experiences of nature's manifold manifestations of life which then served as the sole source of order in human existence. The fugitives of the Sea of Reeds, having lived in Egypt for generations, could not know anything besides this type of order. A manifestation of God in a single historical action must have been to them something unheard and unconceived of. Now one cannot attribute to the escapees from Egypt less of a desire to *be* than their contemporaries entertained; neither can one assume that this group felt being was something within their power to control nor that they could substitute thinking for being. The theophany at the Sea of Reeds must have struck them with utter surprise, something they actually experienced and yet were only half willing to believe. But believe it they ultimately did and then began to draw certain conclusions from it for their own existence. First, the God who manifested Himself in a single action must be *one* God rather than a member in a pantheon of divinities. Second, as a God who had bested Pharaoh and his forces, He must be opposed to the divinities of the Egyptian cosmos or any similar cosmos, and He must be more potent than these cosmic divinities. Thus, a simultaneous worship of the God of Exodus and the gods of the cosmological myth could not be contemplated.

A theophany inevitably raised the problem of a corresponding order of human existence. Insofar as men structure their common life with a view to nature hierophanies of various sorts, they do so by reenacting the myths of creation, destruction and regeneration, being and coming-to-be, and the unity of all life in its multiple forms. This seems to be the most universal, one might almost say, the most "normal" form of order, as evidenced by common patterns occurring in myths all over the globe. A divine manifestation occurring in a single historic action, however, must confront man's ordering mind with an extraordinary challenge. The refugees at the Sea of Reeds experienced God in the single event of their deliverance but that event had gone by. Had God also gone by? If so, is there no presence of a God who shows Himself through historical action. The problem of human order is to relate men and their purposes to that which *is*. How could they who had seen God fleetingly, in a single action, relate themselves to Him? A further difficulty consisted in the lowly station of the escapee group. The historical events recorded in the annals of Rameses II and his predecessors had happened to kings or emperors, but not to ordinary men and women who in these annals had no standing whatsoever. The ragged group of refugees could not possibly have conceived of themselves as "historical" persons. Besides, for generations they had known only Egypt and its order, where the soundness of social life was guaranteed through the identity of Pharaoh with Horus and of Pharaoh's predecessor with Osiris, which made the other divinities, as it were, in-laws of Pharaoh. Thus the theophany of the Exodus combined the experience of a God who was mighty even against Pharaoh with that of a people who were utterly dependent on the divine saving action. This experience did not admit of a social order centering in any kind of identification with God. The conclusion which to us now seems obvious must have been wholly unprecedented and unheard of in the world of Pharaoh's Egypt: the refugee group must exist as a people *under* God. Finally, this theophany had occurred not to an individual person but to a group who identified themselves through an eponymous ancestor, "Jacob and his sons." A response to the theophany could be made, therefore, only in terms of political existence, of a people's unity.

The terms of the response are clearly recorded in the Pentateuch and need not be reviewed in detail at this point. The clan of "Jacob and his sons" acknowledged God, a God of historic judgment and active redemption, as their political sovereign. This meant that the content of their political order, the law, must be nothing but the will of God. Accordingly, the law of Israel differs in form from other law codes in antiquity. The most widely used pattern is that of casuistic conditional formulation: "Supposed a man has robbed and been caught in the act, the same man shall be killed." A certain amount of this can be found also in Israel's law. Mostly, however, Israel's law is cast in the characteristic pattern of an apodictic and unconditional "Thou shalt!" This law represented, as it were, God's terms for the political existence of a people under Him, so that the people could be God's only as they accepted and abided by the law. The pattern is that of a covenant, a mutual promise or commitment in which righteousness (i.e., God's law) was the object of the treaty.[13] Existence, conceived as existence under God, required the continual molding and remolding of the people's will to God's standards. It is in these terms that one could conceive of the continued presence of a God of historical action who became manifest in a single historic event. His presence was the law, as witnessed by the Ark, a box that in many parallel cases was carried around empty but in the case of Israel contained the tables of the law. The entire complex is summarized in the credal formula of Deuteronomy, 6:20 ff.:

> In times to come, when your son asks you, "What is the meaning of the decrees and laws and customs that Yahweh our God has laid down for you?" you shall tell your son, "Once we were Pharaoh's slaves in Egypt, and Yahweh brought us out of Egypt by his mighty hand. Before our eyes Yahweh worked great and terrible signs and wonders against Egypt, against Pharaoh and all his House. And he brought us out from there to lead us into the land he swore to our fathers he would give to us. And Yahweh commanded us to observe all these laws and to fear Yahweh our God, so as to be happy for ever and to live, as he has granted us to do until now."

There was no precedent for this form of existence and no close parallel among other peoples. The strength of the theophanic ex-

[13] According to de Vaux, the apodictical form "Thou shalt!" was a common characteristic in ancient Oriental treaties, which were deposited at a sanctuary and periodically read in public. De Vaux, however, emphasizes the uniqueness of Israel's covenant to which God was a party rather than a mere guarantor. De Vaux, *Ancient Israel*, I, 147.

perience at the Sea of Reeds obviously admitted of no other conclusion, but the people of "Jacob and his sons" must have been quite aware that they ventured out on uncharted seas. An existence under the God of the Exodus was presented to them as a choice, and a most daring one. One can still sense the consciousness of a deliberate choice in the text of Deuteronomy, 30:15, 16, 19:

> See, today I set before you life and prosperity, death and disaster. If you obey the commandments of Yahweh your God that I enjoin on you today, if you love Yahweh your God and follow his ways, if you keep his commandments, his laws, his customs, you will live and increase, . . . I call heaven and earth to witness against you today: I set before you life or death, blessing or curse. Choose life, then, so that you and your descendants may live, . . .

The same form of deliberate choice was observed at the founding of the Palestine amphictyony at Shechem, as reported in Joshua, 24:15.

The Exodus theophany and the people's choice of a political existence under a God of historical deliverance could not escape notice and stimulated an interested curiosity among other clans, tribes, and peoples. It was news fully as much or more than, for example, as a new form of investment is news among people to whom investment is a matter of existence or nonexistence. By comparison, any new variety of divine pantheons, city or family gods of the cosmological variety were not news, because the patterns were essentially similar, and the variety of cults and divinities would not suggest to anybody that his particular cult or pantheon of divinities was invalid. But a cult founded on an historic event, instead of a nature hierophany, was entirely novel, and the riskiness of Israel's choice must have been obvious to all onlookers. As the adherents of the new cult were maintained "in life" they must have attracted proselytes. People who lived in cities, their lives ordered by local deities and priests, protected by royal power directly representing cosmic forces, cannot have been tempted to consider the validity of the cult of Yahweh. But for migrant or desert clans whose tie to the order of being was often merely through family gods, the example of Yahweh's people must have been exciting and deeply disturbing, because it was the cult of a people like they were, helpless, dependent, organized in nothing more powerful than families or clans, and unable to fall back on the might of royalty and mercenary armies.

The core of the new cult was an actual event in history. A cosmic myth, for example, a creation myth, was understood by everyone as a fictitious symbol even though the fiction symbolized the truth of being. A cosmological myth can be celebrated by reenacting again and again the story it relates. But an event that happened once in time and place, "before our eyes," even though experienced as a theophany, cannot be repeated or reenacted. God acted one time and his action can be only remembered. The Yahweh cult, accordingly, was a cult of remembrance, told by generation after generation, of something that happened "before our eyes." The very essence of the remembered action was its positivity. Those who accepted the Yahweh cult, therefore, also embraced an historical past, the past of "Jacob and his sons."

Biblical scholarship distinguishes between the "main themes" of this tradition and its "filling details."[14] One wonders, however, whether it is not improbable that the orally transmitted tradition of an historical past through which God manifested Himself would be conceived first in terms of "main themes," like a student's composition, the elaborating details to be filled in later. We have seen above that a personal identity emerges in the awareness of one's own past and that a personal past is always intertwined with those of one's family and friends. The narrative underlying Yahweh's cult related precisely the type of personal and family occurrences with which everyone is familiar from his own experience. The God who delivered a people from bondage and military pursuit thus could also be experienced as the God of "Abraham, Isaac, and Jacob," a God of individual persons and their families. The fullness of human self-consciousness was thereby related to the divine intervention in history.

The answers to our questions begin to emerge at this point. By

[14] See, for example, Noth, *Überlieferungsgeschichte des Pentateuch.*

the time of the Settlement, the cult of Yahweh had spread far beyond the group who had experienced the theophany of the Exodus and even beyond their descendants. The Settlers were clans, families, and tribes united in and through this cult which involved acceptance of the past of "Jacob and his sons." We need not inquire whether they were blood relatives or ethnically akin to the group that escaped from Egypt, because the fact would be quite irrelevant. What made them into a people or potential people was the common worship of Yahweh, a single God manifested through past historical action. Their law was Yahweh's will, Yahweh led them in battle, he also took the place of an earthly sovereign, and that without any attempt at identification. The people's existence under Yahweh was possible through remembrance of His deeds, and linked to that memory was the memory of the people to whom the deeds had been done, "Jacob and his sons." They had witnessed the divine action, the theophany had occurred "before their eyes." Thus their memories became "our" memories, their eponymous ancestors "our ancestors," their personal experiences the past, as it were, of "our family." This was so not because the experiences struck later generations as familiar ones but rather because the individuals and families to whom they occurred were representative. They were representative because they, men and families "like ourselves," had been singled out by the irruption of God's action into time and the affairs of men.

Once a political community was established on a remote past remembered as if it had happened "before our eyes," it attained a momentum of its own, the momentum of historization. Von Rad believes that the Sinai tradition, originally a cult of God's self-revelation apart from any historical action, was transformed into an historical narrative so as to fit into the form of the Exodus report.[15] The transformation appears plausible but it is hardly plausible that the motive should have been a literary one. Rather one would assume that the Sinai tradition was historized so as to fit into the kind of human existence which corresponded to the Yah-

[15] Von Rad, *The Problem of the Hexateuch*, 31.

weh cult. Even before the monarchy, figures from other cultic contexts had been incorporated into the story. The Yahwist, as was mentioned before, further historized the entire complex by detaching it from various local cult centers and rendering it in the form of a single tale, the historizing transformation even including the creation myth. Once the Exodus theophany had grown into the order of a people living under God on the strength of their public past, history had become a mold of human existence, as such novel not only for "Jacob and his sons" but for the entire human race. Here, however, arise new problems that require separate consideration.

HISTORY AS A MODE OF EXISTENCE

Israel's existence as a politico-military unit can be explained only in terms of the public past that we have described. The modern reader will not experience any difficulty with the concept of a past, but in the late second millennium B.C. a past like that of Israel was a radical innovation. The Egyptian and Mesopotamian civilizations, then practically all the civilization that the human race had developed, based social order on the cosmological myth. In the order of the myth the past was not differentiated from the present and neither was the future. Anything contained in the myth as a story of past occurrings could be reenacted, anything that appeared as a purely human past could be destroyed, and besides, past and future were quite freely reversible. The myth consisted of tales about the gods and their deeds and dealt with such events as, for instance, the Creation. Besides the stories, however, the myth consisted of cultic actions through which a kind of osmosis was effected between the human and the divine. Cultic action touching on divine deeds narrated as of the past brought these deeds out of the past into the present by reenaction. A past which at any time can be converted into a present is no past as we understand it. Many of the mythic tales are dramatic and contained dimensions of both past and future. In cultic action these were not treated as antinomical time indices: the drama's past might appear as the cultic action's future, and the drama's future as the past, as, for instance, in the periodical suffering or death and subsequent redemption of a particular god or a fateful battle between the forces of order and those of chaos. Mircea Eliade has called this feature the reversibility of time.[16]

An aspect of this reversibility is the free destructibility of man's own past. In Mesopotamia and the entire ancient Middle East the most characteristic festival was that of the New Year in which the past of human sin and failure was annihilated. The festival was accompanied by a symbolic dissolution of all order (orgies, slaves giving commands to masters, kings being humiliated by their subjects) as well as symbolic acts simply erasing the past (the scapegoat being driven out into the desert). Therefore, in the order of the myth the past was quite unsubstantial. As nature is periodically regenerated and can return from lifelessness to life, so time appeared capable of regeneration and its regeneration was deemed to wipe out the past. In this order man's existence was experienced not as a movement from past through present into future but rather as a relatively timeless oscillation between order, fluidity, and again order; birth, death, and rebirth; impairment and restoration; being, chaos, and reconstituted being. This movement, in the typical identity of its beginning and end, can be called unhistorical. The suitability of the term "cyclical" is quite doubtful, because that term already presupposes a sense of linear history.

On the other hand, human life and activities under the myth were governed by a variety of times, each appropriate to an activity, an occasion, or a season. There were times constituted by cultic events, times corresponding to certain deities, times applied to agriculture, others pertaining to war, and so on. Georges Dumézil has coined for this the concept of "time as representation."[17] Each time guaranteed the presence of divine forces and powers in an activity vital to human existence. A late formulation of the representative character of various times is found in Qoheleth (Ecclesiastes) 3:1–8:

[16] Eliade, *Cosmos and History: The Myth of the Eternal Return*, tr. Willard A. Trask (New York, 1959).

[17] Dumézil, "Temps et mythes," *Recherches Philosophiques*, V (1935–36), 238.

> There is a season for everything, a time for every occupation under heaven:
>
> A time for giving birth,
> a time for dying;
> a time for planting,
> a time for uprooting what has been planted.
> A time for killing,
> a time for healing;
> a time for knocking down,
> a time for building.
> A time for tears,
> a time for laughter;
> a time for mourning,
> a time for dancing.
> A time for throwing stones away,
> a time for gathering them up;
> a time for embracing,
> a time to refrain from embracing.
> A time for searching,
> a time for losing;
> a time for keeping,
> a time for throwing away.
> A time for tearing,
> a time for sewing;
> a time for keeping silent,
> a time for speaking.
> A time for loving,
> a time for hating;
> a time for war,
> a time for peace.

The book in which this listing of various times is found conveys to the modern reader an impression of despair rather than of ordered security; it was written, though, about 250 B.C., when a wholly different sense of motion in time had already shaped Israel's existence for hundreds of years. All the same, we may still read it as a valid expression of the oscillation from beginning to end and back to beginning that characterized human existence under the myth. Qoheleth is quite explicit on this point: "What is, already was; what is to be, has been already." (3:15) The Hebrew author who already lived in a homogeneous time experienced as history could appreciate the different time of the myth with sharp theoretical understanding which he put in the formula, ". . . and there is nothing new under the sun." (1:9) Qoheleth realized that if there were something "new" it would once and forever break the repetitive and representative movement of various times so that human existence would be radically changed.

That is precisely what happened as a result of the Exodus theophany. The deliverance from Egypt did not fit into a schedule of sacred times, it occurred not on the occasion of some cultic action; the haste characteristically still observed in the Passover celebration recalls a sense of having been wholly unprepared for what was to come. The theophany event then was unexpected and the unexpected is unique rather than repetitive. God quite suddenly burst into the affairs of men, breaking through the cultic order of various times and marking thereby a moment that had no cultic standing in the myth. That moment immediately receded into the past but, in thus fading out of sight and remaining only in memory, it established a past of a kind that had not been known before. Under the myth the past on which men looked back and which was to be erased had been theirs, a past of sin and failure. The divine time, on the other hand, admitted of no definite past but only of a perpetual present. But that fleeting and receding moment of the Exodus deliverance had manifested God, and thus a genuine past had for once been established by God's action. The unique positivity of the fact, the involvement of a theophany in the singular *res gestae* of peoples and rulers, precluded any notion of a cultic reenactment that would convert that past into a present. The sacred fact could only be remembered in its singularity. Something "new" had happened and would always remain "new," no matter how long ago it occurred. The "newness" obviously consisted not simply in the singularity of the event but in that a fleeting fact as such had manifested God and thus stood in irreconcilable contrast to the repetitive times representing the various aspects of existence "under the sun." A past thus constituted by God's action could not be looked upon as destructible in the same sense in which a purely human past might seem destructible. God's irruption into time gave to a single moment receding into the past a kind of substantiality, if that is an appropriate term. One might call this moment an *eternal past*, a moment which, though having occurred in time and incapable of being repeated, lifts the past to the significance of eternity.

The new kind of past induced Israel to live in a new mold of existence in which, for the first time, past and present were sharply differentiated. The theophanic single event could not be converted into a present; it would always remain past, but a past having a life-and-death importance for living men. The full consciousness of this differentiation can be seen in the formulary of Israel's self-identification. Political unity has been variously attributed to common principles, a common language, common race, but Israel's unity was rooted simply in a past event, celebrated again and again in a memory that set off Israel from others. The differentiation of the past from the present entailed further differentiations in the relation of humanity and divinity. Mythical deities had been worshipped as beings acting in a framework of time. Many of these gods were characterized by certain age attributes, some "older" or "younger" than others, both "old" and "young" being understood as permanent attributes, like the age of Dennis the Menace. Many of them were involved in time developments, for example, fluctuations between times of death or sickness and times of life or health, or caught up in complex dramatic sequences. Furthermore, the myth conceived the essential difference between gods and men as that between immortality and mortality. None of these notions could apply to a God who had manifested himself in a singular action breaking into human affairs at an unscheduled and unexpected moment. The God who became manifest through the Exodus deliverance obviously was not subject to any time but was rather a sovereign lord of time, or, to put it differently, a God transcending time. This divine transcendance left man alone involved in time, not in various "representative" times but in time as a general condition of human existence. A time-transcending God, experienced by time-inhabiting man, can be only an eternal rather than an immortal God, a God of timelessness in contrast with the time-bound world of immanence. Furthermore, an eternal God manifested by a pinpointed intervention in time must be a God of purpose, will, and intelligence, rather than merely a god of cosmic potency. As manifested by His action in the past, he must be a God of judgment and redemption.

As an eternal past was constituted by God's breaking into time, a new time experience superseded the old oscillation between a variety of sacred times containing nothing "new." To be sure, even under the order of the myth, kings had their deeds recorded, and these annals contained not repetitive movements but singular events which we today would characterize as a past. But under the myth, the *res gestae* of rulers were not of the essence of social order, they had no standing, as it were, in the osmosis between human activities and divine reality. The Exodus deliverance resembled the *res gestae* of kings in its singular positivity, but it differed from them in that it represented eternity as an historical action of God. So now time became, in a way, an ocean inhabited by men, interrupted by the single island that was thrown up through God's past intervention.

The God who acted once, however, may well act again. Since His first action came unexpectedly, so might subsequent ones. Thus, on the other side from the past, a future opened up. The "opening up" is characteristic of the future, as the "no new thing under the sun" was characteristic of time movements that had no future because they knew of no past. Once a singular moment of past has been established unperishably, some new occurrence of a kindred character might be in store; but the possibilities of such a new occurrence are endless, so that a future is essentially the category of open possibilities. This characteristic openness embraces not only the substance of a new intervention by God but also the time designation: "You will not be expecting us to write anything to you, brothers, about 'times and seasons,' since you know very well that the Day of the Lord is going to come like a thief in the night." (1 Thess. 5 : 1–2) Or, to use the language of Qoheleth, the future, as the eternal past, is precisely the dimension of that which is "new under the sun." This gives the future the quality of a mystery, since what is "new under the sun" cannot come from men or nature but only from God. Later historiographers sought to catch this quality of mystery in the concept of Providence which, however, is inadequate because it connotes among others also the meaning of "foreknowledge" and has tempted men again and again to practice "foreknowledge" in retrospect.

A more adequate conceptualization would have borne some kinship to Nicolaus Cusanus' *docta ignorantia*. Eric Voegelin, analyzing Aristotle's metaphysics, has differentiated *wissendes Fragen* and *fragendes Wissen*, containing both the elements of desire and knowledge, so that the desire for knowledge presupposes both that there is something to be known and ignorance of what is to be known.[18] The *Metaphysics* is concerned with the process of knowledge, but the analysis could apply also to the problem of the future under a time-transcending God who has once manifested Himself by action in time. In the light of this past, man confesses both ignorance of what is to come and knowledge that on some occasions, "as a thief in the night," God again will intervene. The openness of the future imposes on man an obligation to wait on what may come, but the eternal past prevents this "unknowing waiting" from being uninstructed. Existence in history thus is characterized by a new quality that is called hope, a certainty of realities that at present remain unseen (Heb. 11:1); but it is important to note that certainty of "realities at present unseen" stems at least partly from realities remembered in the eternal past. The present, in this perspective, is no mere transition to the future nor a human repetition or reenactment of a divine past, but rather the entire broad and firm ground of human action in a time which, though not sacred, is not lost because it is secured between the memory of past moments of divine irruption and the hope of potential future ones. One practical manifestation of the width and solidity of the present is "the law" which represents enduring sameness in the midst of fleeting

[18] Voegelin, *Anamnesis*, 289.

time and thus suggests divine timelessness. Man, said Boethius in the *Consolation of Philosophy*, in face of temporal mutation seeks to "imitate the ever present immutability of (God's) life," and in this sense Boethius spoke of Providence not so much as foreknowledge but rather as "the never-failing constancy in the present." The other manifestation of the firmly grounded present is the ability of those who live in history established by an eternal past to apperceive phenomena, events, and situations that come to them as ultimately posited by God, by virtue of which attitude they encompass the singular, the accidental, and the unrhymed in the overall meaning of Providentiality and thus can feel "at home" in a seemingly disjointed complexity of ubiquitous change. Kierkegaard's "knight of faith" (*Fear and Trembling*) is a conceptual model of this ability to perceive in the unexpected turns of life the order of the present, experienced "because the man has made and every instant is making the movements of infinity."

ETERNAL HOPE AND "ETERNAL RETURN"

History, human existence in time under a timeless, transcendent God, is de-divinized time—that is, time no longer representing sacred occasions, as under the myth. That does not mean that all time in history drops into the chaos of profaneness as in Eliade's sense. Rather, time assumes a neutral character. In this general ocean of time, the moment of Exodus was and is a sacred point, in the same way in which the spot on which Joshua received a vision was a bit of sacred ground. The sacralizing of a single moment has far-reaching effects on all time, effects which made possible the emergence of a later philosophy of history as speculation on the *eidos* of time as a whole. On the other hand, however, once history became a form of human existence, it replaced that previous order of existence in which sacred times could enact an osmosis with the Great Time of deities, an osmosis through which men could act on and with divine powers and beings. Confronted with a God of eternity, man experienced himself as inhabiting time as a definitely human dimension, with divine grace occasionally breaking into it to "redeem the time." To the de-divinization of time thus corresponds the de-temporalization of God who only as an eternal God can be lord of time. The lord of time is then also the judge of human action in time, as well as the savior whose help in affliction redeems a mankind that can no longer count on cultic osmosis with divinity through a series of sacred times. Human existence in time is therefore an existence in autonomous human responsibility under God, as well as an existence that ultimately depends on divine saving action.

It seems that Israel realized all these implications well before its tradition was written down in literary form. The Ark, the token of God's presence, contained the law. Israel's creed insistently referred to the single-event-past that manifested God in historical action. A long period of kingless existence served to elaborate the political forms corresponding to God's sovereignty. When Israel finally obtained a king, it was made quite clear, as Henri Frankfort has pointed out, that the monarch had been instituted by the people rather than "descended from heaven."[19] Both kings and people knew themselves to stand under God's judgment and to be responsible for their own failures. What is more, the monarchy was merely "an accessory element" rather than the essence of Israel's political existence, for Israel enjoyed nonmonarchical political identity both before Saul and after the exile.[20]

It may be worthwhile to dwell for a minute on the aspect of hope and the particular form that Israel gave it. Hope, as we have seen, is merely the reverse of the sacralized past event and an integral element of history as a mode of existence. In Israel's tradition, hope was first represented by the Lord's promise to the patriarchs. The tradition emerged as the political past of an entity of twelve tribes at the time of the Settlement, and from that point of view the Lord's promise was hope projected back into the past. The Settlement of Canaan, however, did not exhaust the fullness of the promise. Nor

19 Frankfort, *Kingship and the Gods* (Chicago, 1948), 339.
20 De Vaux, *Ancient Israel*, I, 99.

did the Settlement constitute fulfillment of that part of the promise which pertained to land possession, for until David's time a substantial part of Palestine remained in Canaanite or Philistine hands. But from the point of view of David's time, a few hundred years after the formation of Israel, one might look back on the promise to the patriarchs and consider the provision concerning the land substantially fulfilled. Would one then conclude that hope was ended? It is precisely at this point that a new promise took the place of the old one which had matured, as it were. The new promise was made to David and his family: "Your House and your sovereignty will always stand secure before me and your throne be established for ever." (2 Sam. 7:16) Thus hope might be said to migrate from the patriarchs to David's house. The movement did not stop there, for after the capture of Jerusalem, which ended David's line, hope took on a new form, the expectation of the Messiah, and ultimately that of the Second Coming of Jesus Christ. In this form, hope eventually combined with another, the eschatological form.

Eschatology, as A. J. Wensinck has indicated, originally connoted the beginning of a new world period, replete with the death of the gods, a universal catastrophe, and destruction in nature as well as in history.[21] Even though spoken of as a future event, eschatology belonged to what Eliade has called "reversible time," so that eschata already had been and yet also would be. In this sense, eschatology meant a new beginning not only of the entire world but of life, a beginning that might take place every year, season, and even sunrise. The "day of the Lord" in the prophetic books, particularly in Joel, still bears traces of the original "reversibility" which would amount to a pattern of eternal return. As Israel adopted history as its mode of existence, and as time, accordingly, became irreversible, eschatology also took on features of irreversibility and turned into a single metastatic resolution of the world's tensions through events marking the end not of a mere period but

[21] Wensinck, "The Semitic New Year and the Origin of Eschatology," *Acta Orientalia,* I, (1923), 188.

of time itself. In this sense, eschatology appeared as a *telos* of all time, through which *telos* man could experience time as a whole which, even though given over to autonomous human action, also moved toward a certain divinely appointed end. The hope linked to that end, however, was no longer hope concerning periodical renewal but hope beyond time, in eternity.

HISTORY, MYTH, AND POLITICAL ORDER

This analysis has concentrated on the case of Israel's "leap" from a cosmological order to history as political existence, a "leap" that has its counterpart in the movement of the Greeks from the Homeric myths to order in philosophy. When one abstracts from the particular content of the event which in Israel's experience constituted an eternal past, one finds that in other civilizations, too, something like a divinely constituted past was acknowledged, from which time rolled down irreversibly toward the present. Voegelin's studies about historiogenetic speculations prove that even in the cosmological order there was an experience of "history," in the sense that human order and acts of kings were linked to divine interventions in time.[22] The backward projection of royal dynasties to divine origins is history in this sense, as are all genealogies through which irreversible successions of persons and events are established with standing in the divine order of things. It is also true, on the other hand, that a "leap in being" such as that taken by Israel or by the Greek philosophers, never wholly eliminated the primary experience of the myth, and that even in the new order of the "leap" the myth continued to function as a source of public order.[23] In the case of Israel, not all festivals commemorated the events of the Exodus; the Feast of Weeks and the Feast of Tents were more of cosmological than of historical character. So is the celebration occurring on the day of the full moon. To this day, periodic renewal is symbolized in many festivals within civilizations based on history.

[22] Voegelin, *Anamnesis*, 79–116.
[23] *Cf.* Voegelin in the context of the noetic "leap," *ibid.*, 285, 290.

While it is important to realize that history and myth continue together as sources of order, one must not overlook the profound transformation of human existence that was brought about by the leap of Israel as well as by the leap of Greek classical philosophy. No philosophers spelled out the newness of the existence which Israel had learned to live; for this reason we have difficulty in finding suitable concepts by which to designate it. The new existence opened by Greek philosophy can be designated using the terms "noesis" and "noetic," but the Greek language furnishes us with no parallel term for the innovation brought about by Israel's experience of the Exodus. One might think of borrowing a term from Hebrew, the word *'ôlam*, meaning "immeasurably far back or immeasurably far into the future" and whose root, in Arabic (*alam*) connotes "eternity."[24] In this sense one would speak of olamic existence, olamic orientation, olamic consciousness. The olamic existence, then, is a life in awareness of God, the lord of time, and time as human responsibility before God extending to an end characterized by hope in eternity. We have already seen that this form of existence is not incompatible with the awareness of cycles or oscillations in life, with periodical renewals and regenerations, and with special times as representative of special and partial orders. History is the order of a special and unique action of grace, standing out and beside the various rhythms which characterize all that is not "new under the sun." History is always "news," news of a specific past, news of a presence, and news concerning a hope for the ultimate end. At first realized by Israel, it became a universal mode of existence, spread globally by Christianity and Islam, and eventually even by that modern ersatz-religion, Marxism-Leninism.

History as a source of order differentiates various elements which the myth does not isolate: an irrevocable and eternal past,

[24] According to Léon Dufour, " *'ôlam* designates a duration which surpasses human measurement. . . . To make the nature of this duration of which we have no experience understood, the Bible opposes it to the transitory character of cosmic time. . . . A consideration of this type accents the significance of the divine transcendence." Dufour, *Dictionary of Biblical Theology*, tr. P. J. Cahill (New York, 1967), 528.

an informed but yet unknowable hopeful future, a present responsibility before a time-transcending God whose will appears in an apodictic law. From these differentiations arose later perversions which became possible when this or that aspect of the entire complex was emphasized, while forgetting either the whole context or the experience that gave birth to it. An exclusive emphasis on human autonomy in a de-divinized time resulted in an historiography that reduced history to a record of *res gestae* and tended to assume that awareness of this record was tantamount to history as a mode of existence. An equally exclusive emphasis on the significance of the past led to fallacious conclusions about inexorable "laws of history"; focusing solely on the future apart from the experience of divine actions of grace in the past would tend to produce a utopia, a project of hope dependent solely on human political action; viewing the present while forgetting about the "imitation of eternity" reduces that present to a mere "phase of transition."

In earlier chapters of this book we have examined cases of such perversions and have shown their consequences in doctrines regarding political action. In contrast to such perverted doctrines of history, we must bear in mind as a "limit" of consciousness that history as a mode of existence hinges on the all-important experience of a past at which a meeting occurred between time and eternity.

VI □ The Ethics of Existence

SUCCESSION AND PUBLIC IDENTITY

Memory, the emergence of the past into consciousness, is a faculty of the person, tied to the faculty of personal perception. The relation between the positivity of actual facts and the experience of memory is complex and mysterious; whatever happens sinks away into the darkness of oblivion, of having-been but being-no-more, until some of it returns from the depth as conscious experience, and remains from then on as an unperishable constituent of the person. What makes it return is a mystery about which a good many people have reflected; it is clear, at any rate, that the return is not controllable by one's will. Still, memory is linked to one's personal perception, to one's encounter with surrounding phenomena and realities. A public past is also a memory, but obviously a memory of a wholly different kind because what is remembered is known not to have been personally perceived by those who remember and not to have welled up from the depth of one's own years. All the same, persons do call reports of century-old events, deeds, and sufferings "our past," positing some identity that links themselves with those to whom the reported events may or may not have happened. This identity is established by means of a myth called succession. The best-known type is the succession linking ancestors and descendants in an identity abiding in time, of which dynastic succession is only a special application. Not only primitive tribes but also citizens of modern countries speak of their country's "fathers." The succession of generations is often attributed to something called "common blood," but "blood" in this context is a mythical rather than a biological concept, akin to that of "totem." It does not occur to anyone to link in "succession" all those who have type A blood. Equally mythical are similar references to the unifying "factors" of land or language. The content of each succession is invariably a common past, a concrete history acknowledged as "ours" by a multitude of persons. Where a public past is acknowledged, there is succession, the continuous identity of a public realm abiding in time. A common past, as we have seen, is memory of what is significant; not every "Washington slept here" can establish a public memory. What is publicly remembered has some bearing on man's general "desire to know" regarding either being (reality) or right action (ethics). Succession thus implies a certain amount of commitment in that regard; it is therefore not a fact of nature but a function of the historiopoeic mind which records memories as experiences that shed light on the question of being.

Whenever succeeding generations are seen as a continuing, time-abiding identity, the facticity of each particular link in the chain is not what matters. The Exodus tradition was originally imputed to "Jacob and his sons," but later the separate traditions of Isaac and Abraham were added, the whole forming a series of patriarchal generations. Similarly, upon the foundation of the empire of Sumer and Akkad, as already mentioned, a list of succeeding kings of this empire was extrapolated from the records of various Mesopotamian city states which were absorbed into the empire, regardless of whether "succeeding" members of the Sumerian list had actually lived at the same time. The historiopoeic mind is concerned not with the accuracy of facts but with history as an identity-forming myth; it is not disturbed, for instance, by two conflicting genealogies referring to the same historical person. The public past serves not to satisfy someone's idle curiosity about dead facts but rather to provide a *terminus a quo* for a still-continuing succession, by virtue of which the otherwise chaotic flow of time is embedded in the rock of eternity. The question whether it is logical for men to acknowledge as "their past" events that none of them have personally perceived is one to which one would have to reply, with Vico, simply that "men are naturally impelled to preserve the memories of the laws and orders that bind them in their societies."

Through the myth of succession a political community is constituted to abide in time, enduring with sameness through changing generations, assuring the living that the reality in which the "fathers" had their being continues for the "descendants" and that the "fathers' " action and action in the present are governed by the same principles. Renan's definition of a nation, "un plébiscite de tous les jours," completely misses this point. The myth of public succession secures, for the common existence of a multitude, a transcending ground of being, so that men are what they are by virtue of the public identity enduring for centuries. Renan's "everyday plebiscite" suggests that the foundation of common existence poses itself as a brand new problem every morning and that it could be solved by a sheer act of will. If this were so, everything on which we rely as "existing" in the world of history would continuously be threatened by an indefinite multitude of alternatives, each wholly unprecedented and unexpected, and there could be no peace. For the war of weapons is merely one example of sense-killing devastation through ubiquitous and instantaneous change. On the other hand, peace has been realized in concrete communities only because the enduring sameness of the commonly held truths has warded off that destructive flood of the wholly and sweepingly other. Apart from a common past there can be no instituted peace, for the common past alone warrants endurance in time of the truth of existence. Peace then is a product not of arms but of the historiopoeic myth and is threatened not primarily by physical destruction but by a torrent of total and instantaneous change coming from forces that are uncommitted to the public past. It is a community's abiding identity which makes laws possible and meaningful, for without the enduring public identity no obligations would outlive the changes of rulers and generations and nothing but short-lived commands could take effect. Through its public past a community participates in the *logos* which remains the same in the flux of mutability; hence, the community's identity imitates, as Boethius said, "the ever simultaneous present immutability of God's life" which is what one "should rightly call eternal."

POWER AND CHANGE

The abiding identity of succession, which constitutes a zone of peace in the midst of the destructive flux of newness, forms something like an entity, a whole that coheres in a tenacious way. This is what makes possible political power, the ability to control and dispose of, the joint resources of this whole. For an illustration, let us turn once more to the instructive example of Israel. We have seen that the memories of a small group identified by their eponomous ancestor Jacob became the common past of clans and tribes which on settling in Canaan formed a kind of amphictyony. Crushed by the hegemony of the Philistines who enforced total disarmament on Israel, the tribes could not prevent peoples from the East from attacking and practically annihilating one of the tribes east of Jordan, but the event provided a political impulse strong enough to cause Israel to produce a king. Saul's rule, however, was a relatively short episode of a mainly charismatic character not sufficing to secure Israel's allegiance for Saul's son. Thus, after a moment of kingly unification, Israel reverted back to the loose confederate cohesion of before, a people without a ruler but all the same a people capable of sustaining a ruler.

We have a remarkably clear and detailed account of how David the son of Jesse, then king of southern Hebron and a vassal of the Philistines, maneuvered to become king also of Israel. Because Saul's son could not attract more than a handful of followers, there really was no throne waiting simply to be occupied. David perceived, however, that Israel was very much a political reality and as such could be manipulated and captured. He moved with astonishing understanding of this entity and its public past. He married Saul's daughter and publicly punished the murderers of Saul's son; he, who had made his position as a fiefholder under the Philistines, defeated and broke the Philistine power in Palestine; he conquered Jebusite Jerusalem, a neutral city in the Canaanite strip separating the kingdom of Hebron from the lands of Israel, and had the Ark brought there. One symbolic action followed another, each attuned to that past which constituted Israel. Once master of Jerusalem and king also of Israel, David brought the two kingdoms together under the rule of his house which became subject to the order of Israel's public past. The designation "Israel"—Jacob's name—was extended to the combined kingdom as a whole and later, after the fall of the northern part, transferred to the southern kingdom. The divine promise of a blessed future, first given to Abraham, Isaac, and Jacob, was renewed under David as a promise to his royal house. David's clever strategy had indeed realized the potential of political power attached to that entity which a public past had brought into existence, but in the process David himself had to pledge his allegiance to the abiding order of Yahweh.

Following David, the same public past also engendered the kinetic energy of change, through the tension between political expedience and the public past as well as through the tension between Israel's political existence as such and Yahweh's transcendence. The kings and their administrators would pursue certain policies and practices which elicited resistance in the name of the public past. They were rejected as "betrayals" from which a "return" to the foundations was demanded. Other kings then would effect the demanded "return," but each of these "returns" amounted actually to a new interpretation of the public past and a creative renewal of the public order. Other and deeper changes resulted from responses to catastrophical external events: first, the destruction of the northern kingdom, then the capture of Jerusalem and the captivity of its inhabitants, each of these events inducing men sensitive to the public past to reformulate an old meaning in the light of a new situation. In the process, Israel's public past became more and more detached from short-term political applications. All of these changes drew their energy from Israel's public past and abiding identity, the political and administrative machinery providing the obstacle that spurred on what one may call national creativeness. From the abiding experience of the public past also arose an ever-deepening critique of Israel's habits, customs, and administrative practices, formulated by the prophets. Unlike the Socratic critique of Athens which derided the city's public past, the prophets of Israel measured and judged the country by the standards of the public memory:

> When Israel was a child I loved him,
> and I called my son out of Egypt. . . ;
> yet they have not understood that I was the one
> looking after them. . . .
>
> Yet I am Yahweh, your God since the days in the land
> of Egypt;
> you know no God but me,
> there is no other savior. (Hos. 11:1, 3; 13:4)
>
> I remember the affection of your youth,
> the love of your bridal days:
> you followed me through the wilderness,
> through a land unsown. (Jer. 2:2)

As king and people were tempted to "slide back" again and again into habits and customs not befitting Israel's public past but rather the culture of surrounding Mesopotamia, the prophets' hermeneutic of Israel's order probed deeper and deeper until it grew into a penetrating critique of human order, as universally valid as Socratic philosophy.

POLITICAL "EXISTENCE": FOUR CONCEPTS

One needs not merely a name but a concept for something that endures identically in a succession of generations, tends to produce representative rulers, engenders power for common action in history, and fosters an inner energy of change and creativeness. Astonishingly enough, the literature of political theory is quite bare of suitable concepts. Rousseau suggested vaguely that this kind of entity is like a "collective self," possessing a "life and will" of its own, constituting withal a "collective moral body." There is a plethora of imprecise designations for that which politically "exists": nation, society, community, people, country, state. For the purposes of political theory illuminating the order of existence from within, fairly precise terms have been developed and one may argue that that is all that is required. Men, however, have lived not in one political order but in a number of them "existing" side by side, and the phenomenon of this multifarious "existence" has seemed to defy logic and comprehension, although it is a salient experience. For this reason we believe that theoretical concepts acknowledging a mystery at this point come closer to whatever insight we may gain. We should like to examine four such concepts dealing with the problem of a collective or communal "existence."

The Egyptians had a mythical term that symbolized the otherwise unexplainable fact of political existence: the *ka*. According to Henri Frankfort the closest approximation of this word is "vital force," something impersonal which is capable of being present or not being present.[1] In hieroglyphs, only the king's *ka* is pictured, never that of a commoner, although the commoner is supposed to derive his *ka* from the king. The *ka* supports man on earth as well as in the beyond; it is "the experience of power in its direct relation to man"; it is through the *ka* that one can achieve something. One pyramid text reveals that Re, the god, is the *ka* of the king, while the subjects say: "My *ka* belongs to the king, my *ka* derives from the king, the king makes my *ka*, the king is my *ka*." The community, in other words, is equated with a vital energy noticeable in every one of its members, which goes back to the king and ultimately to the god Re, where its why and how remains shrouded in mystery.

Ibn Khaldûn in his *Muqaddimah*[2] coined a concept better left untranslated: *'aṣabîyah*, which, according to Wehr's *Dictionary of Modern Written Arabic* (1961) means: "nervousness, nervosity; . . . zealous partisanship, bigotry, fanaticism; party spirit, team

[1] Frankfort, *Kingship and the Gods* (Chicago, 1948), 62.

[2] Ibn Khaldûn, *Muqaddimah*, Bollingen Series, XLIII (New York, 1968).

spirit, esprit de corps; tribal solidarity, racialism, clannishness, tribalism, national consciousness, nationalism." In Ibn Khaldûn, *'aṣabîyah* connotes a political whole that appears on the historical scene, moves through various stages (bedouin life, sedentary life, decline) from small beginnings to optimal strength and through weakness to ultimate extinction. *'Aṣabîyah* is often translated as "community consciousness" but obviously implies much more—namely, the concrete and unique identity of a political whole, its "existence" with its aspects of vitality and mortality, a concept of common consciousness which still embraces the phenomenal aspects of birth, health, sickness, and demise. A similar concept is Vico's *mente eroica,* the "heroic mind" that animates patricians to band together in society for the preservation of the common good; a "mind" which, however, then wanders from the patricians to the people and eventually to the monarch, so that there is a continuing identity through a variety of constitutions. The eventual decline, according to Vico, comes not from constitutional changes but through the loss of the tension between that "mind" and God, resulting in a spiritually self-centered "barbarism of reflection" which leads to "dissolution" and "madness that wastes the substance of society" at which point people lose their "arms and language." Vico, like Ibn Khaldûn, sees the identity of a political whole as a continuing consciousness or "mind," but finds that this "mind" has something like a life cycle.

The fourth concept is Bodin's sovereignty, the "highest and perpetual power to command over citizens and subjects," which power he assumes to be "above the law," though subject to natural law. Bodin has often been described as advocating absolutism or even worse. No such advocacy can be read into this concept of sovereignty. He states explicitly that it is not the power of anyone who holds governmental office, but rather that which underlies all official powers. Sovereignty is not a possession of either the prince or the people; it is the concept for a whole that cannot be possessed but only imputed either to the prince or to the people or both. Prince and people are both concepts of succession: one cannot identify "the people" with a numerically definite multitude existing at any given time, or "the prince" with a particular king alone. The king never dies nor does the people. Bodin's sovereignty connotes a continuing identity, the "existence" of a community that is prior to human laws and entails powers of obligation. Each person wielding political command then is but a keeper of the perpetual sovereignty which is not diminished by any specific power it confers on these keepers and which continues to "exist" beyond their particular persons. Bodin, too, was aware of the law of vitality of political entities, but his concept on the whole is closer to the Egyptian *ka* than to Ibn Khaldûn's *'aṣabîyah* or Vico's *mente eroica*.

All four concepts reflect the ultimately mysterious character of what modern usage calls "society," the mystery stemming from its continuity in time, its relative independence from human volition and personalities, and its proneness to decay. The four concepts also agree in assuming that political existence is some kind of participation in the divine ground; that the vitality of a political whole has something to do with this; that "there is no power except from God"; and that the appearance of political entities is attributable to Providence. Such overtones are missing in the current concept "society," with its attending association with causal "factors" and its pretense to complete analytical knowability of the object. All the same, modern language offers no ready substitute, so that for the time being we must be content with having circumscribed what it is that begs a name and having indicated why this something seems to be partly knowable, partly ineffable. Along this road it may be possible to push a little farther.

MAN'S "TWO ETERNITIES"

A political community abides in time, stabilizing the sameness of truth in the flux of temporal vicissitudes and thus, as we have seen, "imitating eternity." There is a striking metaphor by Yeats who speaks of "man's two eternities, that of race and that of soul." By "eternity of race" he evidently refers not to the human race which has no entity of existence but to the political community, which not only transcends its individual members but also derives its order from participation in the divine ground. This participation is symbolized by what Yeats at another place calls "artifices of eternity," and "monuments of unageing intellect." What is meant then by "eternity of soul" is the personal awareness of human participation in the divine ground flowing from the experiences of each person's soul, the "sensorium of transcendence," as Eric Voegelin has called it. By juxtaposing the two "eternities" Yeats points toward the tension between them, the possibility of conflict and the difficulty of resolving such conflict in terms of rank that would put one of these "eternities" above the other. It may be instructive to place this tension side by side with that other mentioned by Aristotle when he speaks of the two parts of the human soul, the rational and the irrational and, within the latter, of a vegetative and concupiscent element. Aristotle placed the concupiscent element of the soul below the rational one, the *nous* which is either "itself divine or the most divine thing in us" (*Nicomachean Ethics*, 1177a 15); but he also saw a tension between the soul's concupiscences and the *nous*, a tension in which the *nous* is roughly equivalent to Yeats's "eternity of soul." Forces of vitality, then, are perceived in necessary tension with the "eternity of soul," which tension in this case occurs in a hierarchical setting, the "eternity of soul" being the source of order for the vital desirings. Could one assume that a similar element of less-than-rational vitality accompanies the "eternity of race"? What aspect of community life would appear comparable to Aristotle's concupiscent part in the structure of each person?

What modern translations render as "mind" and "rational" did not connote for Aristotle anything like what we, heirs of the Enlightenment, habitually associate with "rational," namely, a disposition to reduce everything to logical deduction or phenomenal data. Aristotle uses the terms on the one hand as a criterion of differentiation from the myth, myth and philosophy both being "constituted of wonder" but responding to wonder in different ways: the myth through stories about gods, philosophy through concepts of being. Philosophy, however, is moved by wonder as much as is the myth, and its *noetic* consciousness also stems from the experience of man's participation in a divine ground of being. Hence the term *nous* in Aristotle retains a deliberate ambiguity, connoting "what is most divine in man," the divine itself, as well as man's participation in the divine; then again, on the strength of this triple meaning, identifying what is "best" and "highest" in man, for the sake of which man is to be loved, and even is to love himself, with the kind of love which, oriented toward the divine, endures in time.[3]

What about the other pole, Aristotle's "irrational part" of the soul? Moralists have frequently identified it with lusts and appetites, but in a general philosophy of existence one should understand this concept as embracing all the opaque motives, promptings, and impulses that go by the name of habits, prejudices, reactions, passions—in other words the muddy stream of "forces" and "patterns" that we have in view when we approach things through sociology and psychology. They are not capable of lending life the transparency that characterizes the *noetic* consciousness, but Aristotle reminds us that they are capable of heeding the *nous* or refusing to heed it. This tension is the crux of order in human life and order is the substance of peace. If the opaque and vital forces and patterns of man subject themselves to the *ratio* of what is "best" and "highest" in his soul, a person is at peace with himself; if not, he lives in a kind of intramural civil war and self-hatred. Aristotle, then, distinguishes two tensions: that of the soul's rational part toward the divine ground of being, the proper term for which is participation, and that of man's opaque psychic forces toward the soul's *nous*, the name for which is ethics.

Could one identify a similar pair of tensions in man's political order? Let us once more turn to Israel as a representative and suitable example. Israel's "monument of unageing intellect" was the story of Yahweh's deliverance of "Jacob and his sons" at the Sea of Reeds, told and retold countless times, and serving as the basic orientation for a succession of generations, judges, and kings. The

[3] On *noesis, cf.* Eric Voegelin, *Anamnesis: Zur Theorie der Geschichte und Politik* (Munich, 1966).

story illumined life by spelling out the people's participation in the divine ground of history and thus establishing its existence. This illumination, then, is the community's *nous*, the "best" and "highest" element through which a multitude of men were united in a common transparency of being. In this sense the communal existence, represented by various leaders and kings, would constitute for every individual person his "eternity of race," the political existence representing eternal truth. One may note in passing that wherever this relationship of political existence to the divine ground is intensely and emphatically articulated, there also arises the temptation to confuse the community's contingent existence with the finality of the divine truth, to confuse participation with identity, and thereby to eliminate the tension in which the community was founded. Against such tendencies there stood the warnings of sensitive men, men of "vision" and authority, who in the course of centuries again and again called Israel back to that tension toward the divine in which consisted the "eternity of race" in this particular case.

A community, too, has its "irrational" dimension, its opaque "forces" and "patterns" which, though incapable of transparency in themselves, still abide in time and are passed from generation to generation. They are the habits, customs, conventional standards of approval and disapproval, prejudices, superstitions, property relations, gradations of respectability, and other "ways of doing things." Such norms, as Bergson has pointed out, operate through unorganized pressures to which people respond unreflectively. Each obedient response itself adds to the pressures on others, so that psychic and customary patterns are the most tenacious and ubiquitous manifestations through which a political community distinguishes itself. While customs are distinctly evident to the point of being "picturesque," they are incapable of that transparency which provides meaning to existence and action. The transparency of being can reside only in what Yeats has called the "eternity of race," the commonly acknowledged truth regarding God, nature, man, and society. The psychic and social patterns can resist or defy the "eternity of race" or conform themselves to it, so that a community's habits stand in unceasing tension toward the "eternity of race," the name of this tension being justice. Where habits and customs drift away and develop in terms of their own impulsive causality, the community will eventually lose its reason for being and finally, as Vico has reminded us, lose its language and arms, too.

There is also a tension between the "eternity of race" and the "eternity of soul," as Aristotle indicated by his distinction between the "good citizen" and the good man. Under normal circumstances, the "eternity of race" seems to be accorded higher rank, in all probability because it is thought out much more carefully than anything that a single individual can work out in his lifetime, but also because one cannot have a community on everyday notice by critical individuals. On occasion, however, an outstandingly sensitive person experiences what Bergson has called an opening of the soul and attains insights into reality and moral order beyond those underlying the community. His life then manifests a quality that attracts people for whom the previously accepted truths all of a sudden become opaque, a new transparency appears, and the "eternity of soul" confronts the "eternity of race" with an authoritative: "You have heard it said . . . but I say to you!" These are the words of Jesus, but they also characterize a situation that obtained when Xenophanes confronted Homer and Hesiod, Socrates Athens, and Siddhartha Gautama Brahmanism, a tension which Bergson has explored in his *Two Sources of Morality and Religion*, and Jaeger in his *Theology of the Early Greek Philosophers.* It is not the tension of man's irrationality toward the "eternity" of his consciousness, but rather the confrontation of rationality with higher rationality in a mode of gentle persuasion, resulting not in disobedient subordination but in supersession of the lower by the higher authority and a "leap" in the level of existence.

THE REALM

It is at this point that a few suitable terms should be suggested. Hitherto we have spoken of a "community" or a "political entity" or a "people" or "society." These terms are inadequate. "People" is a quantitative concept suggesting a living multitude which at the margin could be counted. Actually, one cannot fix on a multitude as constituting the "people," as the membership of a political entity changes every second through births and deaths. Numbers, moreover, do not convey the quality of *gestalt* or enduring identity, nor that of authority, both of which are implied in the term "people." Cicero identified a people with an association acknowledging principles of true justice, which definition accounted for the authoritative aspect but was subject to Augustine's criticism that it corresponded to no empirical phenomenon. Augustine proposed as an alternative the concept of "an assemblage of reasonable beings bound together by a common agreement as to the objects of their love," which avoids Cicero's idealization, but sets up the unascertainable requirement of agreement and postulates more homogeneity than Augustine himself might have been willing to concede to any existing "people." Earlier, Aristotle, in trying to identify a political community through constitutional forms impressed on the "people" as "matter," had found this definition impracticable; and Polybius drove home the point by pointing to the fact that a people may pass through a whole cycle of constitutional forms without losing its identity. As for Augustine's criterion of a "common love," Ibn Khaldûn described political entities as transferring their "common love" from "bedouin life" to "sedentary life," and Vico's idea of the *mente eroica* wandering from patricians to people to monarch suggested a similar mutation from savage barbarism to the "barbarism of reflection."

If neither the total quantity of component members, nor common principles of loves, nor political forms can adequately define that which politically exists, we must assume something to "exist" which is more fundamental than all of these, more fundamental than even the "people," and of which the "people" would be an attribute. We propose the term "realm" for this time-abiding existential entity, noting that realm implies a unity of consciousness as well as certain geographical limits. A realm is, first of all, a phenomenon of history that is not properly attributable to either logical or psychological or material or environmental necessities nor to be explained in terms of "agreement" or "form" or "principle" or "factor." Vico has rightly claimed the world of history as that of man, which takes it out of the sphere of necessity. Vico was right in stressing that history is that part of reality of which "the principles are to be found within the modifications of our own mind," but neither he nor anybody else has reduced "realms," concrete historical realms, to a human act of free production or creation. Man's historical existence is characterized by chance and choice. Realms arise in the interplay between Providence and human apperception, which accounts for their manifold singularities and their uniqueness. The multiplicity of realms therefore does not require us to take any position; we should approach them, rather, as what are commonly called "facts of life." On the other hand, realms are, each in its way, worlds of political order, and one cannot deal with problems of order in an atmosphere of moral neutrality. There are, then, two approaches to realms. One seeks the intelligibility of order, illuminating from within the experiences on which order is based and the symbols in which insight has been crystallized; this approach cannot do without judgments, because the necessity to distinguish between right and wrong is at the core of political order. The other approach recognizes that order has been achieved among men in a multiplicity of realms. Each realm must be understood from within—an order claiming to represent truth for mankind as such. But precisely because of that, the multiplicity of realms must be confronted as a phenomenon: realms of various shapes and forms in fact coexist, each constituting a world of order for the people within its limits; it makes little sense to argue with this fact or to postulate something different which does not exist.

MYTH, MORES, LIMES

A realm, as we have seen, is multilayered. At the top we find a "We hold these truths . . . ," the *koinon* of Aristotle's *koinonia,* the insights through which being has transparency, which spell out the terms of participation in the divine ground. This common perspective of consciousness renders possible a broad and deep area in which actions and language symbols are commonly understood: a rich soil of taken-for-granted assumptions, associations, and references enabling persons to communicate by gestures, hints, signs, or even silently, and to act toward and with each other with a great economy of decision-energy. On this soil grow common aspirations, the "agreed-upon objects of love" which Augustine pointed out. On it also develop unwritten but highly effective structures, the patterns of custom, conventional judgments, the do's and don'ts usually more strictly obeyed than written statutes. Above all, here flowers confidence, the assurance with which a person moves among his fellow beings, knowing what to expect and on what grounds to engage in cooperative efforts. All this, however, is confined to a *limes,* a spatial boundary. The definition of this boundary may not be possible with precision, but there are areas beyond which a particular order does not obtain. Within the *limes,* however, there is a world of familiarity to which every one of its members "belongs." In other words, there is something like a "whole" of which he as a single person feels to be a "part," moving among other "parts" like him. The whole structure of meaning and familiarity makes for the possibility of friendship, the public friendship of which Aristotle treats in the *Nicomachean Ethics,* a basic openness and benevolence towards all other "parts" even though they be not of one's personal acquaintance. But this entire world of familiarity and conventionality stands in existential tension toward the highest ranking truth which elicits the public effort at justice. The confinement of this order to a certain area circumscribed by a *limes* and to certain persons who are its bearers within this geographical line attaches the order of consciousness to a corporeal and material matrix, so that there is always the possibility of destroying the entire order by destroying the matrix. For this reason, it makes perfect sense to say that a realm *exists.*

For the commonly held truths at the top of this structure, we shall propose the term "myth," stipulating that the meaning of the word in this context shall not be that of a historical variant of order, namely the "cosmological myth," the order that prevailed, as Frankfort put it, "before philosophy." Rather, myth in this context applies to any set of symbols through which a multitude of people, living together, symbolically secure the transparency of life and awareness of participation in the divine ground. In this sense one would have to say that no realm, ancient or modern, is without its myth. Philosophy, noetic consciousness of participation, has made a difference in the quality of life, but no realm has ever been founded by a philosopher or been held together merely by syllogistic propositions. In countries in which the "barbarism of reflection" is widespread by means of instruction, the underlying myths are no longer symbolized by express celebrations and they are hardly recognizable. Such countries resort, on their festival occasions, to phrases and slogans derived from analytical thought rather than to restatements of their myth.

All the same, even there the myth is effective in what most persons take for granted, in tacit assumptions about reality and the meaning of life, about God, man, and nature. Such assumptions are held by the average person not in syllogistic but rather in mythical form. The average American, for instance, takes for granted that each "individual" has a soul, a claim to personal dignity, and an independent mind; he distinguishes "time" from "eternity"; he attributes authority to "the people" but also to "the law"; he believes in an enduring "Constitution"; he pledges allegiance to a "nation under God," all this in the uncritical ways of myths. If it were not for the myth, the mutual comprehensibility of actions and language symbols among the "parts" would atrophy after a while, and in place of familiarity and confident communication there would arise the universal assumption of hostility which prevails, for instance, in desert life. In the course of time, a myth that is not supported by appropriate cultic celebrations may suffer a decline and recede far into the subconscious. All the same, there is a decisive difference between that kind of weakening and the total collapse of the myth, from which results an opaqueness of life that befalls men as a major disaster.

The lower layer of nontransparent motivations, customs, habits, prejudices, we propose to call the "mores" of the realm. The realm as a whole is made up of myth and mores, justice and conventions, the whole and the parts, with multiple tensions prevailing between these aspects, and between the realm as a whole and the divine ground. The individual soul acknowledges as authoritative the myth of the realm, but it also knows of the tension of the person toward God, and of the soul as the "sensorium of transcendence" (Eric Voegelin). On occasion, the illumination of truth in the individual soul turns out to have authority vis-à-vis the public myth, particularly when the myth has been weakened and the mores are drifting guideless by the force of impulses. Then the authority of this or that individual soul may address itself above all to the mores as measured by the truth of transcendence, particularly in a tradition in which righteousness constitutes the chief terms of participation in the divine ground. The individual whose personal sensitivity moves him to a high degree of righteousness then moves into the position of a judge vis-à-vis the decadent mores. In all of this we find no answer to the question of why certain realms appear and exist at a given time and place, why realms are as they are and not different, and, above all, why there is a multiplicity of different realms by virtue of which men exist in communal order rather than one single realm for all humanity. Nobody has come even close to an answer for such questions, and as it seems unlikely that anybody will, it is wisest to leave the diversity and multiplicity of realms in the class of *phainomena*, to be accepted and understood for what they are, without yielding to the temptation of positing potentially different *phainomena* and speculating on what life might be if they existed.

One more word is required about the problem of change. It was obvious to Aristotle even before he finished the *Politics* that it would not do to identify a *koinonia* with a particular constitutional form in the sense that every change of form would bring into existence a new *koinonia*. Realms survive constitutional changes, they also survive dynasties and various ruling classes; they may even survive a period without rulers. A realm presupposes and is subject to a myth, but on occasion a realm may endure a change of the myth, as did the Frankish realm when Clovis converted to Christianity. Similarly, Augustine's "commonly agreed upon objects of love" may change within a continuing realm, as exemplified by Ibn Khaldûn's mutation from "bedouin life" to "sedentary life."

This brings us to the role of the people in a realm. We commonly accord authority to the people, but we have seen that authority derives from the myth which spells out the terms of participation in the divine ground of being. The people, then, are the bearers of the myth at any given time and as such serve as the organ of representation of the public truth, which is what gives authority to the *vox populi*. No authority, however, derives from sheer numbers or from majority, and when the people have become alienated from the myth, when the thoughts they commonly accept and resort to are representative of abstract analysis and arbitrary positions apart from the myth, and the mores are regarded as a law unto themselves, the people cease to represent. Then the bearers of the myth may be concentrated in a "remnant" or even a single person, like Jeremiah in sixth century Judah or Socrates in fifth century Athens.[4] In such situations neither king nor people can speak with authority, and things move toward either dissolution or a renewal of the myth. King, people, government, laws and arms, peace and justice are attributes of a realm rather than its substance. The substance, a public truth in which life becomes transparent and meaningful, is genetically elusive, mysterious, and in a sense "given," particularly because it appears in history as an existent subject to laws of vitality. These laws, however, cannot be traced to biological nature nor to mere morality, but pertain to the area of complex tensions between consciousness and the divine ground, psyche and nous, and to the general relation of things mutable to eternity.

EXISTENTIAL VIRTUE AND PSYCHE

Aristotle's ethics dwells on three aspects of excellence: first, on the moral virtues pertaining to one's relations to one's neighbor,

[4] *Cf.* Eric Voegelin, *Israel and Revelation* (Baton Rouge, 1956), 467.

summed up in the comprehensive virtue of justice; second, on wisdom in the making of contingent choices, the problem of truth in reasoned desire; third, on the complex of attitudes required for the harmony and unity of a human composite, a realm of common existence. Of these three, the most precise vocabulary has been developed with respect to the moral virtues and their complete expression, justice. The second field of excellence is designated by the Greek *phronesis* and the Latin *prudentia*, both of which, however, are very inadequately echoed in the English term "prudence" which no longer implies Aristotle's insights into a state of mind and excellence of character that justifies speaking of "truth" as one decides about matters variable. Least of all has our language any term to render the distinctions and correlations which Aristotle perceived regarding the ethics of existence. Even the awareness that he was doing that has been lost; we distinguish "practical" virtues from "intellectual" virtues, but not until recently did anyone recall to our attention the fact that Aristotle also reflected about "existential virtues."[5] Certainly our modern use of the word "friendship" conveys no idea of what Aristotle was talking about in book V of the Nicomachean Ethics, for who would say today that "friendship seems to hold states together"?

Let us look briefly at *Nicomachean Ethics* IX, 4, one of the salient passages in which Aristotle analyzes friendship as one of the virtues of existence. Reversing Socrates' method, Aristotle finds a model in a man's "relation with himself" by which he hopes to make clear the structure of friendship on a public scale. A man's relation with himself can also partake of the excellence of friendship, which prevails when people "wish and do what is good for their friend's sake." In a similar way, the *spoudaios,* the serious man, wishes and does what is good for his own sake, meaning for the sake of that in him which more than anything else is his essence. This is an attitude of friendship, for the concupiscent part of his soul, his emotions and desires, are lovingly devoted to the "intellectual element" which "is thought to be the man himself."

[5] Voegelin, *Anamnesis,* 128.

The essence of the person is the *nous* of which Aristotle observes in *Nicomachean Ethics* X, 7 that it is "the best part of us . . . whether it is itself divine or the most divine thing in us." In this point, therefore, centers the unity of existence, maintained by the existential virtue of friendship. To the man whose irrational elements are obedient to the *nous*, "existence is good" and he wishes "himself to live and to be preserved."[6] The "goodness of existence," then, spurs the will "to live and to preserve existence" and in turn flows from the attunement of all parts of the man to the divine ground through the *nous,* which "by its very nature rules and guides us."

At this point Aristotle ties his analysis to the historical concreteness of existence in order, for the *spoudaios,* he says, "wishes for this only on condition of being whatever he is," and it is the "thinking part of each individual that constitutes what he really is." The *nous*, then, is the source of order through participation in the divine ground, but this participation is concrete, historical, embodied in a singular person whose individual existence is, in a sense, an ineffability. To wish for the good is not serious if it relates not to the particular and ineffable existence in time and place but rather to some abstract being, a phantasma of no potential existence. "No one chooses to possess the whole world if he first has to become somebody else." The entire excellence of doing and wishing what is good is, then, embedded in the here and now, the thusness of substances for whose existence there is no accounting. Behind the truth of right decisions in contingent matters there is always a concrete existence at the point where given historical coordinates cross and meet.

Aristotle drives the point home by referring to the coordinates of past and future. The *spoudaios,* he says, enjoys "living with himself," for his existence which is bound together by friendship between the rational and irrational elements has the depth of "de-

[6] This insight has been formulated by a modern writer. "Joy is praise of the whole and cannot exist where there are ulterior aims." Thornton Wilder, *The Eighth Day* (New York, 1968), 186.

lightful memories of past acts," and consequently "good hopes for the future." And in the depth of the years the mind is "well stored with subjects of contemplation." Finally, in the same way in which friends grieve and rejoice with each other, the *spoudaios* is at one with himself in the stirrings of his emotions; everything within him is attracted by the same things at all times. Over against the *spoudaios* Aristotle then sketches a portrait of the "unserious" man whose appetites for some things are at war with his rational desires for other things. He loves not what is best in himself and constitutes his self, thus "shuns himself," and consequently his "soul" is rent by faction." Thus torn, he cannot enjoy his life, for he remembers "many a grievous deed, and anticipates others like them." As a result his will to life is weak and may decline to the point of self-destruction.

Because Aristotle from the outset applies his entire discussion of friendship to political communities, we must consider this particular analysis relevant to the problem of political existence and order. In spite of its terseness and briefness, its range is remarkable in that it relates the noetic consciousness of participation in the divine ground, the psychic forces of desires and emotions, the historical dimensions of past and future, and the vitality of the will to preserve a concrete existence "whatever it may be." This vital energy, of course, is the same to which Ibn Khaldûn referred by his concept *'aṣabîyah,* and Vico by his *mente eroica,* which Bodin perceived behind *sovereignty,* and which in history has "prorupted" in kings and peoples, laws and customs, and the instruments of self-defense. The phenomenon of collective vitality has struck many thinkers as something mysterious. By contrast, we seem to take for granted vital energy in the body-soul composite of particular individual persons. Aristotle, more than twenty centuries before Freud, found that even particular persons may succumb to the possibility of a death-wish, a self-destructive intent replacing the will to life, if and when their inner unity is not preserved by the excellence of friendship. Behind the vitality of existence there lies a complex "self" which is enjoyed only as there is a past delightful to remember and a future of good hopes. A self is composed of rational and irrational elements; where these parts are "rent by faction" they negate each other so that life is not attractive.

Thus, behind the vitality of existence there is a psychology of memories, mutual attractions, unified feelings, hopeful impulses. Such psychic forces do not explain vitality, but they obviously must be present if existence is to be sustained by vital power. Aristotle's analysis centers these problems of "friendship" in the "intellectual element," the consciousness of a higher ineffability through which man is rightly ordered. Here the analysis returns to Aristotle's previous findings: Only a friendship maintained for the sake of the good in one's friend is enduring, while friendship for the sake of utility or pleasure is subject to inevitable disappointments, complaints, and quarrels which, of course, would disturb the "wish to live with, and the capacity to have the same tastes as, another." The memories, to be good, must be memories of moments in which the order of human existence became manifest as participation in the divine ground. Where friendship cements an entity of political existence and engenders the wish to preserve it, "whatever it may be," there also is found *homonoia*, the capacity to be of the same mind, which renders possible the making of laws and taking of action in history. *Homonoia* is the ethical premise of a society's common action in history and has a constancy transcending any generation of living people in so far as its bearers are *spoudaioi,* men whose souls are open to the divine and whose strivings are therefore constant. The soul that is open to the divine and, for the sake of the divine, open to others who are "equal," observes that existential virtue which sustains "selves," affirms concrete existences which are preserved as they are enjoyed. This goes for individual persons as well as communities.

Aristotle's ethics thus covers three groups of virtues: (a) the moral virtues, excellencies regarding one's conduct toward one's neighbors; (b) the dianoetic virtues, excellencies regarding the human quest for truth; and (c) the "existential" virtues, excellencies that form and maintain existence, both social and individual. The latter are explicitly stated to center in man's orientation toward the divine and love of that in man which is closest to God and through which men participate in the order of being. Aristotle's concept of friendship has not been preserved in modern language. Aquinas also divides virtues into three groups, of which the first two, intellectual and moral virtues, correspond to Aristotle's explicitly named types. The third, consisting of faith, hope, and charity, might be considered a Christian version of Aristotle's "existential virtues." Augustine, however, had so sharply divided the natural from the supernatural order that the theological virtues were wholly reserved to the latter as God's supernatural gifts through revelation. Aquinas therefore speaks of prudence, justice, fortitude, and temperance as "political" virtues through which man can hope to conduct himself well in the this-worldly order of society.

It is in Aquinas' treatise on law, however, that we find further echoes of Aristotle's insights under a different name. Aquinas sees the natural law, the participation of human reason in God's eternal will and rule, as the sole constitutive force of any social order. Sheer power can issue decrees flowing from a mind that is not open to the highest reason, which is the natural law. However, such decrees have no force of obligation, so that a community united by law is rooted in man's love of that which in his mind is highest and which participates in the divine order of being. This starting point is identical in Aquinas and Aristotle. From there, Aristotle moves toward the will and pleasure of living together, the resulting "same-mindedness," the "at-homeness in existence" (Thornton Wilder's term), and the enjoyment of common living. Aquinas ostensibly and explicitly turns to the problem of obligation, the validity of humanly posited laws, and the legitimacy of authority. Alongside these considerations, however, the concept of habit plays a key role in Aquinas. It seems that this concept covers much of what Aristotle means by "friendship," the strength of what is familiar and homogeneous, the common premise that is appropriated into each particular life, the sameness of judgment and patterned conduct, all that which Burke adumbrated by his term "prejudices"—in short, the personal affirmation and enjoyment of what one shares with others. Aquinas' emphasis on habit, as Aristotle's on friendship, links the order of consciousness to the emotive patterns, the impulses and sustaining feelings, the ways of doing things in everyday routine through which an order of participation in the divine ground has a concrete existence in the practical life of a peculiar people. In the words of T. S. Eliot:

> History is now and England,
> With the drawing of this Love and the voice
> of this Calling.

The decisive difference between Aristotle's and Aquinas' insights into political existence and modern constructions is found in the relationship between the order of consciousness and the psychohabitual and emotive reality of community life. Aristotle and Aquinas attributed to the order of consciousness through participation in the divine ground the capacity to elicit friendly and community-furthering psychic forces, so that they would put the order of consciousness at the top, next the will to preserve each other, then the similarity of judgments and attitudes, and finally the enjoyment of common existence. This order was not reversible, because it is the love for what is divine that orders not only consciousness but indirectly also the habitual attitudes, emotions, and practices. Since Hobbes, however, this insight has been set aside. Hobbes placed passions first and foremost and moreover postulated the passions of a fictitious unsocial man as the basic impulse from which the mind supposedly was to derive the elements of order. It is clear that order oriented toward this basic self-centeredness must lack precisely the element of friendship, the warmth of traditionally enjoyed community, which Aristotle and Aquinas both stressed. This deficiency did not escape Hobbes; later it also struck Rousseau, Saint-Simon, and Comte, all of whom sought to fill the gap of community-sustaining emotions and psychic forces by a civil theology, thereby reversing the above mentioned order. In other words, at the top they placed a power structure established on the foundations of prime passions, and subordinate to this they introduced a purely utilitarian religion.

One cannot consider the modern civil theologies as new versions of the civil theology mentioned by Varro, against which Augustine directed his polemic. Varro's civil theology was simply the cosmological myth surviving in the political cult of Rome which, celebrated side by side with the "natural" (i.e., philosophical) theology of Plato and the schools, formed a somewhat superannuated version of human participation in the divine. By contrast, the modern civil theologies have nothing to do with participation at all. They are merely an afterthought of ideological postulates and propositions, after their authors had realized that what they called for would, if translated into practice, totally lack the existential virtues of friendship, communal solidarity, and public goodwill. Having posited their power structures in a cold, calculating mind, they then added something which they hoped would warmly attract man's psychic forces. The civil theologies of Hobbes, Rousseau, Saint-Simon, and Comte are "ersatz-existentialist" "ersatz-virtues," contrivances aiming at the molding of manageable subjects to the bidding of powers elevated to the rank of "mortal gods."

VII ☐ True and False Prophets

THE REVOLUTIONARY ANTIMYTH

Marx invented the concept of "radical revolution," a revolution that would not "leave the pillars of the house standing." The metaphor of bringing down a house to the last pillar should not be read as referring merely to institutions. "Radical" for Marx meant going "to the root of things," and the root of political order is found in the truths men hold in common concerning God, man, nature, and history. Marx aimed straight at the heart of the Greco-Judaean-Christian foundation of political order when he asserted that more than anything else, man *is* labor, that he alone creates his own life, and that the coming-to-be of man goes on in history through a succession of revolutions culminating in the socialist revolution. As much as Nietzsche, Marx sought to destroy the common acceptance of a divine creation and a created human nature, in view of which assumption political order in the West had been conceived as the order of *acting* within a cosmos of natures, rather than as a project of *making* both man and the world. The "radicalness" of Marx's revolution thus consisted not merely in his attack on private property but even more in his assault on the myth that has instructed public order in the West. Imitating his master, Lenin also aimed at something more fundamental than mere private property, Tsarist government, or market economy institutions. More than other Marxists, Lenin had an exceptionally keen eye for who or what was the proper enemy of the revolution. Overthrowing factory- and landowners was "easy," he said in 1920; the real fight, however, loomed ahead only after that overthrow: it consisted in a "protracted struggle" against the "terrible force of habit of millions and tens of millions." There, in the hearts of illiterate men, survived the order of Russia's traditional myth, manifesting itself in their mores and displaying continued power to give shape to countless lives.

Marx and Lenin thus confirm our findings that realms of political order are rooted in public myths concerning man, nature, God, and the meaning of life and that they take practical effect in patterns of habit, where the order of consciousness and nonconscious vitality meet in concrete ways of life. Their attack on the roots of order, however, had a totally negative character; it could destroy but not provide any new illumination of life. The Marxist-Leninist failure in this respect may demonstrate merely the impossibility of creating an ordering myth by willfully designing an intellectual formula. Beyond that, however, Marx's assertions about man and history simply had no relevance to the experiences and situations of everyday human life, to birth, death, marriage, friendship, love, contrition, conciliation. It might instruct a revolutionary enterprise in terms of historical meaning and practical goals of strategy, but it could not serve as a new myth ordering human existence.

A myth, as Aristotle pointed out, "is made up of wonders" about all of the reality in which man finds himself participating and about all the ways of his participation through body, soul, and mind. Marx's concept of man and history was not "made up of wonders"; it amounted to nothing but a polemical formula, pugnacious in its sharp reductionism and incapable of providing guidance for daily living. Properly speaking, Marx's was an antimyth. Similarly, Lenin's attack on the Russian pattern of habit offered no substitute. Insofar as lay in his power, he would replace the order of habit, in which each man and woman could experience a personal participation, by sheer organization from above. The unconscious or semiconscious "way of life" appeared to him as the devil's own temptation; he never tired of decrying *stikhiinost'* (spontaneity) and calling for its replacement by *soznatel'nost'* (consciousness), the latter term connoting conduct wholly governed by the party line. In practice, Communist rule thus would fight against the mores whose familiarity and deeper meaning made for mutual confidence and friendship, offering in their place nothing but the army-like discipline of party and factory. Germany's National Socialists, it is true, meant to create something like a myth but, like the Communists, offered no more than polemical formulae instead of notions born from wondering about life, couching them in empty if mythical sounding words like *Blut* and *Boden* (blood and soil), which illuminate nothing. They claimed that theirs was a "movement" rather than an organization, but in practice the movement's sole substance turned out to be unconditional subservience to the *Führer*—in other words, a despotism without legitimation. Without exception, modern total critiques of society have offered nothing more than radical negation, a negation stemming from discontent rather than affirmation, capable of demolition but not of construction, closing minds and souls to what exists, without opening them to a higher truth.

TOTALITARIANISM'S PERMANENT ILLEGITIMACY

The characteristic of our times, says Camus, is murder issuing from the logic of ideologies, murder deliberately espoused by regimes of nihilists when they attain control of countries and peoples. In the eyes of a witness and victim of one such regime, underlying such practices is ineluctable fear. "I have been condemned to fear for the whole of my life," says A. Kuznetzov. "From the age of 5 I have been living in a state of fear. . . . This is not just my personal lot; it is the fate of all who are born in this Russian land. . . . All of them, those who command and those who are regimented, those who punish and those who are punished, are afraid. Because they are all afraid of each other. And those who fear most of all are the dictators themselves."[1] Fear becomes the general climate of coexistence when legitimacy of political order is lacking; it is then that murder and deceit must be expected at any time. Regimes born from gnostic ideological total critique of present-day society have not established the legitimacy of their rule, hence they are driven to rely largely on systematic intimidation, which at

[1] *New York Times*, August 17, 1969.

times turns into overt terror and always requires spying and denunciation as a basis of government.

These facts in themselves, however, do not answer the question whether a revolutionary party centering in the total critique of society is or is not endemically unable to create a new legitimacy. Marxism-Leninism, to take the most prominent example, holds out to the people the confident prediction of a society without classes, state, law, and economic scarcity, free from disharmony, oppression, war, and all evil, which has been praised as "the most sublime goal" ever conceived in history. There can be no question that this vision has great power to attract and commit people, as witnessed by the millions who enlist in Communist ranks and the many more who willingly place themselves at the service of the party regime. In their eyes, this goal provides a full and sufficient justification for any degree of subordination the party may require of them, as well as of doctrines, strategies, and tactics which otherwise might appear to them absurd, devious, or repulsive. Thus, at least for party members and active supporters, the expected future serves as a legitimating cause. Could it not come to be accepted in the same way by an entire people, so that totalitarianism would then evolve into legitimate government?

Legitimacy is manifestly not wedded to sheer tradition. New legitimacies have formed from time to time. On the other hand, it also seems obvious that not every idea is capable of serving as a legitimizing concept, so that legitimacy moves within certain limits of possibility. A political order, as we have seen, extends all the way from the deepest insights into the ground of being to the pattern of daily habits, customs, and prejudices, linking people who must coexist economically by bonds of common truths and public friendship. A ruler or regime is legitimate when representing truths about being which are held in common and not flying in the face of possible pattern of habits, thus evoking the "public faith" that links ruler with ruled, and all the various parts of a body politic. A total critique of society that has nothing to say about being except in terms of a movement toward a remote future therefore cannot produce a legitimate representative ruler. This is so not because it is concerned with the future but because it postpones being to the future. The dimension of the future cannot be denied its place in politics.

Bertrand de Jouvenel rightly reminds us that the practical meaning of political order is to render "projects" possible. Projects point toward the future, as does every kind of "making." Citizens, within the framework secured by political order, engage in projects, as does every government when it concerns itself with public services, reforms, or military action. What enables private and public concerted action to pro-ject into the future, however, is precisely a certain sameness of existence and the fundamental sameness of being which links present and future. Thus, the future of "projects" is one thing and the future coming-to-be of reality as predicted by the ideologies, another. In the view of the latter, present and future are not united by the sameness of being or existence but only by the preparatory character of the present as the transition to the predicted future goodness. For the now-living generations, "coming-to-be" conveys no meaning other than "not yet." No order of existence can flow from such a notion; it provides men in their day-by-day lives with no orientation or measure and thus cannot translate into habits, customs, or taken-for-granted ways of looking at or doing things. Ideologies centering in the total nihilistic critique of society can justify order only for their adherents, and for those only a battle order, the order of hostility rather than friendship, the deceits of war rather than public faith. Modern academic philosophy may dissolve being into becoming, but when it is a question of acting and choosing, within the order of customs or laws, only the orientation toward the order of being can constitute a public orientation. A nihilistic ontophobic, total critique of society bars its adherents from any possible legitimacy and can persuade them only to accept strategy in the place of an order of existence.

THE "LIMITS" OF EXISTENTIAL VIRTUES

Camus saw the remedy for "logical murder" in the rebel's acceptance of "limits." His concept brings to mind the often-heard complaint that totalitarian movements might be acceptable for their "idealism" if they could refrain from their "excesses," a view that engenders the never-dying hope that these movements, at a certain stage of development, might in fact rid themselves of "revolutionary excesses" and "become normal." Murderous practices of political regimes, however, flow not from gratuitous zealotry but from disorders of consciousness. Intellectual and spiritual destruction of reality entrains physical destruction of humanity. The total critique of society that negates without affirming issues in nothing but "irreconcilable struggle." Must we, however, then rush to the conclusion that every total critique of society is to be shunned? A political science dating its ancestors from Socrates will not settle for that simplistic answer. Yet the term "limits" is too suggestive of external restraints imposed on unrestrained strivings. The problem of a critique of society is fundamentally the same as that of political order: it must be underpinned by "existential virtues," the attitudes toward the political whole and the whole of life which in their loving affirmation alone guarantee rationality.

A critique of society, even though total, still addresses itself to a living community of men and women who will not disperse because of an intellectual formula. There they are, destined to spend the rest of their days in a common framework of order. The critique of society must affirm the concrete fact of this community. An intellectual who fashions a formula of abstract perfection is likely to separate himself from his fellow beings, regardless of how lofty his conception may be. Beliefs about public order must have something of the quality of a mother's "belief" in her wayward boy, an activity of intellect and consciousness that is capable of sustaining the given condition of belonging-to-each-other. This primary condition cannot and must not be unwilled by an intellectual fiat. The critic who forgets that he is a citizen produces not a changed order but sheer disorder. Furthermore, all social order is historically-geographically concrete; it is characterized in its uniqueness by time, place, and a given past. Aristotle's *spoudaios* wishes for the good "only on condition of being whatever he is."

The critic's wishes for the good likewise must be for a given people, "on condition of being whatever it is." No other people can be wished into existence in its place. Humanity as such has no existence as an entity. There is a humankind common to all peoples which enables us to compare cultures and governments, but there is no recognizable form of human existence apart from the concreteness of given realms and peoples. What is more, the concreteness of human existence commits the critic not to overlook the practical, mundane, earthbound concerns which ultimately are what political order is about: it is *this* house with *this* plot, *this* town in *this* climate, *this* family with *this* ancestor, *this* country with *this* past in which political order alone takes effect. The contemporary concept "environment" completely misses this point, in that it presupposes an abstract subject thrown accidentally into a concrete "environment" with which it "interacts." There is no "environment" because there is no man apart from historical and geographical concretion. A total critique that moves in ahistorical abstractions, whether of the future, the past, or the present, overlooks human actuality for a nonexisting "individual," disregards the accretions of past living as irrelevant and obnoxious, and thus already does manyfold intellectual violence to living men.

The affirmation of existential virtue must embrace not merely the concrete community but also the whole of life in which men find themselves participating. In our civilization, formed as it has been by philosophy, this means that the political critic must refuse to cut off himself and his fellow beings from the transcendent dimension of life. After all, we have Marx himself as a witness that "everything palpable in practical life" suggests to man the reality of a divine creation. Political order is the order of practical life. Practical life takes shape around notions of a hierarchy of being, and particularly about the highest-ranking being, as Aldous Huxley's *Ape and Essence* (1948) has demonstrated in stark frightfulness. Affirmation of the whole of reality, including the dimension of transcendence, is not tantamount to insistence on an established religion. There have been total critics of society who assailed religious beliefs, but when they did so in a spirit of philontic affirmation rather than ontophobic negation, they neither wrought intellectual destruction nor inspired destructive political practices. The total critic who speaks from insight into the transcendent ground of being rather than in the name of nothingness, speaks as one "with authority." The total critic who lacks authority also lacks the power to sustain or renew community.

In the following sections we shall examine three examples of authoritative total critique: the Hebrew prophets, Socrates, and Augustine, whose wholesale attacks on their societies led not to "logical murder" but rather to "leaps in being."

The Prophets of Israel

It has been said that the prophets of Israel are unique in history. It is true that nowhere in antiquity but in Israel do we find a political order in which the political existence knows itself to abide in tension toward the divine will. The prophets were the mouthpiece of that tension, suffering it in their own person with intense agony as well as proclaiming it to the people. The problems of a critique of Israel were complex because the people not merely fell short of the standards of righteousness demanded by Yahweh but also yielded partly to the temptations of a wholly different order that promised to them the security of a mythical union with cosmic divinities. It is customary in modern literature to castigate the Baal cult for its moral inferiority, its orgiastic rites, temple prostitution, and fertility festivals. The prophets' total critique of Israel existence, however, emphasized chiefly another aspect: the mundane insecurity of Israel's order with its tension toward a God of righteousness, as contrasted with the implicit security of a cult of nature and power divinities. Prophets were supposed to be warners and monitors. The prophetic literature has developed certain criteria of distinction between "false" and "true" prophets—that is, between a prophetic critique which, though total, was the voice of order and another critique which, though partial, was the voice of disorder. The problems of total critique, as well as those of the distinction between true and false prophets, emerge clearly in Jeremiah, 14:13–18:

> "Ah, Lord Yahweh," I answered "here are the prophets telling them, 'You will not see the sword, famine will not touch you; I promise you unbroken peace in this place.' "
>
> Then Yahweh said to me, "The prophets are prophesying lies in my name; I have not sent them, I gave them no orders, I never spoke to them. Delusive visions, hollow predictions, daydreams of their own, that is what they prophesy to you. Therefore, Yahweh says this: The prophets who prophesy in my name when I have not sent them, and tell you there will be no sword or famine in this land, the same prophets are doomed to perish by sword and famine. And as for the people to whom they prophesy, they will be tossed into the streets of Jerusalem, victims of famine and the sword, with not a soul to bury them; neither them nor their wives, nor their sons, nor their daughters. I will pour down on them their own wickedness."
>
> "Say this word to them,
> 'Tears flood my eyes
> night and day, unceasingly,
> since a crushing blow falls on the daughter
> of my people,
> a most grievous injury.'
> If I go into the countryside,
> there lie men killed by the sword;
> if I go into the city,
> I see people sick with hunger;
> even prophets and priests
> plough the land: they are at their wit's end."

A similar note is struck in Jeremiah, 23:11–15, Ezekiel, 13:2–16, Isaiah 28:7. The true prophets accuse the false ones of (a) prophesying not by the will and command of God but by their own fancies and wishful expectations, (b) assuring Israel of prosperity, harmony, and security when this could not be Israel's lot, (c) not causing the people to turn from evil, and (d) speaking lies. The background for these charges was not only a widespread inclination in Israel to adopt cosmological cults either of Canaanite origin or borrowed from Assyria or Egypt but also the moral decline in Israel's daily life. As they inveighed against the cosmological cults, the prophets might possibly be regarded as bigoted zealots who intolerantly thundered against people who adhered to the "God of their choice." Intolerance, however, was generally speaking quite alien to the ancient world. In the multitude of different cults to which various city states or larger realms adhered, nobody denied that the ones others worshipped were also gods. Nor did the true prophets assail the cosmological religions of Assyria or Egypt in the way in which Augustine later on devastated the Roman religion in the *City of God*. The charges of willfulness, false judgments, and lying are directed not against representatives of other divinities but against other prophets of Israel. Since the Settlement Israel's existence had been founded on the cult of Yahweh, the God who delivered "Jacob and his sons" from Egypt and whose will was spelled out to Moses in the Covenant at Sinai. The consciousness of reality on which Israel's order was built had moved beyond and above the cosmological myth of the environing world. This "leap in being" could not be reversed at will; after it had occurred, the cosmological myth could not again become the order of Israel. The road back had been closed forever. If the mundane insecurity of an existence under Yahweh would cause some people in Israel to look with envy on those who adhered to Baal, an attempt to return to that level would not result in restoring the order of Canaan.

For Israel the alternative, Yahweh's order or Baal's order, did not exist; it was either Yahweh's order or no order. If the people insisted on dropping out from Yahweh's order, the result would be a fall into chaos, the chaos of concupiscence, alienation, and anxiety. Those prophets who condoned the people's flirtation with Baal and Tammuz had therefore cut themselves off from the only source of order available to them. This is why they were speaking from the "deceit of their hearts," from the promptings of their creature desires and fears. Jeremiah's charge that the false prophets had a distorted vision and substituted their own wills for that of Yahweh—thus losing their capacity for judgment—is therefore an accurate assessment of existence alienated from the source of order.

The prophets' total critique of Israel consisted of three themes:

(a) lament over the separation between Israel and Yahweh, the source of order, (b) denunciation of Israel's habits for the evil practiced by high and low, and (c) the prediction of political disaster for Israel, a prediction which the prophets' opponents often attacked as defeatism or even treason. The prophets' critique clearly did not envisage some phantasmal society in lieu of Israel but charged Israel with defection from its own order. A people basing its existence on trust in a God of righteousness can never be assured of external security, because it must always remain aware of its imperfections, its propensity to fall short of God's demands. Moreover, the covenanted mutuality did not admit of a policy by which Israel would seek to secure its own existence chiefly by its own means of power and that of its allies. From the very beginning, the relationship between Israel as a political unit and Yahweh included the possibility of military defeats, humiliations, and, at the margin, political catastrophe, for it included the possibility of the people's utter failure to meet God's moral demands. The prophets were compared by Ezekiel (33:2–6) to sentries or watchmen posted to warn the people against approaching danger. Therefore, a prophet who did not "declare Jacob's crime to his face and Israel's to his" could not truly be "full of strength [of the breath of Yahweh], of justice and courage" (Mic. 3:8)—that is, represent the truth of Israel's order. The philo-ontic total critique of the true prophets postulated not Israel's destruction but rather spelled out the substance of Israel's existence. The prophets anchored their critique in Israel's public past and denounced the departure of the people's mores from that foundation. They desired to preserve and restore, and when the predicted catastrophe finally overtook first one and then the other of the two kingdoms, their total critique survived both catastrophes and became the rule and measure of Israel's postexilic existence.

Socrates and the Sophists

Socrates' total critique of Athens had a structure different from the prophets' view of Israel, even though there were some similarities. Most immediately, Socrates indicted the way of life, the attitudes and orientations of his fellow Athenians. His charges bear a certain resemblance to those of the prophets: he denounced the people of Athens for pursuing power, wealth, and material pleasures. He sought to induce individual persons to a conversion, a return, as the key to the good life. Return in this case, however, did not mean, as it did in Israel, return to the public past as the sole valid source of order. Athens' public past, officially recognized, was the myth represented by Homer. That myth had been under the philosophers' attack for some time and the validity of its order had been under a certain cloud. From Ionian to Eleatic philosophy had come visions of new insights into the order of being, which had attained a certain public status in the tragedies. Thus, the return to the divine ground of being which Socrates sought to induce could not be a return to Homer and Hesiod. All the same, Socrates was admonishing the Athenians in the name of God, as did the prophets.

Socrates, however, faced a second critical task: removing the debris of the discredited Homerian myth in order to clear the field of vision for the perspective of true order. In addition, Socrates had to oppose certain rivals who also hurled a total critique against Athens, the Sophists, who appeared on the scene with recipes for critical science, practical skills, and public success. Socrates' relation to them resembled that of Israel's true prophets to the false ones. Jeremiah and Ezekiel, however, left us mere hints concerning the criteria of distinction, while Socrates proved that the Sophists were false prophets and made this proof the main vehicle for communicating his insights to the Athenians. To most Athenians, however, Socrates' total critique appeared not as a return to but rather a departure from, true order, as a proclamation of unheard-of gods, and thus as sedition and impiety. Similar charges had been brought against some of Israel's prophets, but the prophets always had at their disposal the powerful weapon of the Exodus tradition, to which nobody in Israel denied supremacy. Socrates could not appeal from the Athens of his day to a public past embodying Athens' true order. All the same, his total critique, like that of the prophets, was not the assault of a revolutionary enemy, but the sentry's warning to his own people, coming from a loving and anguished heart.

Socrates proved the Sophists to be false prophets by demonstrating (a) that virtue is not a mere ornament of respectability but rather a prerequisite of true being, because the good *is*, irrespective of our opinion; (b) that not man but God is the measure of human thoughts and actions; and (c) that political order is a matter not of wealth and success but of participation in the order of being as well as participation in the concrete reality of Athens. The latter point may call for a few observations. Felix Heinimann has drawn attention to the Sophists' disposition to derive order from "nature" and to oppose this order to that of the community.[2] This implied carrying on political speculation in a spirit of nonparticipation, existential detachment from the historical community. The Sophists' approach was new in Greece. It amounted to a total critique not only of Athens and the Homeric myth but also of the two centuries of philosophy preceding Socrates. Heraclitus had taught that all human laws draw their nourishment from the divine law, a teaching coming close to that of St. Paul which maintains that "all government comes from God" (Rom. 13:1). Socrates' argument against Protagoras revolved around the question whether order (virtue) is something immanent that can be made to develop like any skill or prowess, or rather flows from man's openness toward the divine source of order. In this argument the Sophist Hippias intervened with the following remark:

> Gentlemen, he said, I count you all my kinsmen and family and fellow citizens—*by nature, not by convention.* By nature like is kin to like, but custom, *the tyrant of mankind*, does much violence to nature. For us then who understand the nature of things, who are the intellectual leaders of Greece and in virtue of that fact are now assembled in Athens, the center and shrine of Greek wisdom and in this the finest house of that city, it would be a disgrace if we produced nothing worthy of our fame but fell to bickering like the lowest of mankind.[3]

[2] Heinimann, *Nomos und Physis: Herkunft und Bedeutung einer Antithese im griechischen Denken . . .* (Basel, 1945). *Cf.* also Voegelin, *The World of the Polis* (Baton Rouge, 1957), 53–66.

[3] Plato, *Protagoras*, 337 d–e. Italics mine.

Hippias here invokes "nature" compared with which all historical political communities are "tyrannies," an idea that recurs in Meslier's and Morelly's wholesale condemnation of all historical societies in the eighteenth century and echoes in J. S. Mills's devil concept of the "tyranny of the majority." Hippias, the foreigner from Elis, sitting in Athens in a group mixed of Athenian citizens and foreigners, calls all of them kinsmen and fellow citizens, members of the community of those "who understand the nature of things, who are the intellectual leaders." Thus he invokes a fellowship not of shared life in a concrete historical setting, but of intellectuals who have removed themselves from all concrete human communities and profess a loyalty to the world of thought which they have built up in their minds. For Hippias, "nature" is something like an Archimedian point from which the intellectual in Promethean superiority can move the world, from which historical communities appear not as an undertaking in common living in which one is to participate, but rather as an "object" of research or a "project" for revolution. With this attitude, Hippias finds nothing incongruous in his claim to political authority in Athens, where he is a foreigner—that is, a man not committed to participation, but rather a bystander looking on political life as something of no concern to him. Socrates, by contrast, mentions the practices of Sparta, the "best governed city," where councils on grave problems are always closed to foreigners—that is, to noncommitted bystanders. He proves the Sophists to be false prophets because in every way they deny themselves to participation, both the participation in the divine ground of being and participation in the concrete life of the historical community.

Socrates, the true prophet, draws his total critique of Athens from the deep well of loyal commitment. In Athens' wars, he fought with great bravery as a citizen-soldier. He accepted the mission to bring to conversion the youth of Athens, but he considered his mission in the restrictive sense of "I was sent only to the lost sheep of the house of Israel." His crowning act of loyalty was to suffer the execution of an unjust death sentence in obedience to his city's laws, even though escape was offered to him. Socrates' total critique thus must be seen as flowing from the participating life in which the soul experienced, and the mind became aware of, both the divine source of order and the concrete historical realm in which life was cast. In Israel as in Athens, the true prophets identified themselves with their people's life even when they castigated it with their total critique. The most intense expression of this participation is Jeremiah's lament:

> The wound of the daughter of my people wounds me too,
> all looks dark to me, terror grips me. . . .
> Who will turn my head into a fountain,
> and my eyes into a spring for tears,
> so that I may weep all day, all night,
> for all the dead out of the daughter of my people?
> (Jer. 8:21, 23)

It is hard to imagine Marx overflowing with tears for his people, or Bakunin fighting as a loyal soldier in his country's wars, or Lenin obediently submitting to an unjust death sentence. The false prophets, Sophists and modern ideologists alike make their home in phantasmal "possible worlds" and confront their city, their country, and this entire reality as strangers from another world.

Augustine and the Manichees

Among the various total critiques of society, could any one be called more radical than that of Augustine? He arose to refute charges that acceptance of Christianity and unfaithfulness to Rome's ancient gods had brought political catastrophe on the city, but he drove home his refutation of this charge by a counterattack exposing Rome's gods as false gods, unreliable in both peace and war, unsuited to inspire anyone to the good life, and drawing their life at best from the one true God who governs the entire world and is not privy to any particular country. Not content at this point, Augustine assailed the entire concept of life on which Rome was founded, derided and rejected Rome's public past, exposed the dubious value of Rome's historic achievements and the pretensions of

Rome's vaunted virtues. The thoroughness of his critical devastation by far surpasses that of Marx. Moreover, because he conceded that, relatively speaking, Rome was the best among all empires, his critique applied *a fortiori* to all political entities. He denied on principle that any political community could achieve true peace, justice, and order such as would be required for man's happiness. For among men, he said, two principles of associative love are active: "the love of self, even to the contempt of God," and "the love of God, even to the contempt of self," the first resulting in "litigations, wars, quarrels, and such victories as are either life-destroying or short-lived," so that at best a political community can attain but a very modest modicum of order. Augustine thus became the first political thinker who systematically dealt with the problem of alienation, the assumption that something in human existence structurally prevents man from appropriating as his own the premises and principles of public order. If man is existentially alienated from any concrete order in history, his being must necessarily be split and thus point beyond all historical communities to a complete and integrated life yet to come. The dialectic of alienation is necessarily eschatological.

Like Socrates, Augustine had to fight on two fronts, against the traditional myth on which Rome's pagan order was based and against false prophets who likewise assailed Rome's tradition but extended their total critique to the entire creation, the world of existence and experience. Augustine's break with the Roman tradition was more radical than that of Socrates who, after all, could fall back on the beginnings of an order perceived by philosophers and acknowledged by Athens in the form of the tragedies. Augustine spoke to Rome in the name of truths which had no *point d'appuy* in Rome's tradition before his own lifetime. He rejected not only Rome's "civil theology" but also the "natural theology" of the Greek philosophers to which many leading Romans had paid a certain allegiance. Had he been brought to trial like Socrates, a good case could have been made to sentence him for subversion of everything that Rome had stood for in the past. What he said might have been read as an argument for the complete dissolution not only of Rome but of any alternative political entity. That it was not to be so read is due to Augustine's fight against those who, declaring themselves strangers in this whole world of creation, advocated either utter indifference from or essential resistance to any public order, in other words, against an ontophobic total critique culminating in antinomianism. Augustine, like Socrates, made his main points by demonstrating that this was the total critique of false prophets. His main argument lay against the Manicheans, although he had to contend in a few engagements with the Neoplatonists and their influence on such Church fathers as Origen and Tertullian from whom could come the statement: "nec ulla nobis magis res aliena quam publica." (Nothing is more alien to us than public affairs.)

The problem of alienation furnished the battleground on which Augustine attacked and overcame the false prophets. At the core of the Manichean doctrine was the notion that not only society but nature constituted an environment wholly alien to man in which there could be no participation. Nor could man participate in the divine ground of being for the ground of being was not divine but demonic. The cosmos appeared to the Manicheans as an antidivine stratagem of dark powers, who in and through this creation imprisoned parts of the divine light. The light, however, was imprisoned and had no place in this world. Thus no good has any reality that could be experienced. Not only man's body but also his soul are diabolical products. God is radically transcendent to the point of being alien to the whole cast of existence, so that the knowledge of the divine is wholly speculative and unsupported by experience, reason, and even general revelation. Manichean nihilism exceeds by far that of Gorgias the Sophist against whom Socrates struggled but who could, after all, never hope to appeal to more than a few blasé intellectuals. Manicheism developed a complex but comprehensive doctrine, a code of action, and even organization and thus became one of the world religions.[4] Its consid-

[4] *Cf.* Stephen Runciman, *The Medieval Manichee* (Cambridge, Eng., 1955).

erable though antinomian political power inevitably came into bitter conflict with political communities based on some symbolism of participation in existential reality.

The Manicheans' rules centered in the notion of the sin of existence. Augustine countered that there could be no notion of sin except in a nature whose property it is to abide with God; that the good God produced a good creation, that everything created is good by nature, including man's body; that sin resides not in the nature of created beings but in the proud will that refuses to acknowledge the Creator; and that man's misery is thus nothing "but his own disobedience to himself," an argument very close to that of Aristotle in the *Nicomachean Ethics*. Being, says Augustine, is not a deception; it is real, and ultimately good. "I am most certain that I am, and that I know and delight in this." By this un-Cartesian formula "I am, I know, I love," Augustine proclaims a great Yes to whatever exists, a Yes not only to soul or *pneuma* but to body, mind, and soul, to the concreteness of existence, the particular family, city, or country, the earth, sky, and sea that surround us, the concrete time and place of each existent. Man's nature, created good, has been vitiated by his sinful opposition to the Creator, but the resulting distortions of body, mind, emotions, and soul do not condemn existence. They impart to human existence a yearning for completion and return, which is precisely the dialectic of alienation. Augustine discovered in history scattered evidence indicating an eventual fulfillment of this yearning, a return to God as the climax of man's peregrination "abroad." But, he insisted, it is not in history, in the setting of concrete times and places, that the fulfillment will come. He even removed the temptation to look for a future of the "thousand years" in which "Satan would be bound" and "Christ rule with his saints" (Rev. 20:2–4), affirming that Christ was ruling with his saints *now*, in the time of his first coming, and that it was idle to look to the temporal future for the millennium.[5] In other words, life is what it is; man's existence is altogether historical and cast into the setting determined by time, place,

[5] St. Augustine, *The City of God*, book XX, chapter 9.

environment, the forces of his emotions, the traditions of his people, the historical illumination of his mind. The unfulfilled yearning for God is a feature of this existence and while history points to its ultimate fulfillment, that will not come until the "eighth day," beyond time. The eschatology of alienation belongs to eternity rather than to history. Paradise is and remains lost, as far as history is concerned.

Camus was among those who have spotted "metaphysical revolution" as the source of modern disorder. He found that rebellion, while necessary for the occasional assertion of human dignity, ought to acknowledge a "limit."[6] Camus himself did not go beyond acknowledging the need for a "philosophy of limits." Augustine, however, developed such a philosophy. "That the world is, we see; that God is, we believe"; and further, "Assuredly the world was made, not in time, but simultaneously with time." In this creation, which is good because it stems from a good God, evil has no positivity: it is but the loss of good. Hence evil has the negative character of nothing, but existence is positive, even though it may be injured. Augustine's affirmation of nature and natures, of existence with its material and corporeal concreteness, which in its suffering from inner disunity carries a "strong proof of the goodness of the nature," has established one of Camus' limits. The other has been set by Augustine's philosophy of time, the created medium in which we have our existence, such as it is. Thus it is foolish to look for some other kind of reality in time; that completion of life toward which the historical fragmentation of human nature is pressing will be accomplished beyond time, beyond history, in the kingdom that is "not of this world." Meanwhile, though man's nature is badly distorted and enslaved by inferior impulses, Augustine says Yes even to this condition. "For so long as we wear the infirmity of this life we are rather worse men than better if we have none of these emotions at all." Augustine subjected all of political order to a total critique more incisive than that of any modern ideologist, but his tracing of corruption to the human soul kept his critique from re-

[6] Camus, *L'homme révolté*, part V.

sorting to the phantasm of a Second Reality, either a notion of a nonexistent spiritualized man or a dreamland of communities without laws.

Augustine's philo-ontic total critique never left out of sight the ultimate importance of the concreteness of existence, the particular body, particular soul, particular parents, the particular bit of ground, the particular people, of men who while transcending all these historical givens yet have their substance only in such determinateness. In spite of his devastating criticism of Rome and all political entities of this world, Augustine yet returns to the necessity of government in general and the inescapability of particular realms in particular times and places. Having derided the historical empires for their "short-lived victories" and their "inflated prides," he yet adds: "But the things which this city desires cannot justly be said to be evil, for it is itself, in its own kind, better than all other human goods." The creature, in order to enjoy whatever goods are available, needs peace. Peace is the business of the historical extant realms, each constituted not according to an abstract principle of perfection but rather by the "common love" which prevails among its people. Nor are all realms of equal rank and among the purely mundane requirements of good politics, the virtues acknowledged by the Romans must still be given a high grade. Augustine goes even further. Having observed, "Miserable is the people which is alienated from God," he adds, "yet even this people has a peace of its own which is not to be lightly esteemed."

The Manicheans' critique amounted to "metaphysical revolution"; it was a rejection "without limit" of existence in the world as known to experience. Augustine, by contrast, spoke as the faithful watchman for his people, and he spoke in the name of "the Lord who hates nothing that he has made." Never does he draw from the imperfections of human existence an alleged title to destroy whatever order fallen man is capable of achieving. Even though men here are "restless, till they find rest in God," concrete existence in this world is never to be regarded as trivial or merely provisional. It is pregnant with "real possibilities" which Augustine discovered much more imaginatively than any progressivist of the Enlightenment, but which he never was in danger of confusing with phantasmal "possible realities."

Israel's prophets, Socrates, and Augustine furnish examples of philo-ontic total critique that is neither nihilistic in thought nor destructive in practice. One might be tempted to enter into a systematic comparison of these examples with the cases of ideological total critique presented in the first few chapters of this book and to derive from that comparison a kind of "ethical code for total critics." That temptation, however, must be resisted. An attempt has been made to analyze the spirit from which each of the total critiques flows, and the attentive reader will enter into this spirit in each case and will then draw conclusions of his own. The objective of an investigation of this kind is not to provide ready-made recipes but rather to foment a process of returning awareness of what it is that feeds the widespread disorder of our age and what and where are the sources of our order.

Subject Index

Name Index